# BEYOND THE NARRATIVES

# BEYOND THE NARRATIVES
Essays on Occultism
and the Future 2004–2017

*John Michael Greer*

**AEON**

First published in 2020 by
Aeon Books Ltd
PO Box 76401
London W5 9RG

Copyright © 2020 by John Michael Greer

The right of John Michael Greer to be identified as the author of this work has been asserted in accordance with §§ 77 and 78 of the Copyright Design and Patents Act 1988.

All rights reserved. No part of this publication may be reproduced, stored in a retrieval system, or transmitted, in any form or by any means, electronic, mechanical, photocopying, recording, or otherwise, without the prior written permission of the publisher.

British Library Cataloguing in Publication Data

A C.I.P. for this book is available from the British Library

ISBN-13: 978-1-91280-759-8

Typeset by Medlar Publishing Solutions Pvt Ltd, India
Printed in Great Britain

www.aeonbooks.co.uk

# CONTENTS

| | |
|---|---|
| INTRODUCTION | *vii* |
| **DRUIDRY** | |
| Phallic religion in the Druid Revival | 3 |
| William Blake and the Druid Revival | 19 |
| The myth of Einigan | 31 |
| The Coelbren of the Bards | 43 |
| The fourth quaternio | 61 |
| **RELIGION AND OCCULTISM** | |
| The god from the house of bread | 75 |
| The hidden church of the Golden Dawn | 85 |
| The place of mingled powers | 97 |
| **POLITICS, WAR, AND MAGIC** | |
| Getting beyond the narratives | 119 |
| Magic and the end of history | 139 |
| Asymmetric tactical shock: a first reconnaissance | 153 |
| Fascism and the future | 165 |

## THE ROAD AHEAD

| | |
|---|---|
| How civilizations fall | 183 |
| The long road down | 199 |
| The falling years | 213 |
| The Next Ten Billion Years | 227 |
| The coming of the Post-Axial Age | 235 |
| Toward the deep future | 259 |
| | |
| *INDEX* | *269* |

*INTRODUCTION*

The second decade of my career as a writer began with a seismic shift that still has me struggling to catch my balance. At the winter solstice of 2003, as a result of a cascade of absurd events that no novelist could get away with, I became the seventh Grand Archdruid of the Ancient Order of Druids in America (AODA), an initiatory organization teaching Celtic nature spirituality which was founded in 1912. When I joined it, it had fewer than a dozen members left and was teetering on the edge of extinction, and I still suspect now and then that the other members elected me to the Northern Chair because it was less work than going to the trouble of shutting the order down.

Be that as it may, I threw myself into the work of reviving a nearly moribund Druid order, getting a website and an email list up and running, revising its long-neglected study program, and writing a book to introduce its teachings to a wider audience. After the frustrations and failures of the previous decade, I had no great ambitions; I hoped at most to attract enough members to the order to give it a new lease on life, and took it for granted that my new title would do no more for my writing career than previous involvements had done.

I was wrong on all counts. The book I wrote to present AODA's teachings to the general alternative-spirituality scene, *The Druidry Handbook*, became one of my bestselling titles, and the order attracted a steady stream of new members. Even more unexpectedly, when I launched a blog—*The Archdruid Report*—and started weekly posts discussing the environment and the future of industrial civilization, it took off beyond all expectation, rising to a peak readership of a third of a million readers a month. I started getting speaking gigs, first in the Neopagan community and then, to my astonishment, at conferences called to discuss peak oil and the environmental crisis of our age.

The outcome was that my writings began to stray into territory very far from the Hermetic occult philosophy that was the focus of my first decade. The essays included in this volume chronicle some of the themes I explored as a result: Druidry, Jungian psychology, politics, history, and the shape of the future in a society in decline. I hope they will provide inspiration as well as instruction to my readers.

—John Michael Greer

# DRUIDRY

# Phallic religion in the Druid Revival

*On the first of May, 1994, I was initiated into the Order of Bards, Ovates and Druids (OBOD), and began work on the lessons of OBOD's correspondence study program. I finished the course in 2001, and in 2003 received that year's Mount Haemus Award, OBOD's way of recognizing scholarly merit among its members. Each Mount Haemus Award recipient is expected to write a scholarly paper on some subject relevant to Druidry. Mine was perhaps a little more colorful than most, but it touched on themes that would turn out to be important in my later research into Druidry and the history of Western occultism.*

Like any other anniversary, the fortieth anniversary of the founding of the Order of Bards, Ovates and Druids offers an opportunity to glance back over the past and sum up a few of its lessons. While the history of OBOD itself has much to interest the scholar as well as the practicing Druid, I propose to look back a little further in the history of the Druid Revival, and note some of the factors that have made our modern Druidry what it is. Any such assessment needs to start by noting the sheer improbability of the Druid Revival itself. A handful of scrappy documentary references to an all but forgotten ancient priesthood—none of them written by members of that priesthood and half of them contradicting the other half in almost every particular—have managed somehow to inspire 300 years of efforts to turn a bare rumor of archaic wisdom into a living spiritual tradition relevant to contemporary concerns.

Of course no two of these efforts have had the same results. Jacquetta Hawkes once famously remarked that every age has the Stonehenge it desires—or deserves;[1] the same could be said with at least as much justice about the Druids. Yet the attention paid to the ancient Druids has too often been paired with a remarkable lack of curiosity about those Druids whose lives and teachings are many centuries closer to us. For many people, images such as the much-reprinted photo of the young Winston Churchill blinking owlishly amid a throng of elderly Druids in false beards seem to have defined the entire Druid movement before 1970 or thereabouts. Yet behind the false beards, some remarkably strange things took place, and at least some of them have lessons of value for scholars as well as practitioners of Druidry today.

One example stands out a little more prominently than most, if I may so express the matter. The facts of the case are simple enough to state: During the latter part of the reign of Queen Victoria, there was a Welsh archdruid who believed and publicly taught that Jesus Christ was a phallic symbol. The archdruid's name was Owen Morgan, and under the name and title of Archdruid Morien he presided over the Druid gorsedd of Pontypridd. A gorsedd is a community of bards.

Owen Morgan's astonishing career had its roots, like so many other phenomena of the Druid Revival, in the work of that force of nature Edward Williams, better known by his *nom de bardisme* Iolo Morganwg. Poet, opium addict, first-rate scholar of medieval Welsh literature, and one of the brightest stars in the glittering firmament of nineteenth-century literary forgery, Iolo had in addition the invaluable gift of believing utterly in his own fabrications. Having concocted a fine set of rituals and traditions for gorseddau of Welsh bards, he proceeded to organize a gorsedd anywhere anyone showed the least interest in having one. Merthyr Tydfil, not precisely a large city at the time even by Welsh standards, at one point in the nineteenth century boasted no fewer than three independent gorseddau.[2] On one of Iolo's many journeys through southern Wales, the town of Pontypridd in Glamorgan received his

---

[1] Cited in Piggott, 1975, p. 191.
[2] Raoult, 1983, p. 58.

eccentric benediction, and began its journey toward the far reaches of British religious history.

In its first years, little distinguished the gorsedd of Pontypridd from other local gorseddau that sprang up in Iolo's wake all over Wales, but its archdruid Evan Davies (1804–1888), better known by his Bardic name Myfyr Morganwg, proved to be a resource few other gorseddau could match. Some sources refer to Davies as a watchmaker by trade, others describe him as a Protestant minister; it's entirely possible that he was both, serving as a lay minister in one of the many Welsh Protestant sects of the time while earning his living in a more prosaic fashion.[3] But Fate had marked him out for a more interesting career.

Sometime in the 1860s, after what a contemporary acquaintance described as "thirty years preaching of Christianity,"[4] Davies abandoned his church and announced the revival of the ancient Druid mysteries of his forefathers, with himself as archdruid. From that time until his death in 1888, he and his fellow Druids celebrated the solstices and equinoxes beside the Pontypridd rocking stone with a distinctly Paganized version of Iolo's gorsedd ceremonies. However eccentric this may seem, it attracted followers not only in Wales but across the Atlantic in America as well.[5]

On Davies's death, his mantle passed to Owen Morgan, a prolific writer for the popular press who took up his teacher's cause with enthusiasm. He quickly turned his literary talents to the Druidic cause, producing a tome entitled *The Light in Britannia*. The scale of this magnum opus of Pontypridd Druidism may be judged by its subtitles: *The Mysteries of Ancient British Druidism Unveiled; The Original Source of Phallic Worship Revealed; The Secrets of the Court of King Arthur Revealed; The Creed of the Stone Age Restored; The Holy Greal Discovered in Wales.* Historian of Druidry James Bonwick referred to it as "among the most candidly expressed books ever printed,"[6] and indeed it is. Unfortunately for Morgan's hopes of literary fame, all this unveiling, revealing, and discovering had to do with the ultimate terra incognita of Victorian culture, the region midway between the navel and the knees.

---

[3] Raoult describes Davies as a watchmaker, while Bonwick (who knew him personally) calls him a Christian minister; see Bonwick, 1894, p. 3, and Raoult, 1983, pp. 86–89. Numerous elements in Davies's biography would repay further research.
[4] Bonwick, 1894, p. 3.
[5] *ibid.*
[6] Bonwick, 1894, p. 4.

To do him justice, Morgan was anything but coy about the matter. He began his book with a note warning the incautious reader to expect explicit talk about phallic worship. The first page launched straight into a discussion of the masculine and feminine principles of Nature. Within a few more pages Morgan was talking about the vulva of the goddess Venus and outlining the sexual mysteries central, at least in his opinion, to every religion worth the name. Before long the Sun was revealed as the son of the masculine divine principle Celi; the Earth likewise as Venus, the daughter of the feminine divine principle Ced; and the fertilization of the Earth by the Sun takes place in exactly the way one might expect. Speaking of the feminine principle, Morgan wrote: "Her feet were represented, open like a triangle, toward the sun rising at the summer solstice and winter solstice respectively; the apex of the fork would be on the equinoctial line, facing the virile sun in spring rising due east."[7]

In the time of Queen Victoria, this sort of image was startling enough, but Morgan was only just warming to his theme. Every mythology around the world, he believed, can be explained by the same combination of astronomy and sex, and every obscure name can be interpreted by transliterating it into the nearest Welsh equivalent and seeing what results. With Morgan, what results is fairly predictable. The name of the planet-god Saturn, for example, is in Welsh *Said-Wrn*. *Said*, according to Morgan, means the phallus, and *Gwrn* (here grammatically mutated to *Wrn*) is an urn, which is of course a vaginal symbol. Yet Morgan does not fail to note Saturn's status as the planet of old age, time, and fate: "Gwrn, or Urn, was the vessel into which, in ancient times, the ashes of the Druidic dead were deposited, and the name Said-Wrn (Saturn) implies that the virile power of the personified Sun has disappeared, and that his *membrum virilis* is now dead, or unable to reanimate the seeds in the Urn, and its former force is itself now exhausted in the earth, considered as an Urn."[8]

When he proceeded to explain that "Aaron entering into the Holy of Holies and the presence of the Ark of the Covenant, signified the same thing as Noah entering into his Ark,"[9] the attentive reader must have guessed readily enough that Morgan's phallic theology had, so to

---

[7] Morgan, n.d., p. 33.
[8] *op. cit.*, p. 15.
[9] *op. cit.*, p. 41.

speak, thrust its way into the Old Testament. Morgan devotes pages to the task of exposing the Ark of the Covenant as the symbolic vulva of the Earth goddess.[10] A full chapter expounds the solar and sexual mysteries of the Tabernacle erected by the Israelites in the wilderness.[11] Another interprets the ritual of the Day of Atonement as a symbolic orgy of astronomy and sex, in which the high priest enters the Holy Place and is reborn from it, or, in Morgan's own inimitable prose, experiences a new birth "through the hairy eastern outlet of the Virgin of Israel."[12]

It's only fair to point out that Morgan's theology had a metaphysical dimension as well. The two primal divinities of his system, Celi and Ced, were respectively the male and female aspects of the unknowable First Cause. The Sun and the Earth were the primary symbols and emanations of Celi and Ced, and every other phallic and vaginal symbol in the cosmos (including, of course, phalluses and vaginas) reflected the mystic interplay of virile Sun and fertile Earth. Thus Morgan devoted pages to seasonal and astronomical symbolism, including that durable theme, the impact of the precession of the equinoxes on ancient mythologies.

The centerpiece of Morgan's entire project, however, was his demonstration that Christianity itself was simply a restatement of the ancient wisdom of sex and the turning heavens. In Jesus Christ, the god who rose again, Morgan once again discovered the holy symbol of the masculine powers of nature. The corresponding feminine symbol was none other than the Church, the Bride of Christ.[13] But this parallel symbolism was far from the only relationship Morgan traced between Christianity and the ancient Druids. He argued, in fact, that Jesus had intended to replace the priesthood of Aaron among the Jews with the priesthood of Melchizedek, which latter was nothing other than Druidism pure and simple, learned by Jesus during his boyhood visits to Britain.[14]

For Morgan, in other words, Jesus was not only a phallic symbol and the reborn Sun of the winter solstice, he was also a Druid missionary. Morgan thus handled the conversion of the Druids to Christianity, a staple of Druid Revival literature before and after his time, in his own distinctive style, claiming that the "conversion" was simply a matter of

---

[10] *op. cit.*, p. 7 ff.
[11] *op. cit.*, pp. 207–224.
[12] *op. cit.*, p. 324.
[13] *op. cit.*, p. 31.
[14] *op. cit.*, pp. 325–328.

changing names, since the Christian priesthood was none other than transplanted Druidry, and Christian doctrine simply a restatement of the universal wisdom of astronomy and sex using slightly different symbols.[15]

This was Owen Morgan's phallic Druidism. It may seem odd from a modern perspective to use a one-sided label such as "phallic religion" to describe Morgan's theory, but it's a thoroughly Victorian oddity. The most widely respected medical textbook on human sexuality published in England during Queen Victoria's reign, Dr. William Acton's massive tome *The Functions and Disorders of the Reproductive Organs* (1857), mentions women twice and vaginas not at all.[16] For Acton, as for most male Victorians, "reproductive organs" meant penises and testicles. Vaginas were utterly taboo—a taboo so rarely breached that when the scandalous avant-garde French painter Gustave Courbet painted a woman's genitals and titled the painting *L'Origine du Monde* ("The Origin of the World," 1866), the rich private collector who commissioned it kept it in his dressing room with a veil hanging in front of it.[17] Thus learned Britons of the time, or at least learned male Britons, spoke of phallic religion rather than genital religion.

Remarkably, though, they found room in their theories of primitive religion for vagina-goddesses as well as penis-gods. This probably explains why books on the sexual dimension of religion were considered pornographic all through the nineteenth century, not only by moral reformers, but by sellers and buyers of pornography as well. Thus Richard Payne Knight's *A Discourse on the Worship of Priapus*, an academic treatise originally published in 1786, saw print again in 1865 at the hands of J. C. Hotten, one of the premier publishers of Victorian smut.[18] In the same way, plenty of other scholarly eighteenth- and nineteenth-century works on sexual themes in mythology and religion graced the shelves of Victorian London's pornographic bookstores. It was the one way many of them could get into print at all.

Yet this literature had been considered serious scholarship less than a century before *The Light of Britannia* saw the light of day. Many luminaries of late eighteenth-century scholarship turned their efforts to

---

[15] *op. cit.*, p. 327.
[16] See Marcus, 1964, pp. 12–33.
[17] Showalter, 1990, p. 147.
[18] Sigel, 2002, p. 72.

unraveling the origins of religion. The Deist and skeptical temper of the time guaranteed that direct revelation by the Christian god rarely figured in their accounts. Instead, most of them found the sources of myth and ritual in nature, and the origins of religious creeds in overly literal misunderstandings of a symbolic language once meant to communicate the truths of natural philosophy.

The book by Richard Payne Knight just mentioned provides an excellent specimen of this literature, and one that, as will be shown shortly, has more than a casual connection with our theme.[19] Knight himself was a scholar of independent means, whose interest in ancient Greek literature extended to those portions not usually translated into English even today. Like many learned gentlemen of his time, he also read with interest the translations of Sanskrit religious literature then just beginning to arrive from Great Britain's newly acquired Indian colonies. Ancient Greece and modern India alike posed a challenge to some of the fundamental certainties of the Christian West, for each presented the spectacle of a profound and mystical spiritual tradition in no way inferior to that of Christianity, that not only cohabited with an ebulliently enthusiastic attitude toward sex, but thrust explicit sexual imagery into a religious setting. To Knight, as to many other liberal scholars of his time, the splendid nakedness of the Greek gods and goddesses seemed to share a common symbolic and religious language with the erect lingams and erotic carvings that decorated countless Hindu temples.

In his work on the phallic religion of the ancients, Knight attempted to interpret some of this language. He argued that in ancient times, the supreme god was believed to divide into a male aspect of all-engendering spirit, symbolized by the penis, and a female aspect of receptive matter, symbolized by the vagina. These two appeared in the world of human experience as the life force and the substance of the Earth, which produced all living beings through their mating. Every phallic image in ancient art, Knight proposed, was a sacred symbol of the creative force of the divine, while every vaginal image represented the equally holy receptive and material dimension of divine creative power. Nude figures of male and female deities had precisely the same meanings, while images of sexual intercourse referred to the cosmic creative process through the metaphor of its most obvious human expression.

---

[19] See the discussion of Knight in Godwin, 1994, pp. 1–26.

This metaphysical symbolism led to surprisingly chaste interpretations of ancient and Eastern erotic art. Knight thus described one scene from the carvings at the Hindu temple at Elephanta: "... the action, which I have supposed to be a symbol of refreshment and invigoration, is mutually applied by both to their respective organs of generation, the emblems of the active and passive powers of procreation, which mutually cherish and invigorate each other."[20] The possibility that the sculptor's robust depiction of mutual oral intercourse might have had a less rarefied meaning, whether or not it entered Knight's mind, appeared nowhere in his prose.

Knight's work was closely paralleled by that of several contemporary scholars, most of whom published in the pages of *Asiatic Researches*, at that time the cutting edge periodical in the field of comparative religion. Still, his phallic theology was far from the only novel theory of the origins of religion available to literate readers in Owen Morgan's time. Another set of theories, popular in some circles even today, argued that the secret meaning hidden within the myths and religious teachings of the past was not sexual but astronomical. A number of the *philosophes* of pre-Revolutionary France, including Nicholas Boulanger, Charles-François Dupuis, and Constantin François de Volney, lent their support to this interpretation, which was taken up in turn by the English scholar Sir William Drummond in his *Oedipus Judaicus* of 1811.

The astronomical theory of religion argued that the reality behind the complexities of myth and doctrine was simply the movement of the Sun and the changing seasons over the course of the Earth's annual cycle. Every god was either the Sun or some other celestial phenomenon, every goddess the Earth or some sign of seasonal change. Some aspects of the theory made quite a bit of sense, and indeed make sense today; it puts no great strain on the imagination to compare Heracles in his lion's skin and his twelve labors to the Sun's annual path through the twelve stations of the zodiac.

Other solar interpretations of mythology required a good deal more in the way of suspension of disbelief; in some cases, as J. R. R. Tolkien commented in a different context, disbelief had not so much to be suspended as hanged, drawn, and quartered.[21] Like most theories of mythology, then and now, the solar theory also adopted interpretive

---

[20] Cited in Godwin, 1994, p. 9.
[21] Tolkien, 1966, p. 50.

rules so broad that anything could be read as a solar myth, and hostile critics accordingly had a field day coming up with parodies. Drummond's *Oedipus Judaicus* attracted perhaps the best of these, Rev. George Townsend's *Oedipus Romanus*, which purported to prove that the twelve Caesars whose misdeeds were chronicled by the Roman historians Tacitus and Suetonius were simply the twelve signs of the zodiac under yet another symbolic disguise.[22]

Such parodies, and a torrent of less amusing criticism in tones ranging from solemn to shrill, descended on the heads of proponents of the solar theory because they failed to restrict their talk about religion to other people's faiths. An analysis of Christianity as solar myth was part and parcel of the solar theory from its earliest days, with Christ in the midst of the twelve apostles providing only the most obvious set of solar symbolism in Christian mythology. For many of the solar theorists and their defenders, this redefinition of Christianity as just another Pagan Sun cult was the whole point of the exercise, a calculated strategy in the Deist attempt to break the grip of dogmatic religion on the Western mind. Much of the literature of phallic religion had the same aim in mind; thus Richard Payne Knight's writings made blistering references to "the sour mythology of the Christians," and his *Discourse on the Worship of Priapus* defended the sexual religion of the ancients on the grounds that it had avoided "two of the greatest curses ever to afflict the human race, dogmatical religion and its consequent religious persecution."[23]

All this literature, the solar as well as the sexual, forms a crucial backdrop to Owen Morgan's project. Morgan cited Richard Payne Knight and *Asiatic Researches* frequently in *The Light of Britannia*, and all the themes of Morgan's work can be found detailed in the earlier literature. His metaphysics, with its transcendent divine being dividing into male and female aspects, is straight out of Knight, who also seems to have provided the inspiration for Morgan's sexual interpretation of mythology as well. Yet the solar theory is not lacking in *The Light of Britannia* either; Morgan's Jesus is solar and phallic at once.

Morgan's borrowings from earlier scholarship were not limited to these sources. His habit of using Welsh as a key to hidden meanings of words in other languages was borrowed from a forgotten classic of the

---

[22] See the discussion in Godwin, 1994, pp. 45–46.
[23] Quoted in Godwin, 1994, pp. 3 and 11.

late eighteenth century, *The Way to Things by Words*, which was written by John Cleland and published in 1766.[24] Cleland was also the author of *Fanny Hill*, and therefore could be considered something of an authority on phallic matters, but he was additionally an enthusiastic if wildly inaccurate etymologist and a strong believer in the profound wisdom of the ancient Druids. He argued, for example, that the Christian Mass got its name, not from the closing words *Ite, missa est* of the Roman ritual, but from the mistletoe of the ancient Druids: a remarkable foreshadowing of Morgan's own Druidic Christianity.

It is worth noting that Morgan was not quite the first person to couple the solar and phallic theories of religion with the ancient Druids. Richard Payne Knight himself commented on the phallic menhirs of prehistoric Britain,[25] and one of his more eccentric successors, Henry O'Brien, dedicated his book *The Round Towers of Ireland* (1834) to a theory that identified these structures as phallic shrines erected by ancient Irish Buddhist Druids.[26] Nearly every possible ancient religious tradition, however poorly understood at the time, was grist for the mill of nineteenth-century theorists of religion, and so Druids appeared here and there as one more solar or phallic priesthood.

Yet the most interesting thing about Morgan's borrowings was the way he reshaped and redirected the sources he used. Solar and phallic theories of religion alike used connections between Christianity and older Pagan faiths in the service of an unstated assumption, one that was shared by most people in Great Britain in the eighteenth and nineteenth centuries. The phallic religion literature attempted to show that Christianity was just another version of Pagan sex worship, and could therefore be dismissed from serious consideration. The solar religion literature, in turn, attempted to show that Christianity was just another version of Pagan Sun worship, and again could therefore be dismissed. Most Druid Revival literature from before Morgan's time, by contrast, attempted to show that the old Druid religion was just another form of Christianity, and could therefore be tolerated. The assumption underlying all these claims was that Pagan nature worship was not a valid form of religion. Thus opponents of Christianity could attack its validity by showing that it was nothing more than Pagan nature worship, while

---

[24] Piggott, 1975, p. 164.
[25] See Godwin, 1994, p. 10.
[26] *op. cit.*, pp. 19–22.

defenders of Druidry had to catch Christianity's coattails in order to claim some sort of religious respectability.

What made Morgan's solar-phallic Druidry so distinctive was its refusal to accept this assumption. Morgan was thoroughly familiar with the solar and phallic theories of religion; he also knew the earlier Druid Revival writings, and drew extensively on all three literatures. At every opportunity, though, he stood the preconceptions of these earlier writings on their heads. If, as the phallic theorists proposed, all religions were fundamentally about sex and fertility, Morgan took this to mean that sex and fertility were holy. If, as the solar theorists argued, all myths described the turning seasons and the cycles of heaven and Earth, Morgan saw this as evidence that the seasonal cycle was profoundly spiritual. And if, as all three literatures insisted, Christianity and ancient Druidry shared core elements, Morgan saw that as proof that Christianity was valid, because it restated the old profound mysteries of man and woman, Sun and Earth, seed time and harvest under a slightly different symbolism: because, not in spite of. For Morgan, Pagan nature worship was the only true religion, and Christianity was valid because, and only because, it unknowingly preserved the old fertility mysteries.

This last comment points toward the final difference between Owen Morgan and the scholars who provided him with the raw material for his Druid teachings. Richard Payne Knight devoted many pages to a sexual analysis of myths and symbols, but neither his writings nor any other source suggests that he even considered founding a religious movement to spread his gospel of the phallus. Drummond's *Oedipus Judaicus* poked fun at the claims of revealed religion, yet he offered nothing but Enlightenment skepticism in its place. Morgan, on the contrary, was neither a disinterested scholar nor a skeptic. He had discovered, or so he believed, the true religion of the ancient Druids, which was also the true and undistorted Christianity of Jesus; he presented that teaching to the world at large for its enlightenment, and he celebrated the rites and mysteries of phallic Christian Druidism beside Pontypridd's rocking stone until the end of his life. Thus Knight's scholarship became Morgan's religious revelation; what Knight preached, Morgan practiced.

This curious tale has at least two claims on the attention of today's Druids, aside from the simple and wholesome attractions of ordinary prurient interest. First of all, the process that gave rise to his phallic theory of Druidry—the transformation of scholarly research into living spiritual tradition—neither began nor ended with Morgan. In a very important sense, the entire Druid Revival from its beginnings to the present day has its roots in the same process. The eighteenth-century antiquarians who launched the Revival and founded the first Druid orders of modern times drew their inspiration, and many of the details of their Druidry, from what was then cutting-edge scholarship in the field of ancient Celtic religion. Each generation of modern Druids in turn has taken the legacies handed down to them and enriched them with material from the scholarship of their own time.

Just as Owen Morgan depended on the work of Knight, Drummond, and other theorists of fertility religion, Iolo Morganwg built his Druidic edifice on a foundation provided by the researches of the Gwyneddigion Society into early Welsh literature, and today's Druidic literature on the Ogham alphabet would never have been written without the hard work of scholars such as George Calder, the translator of the *Auraicept na n-Eces*.[27] The same process continues today; one of the major American Druid organizations nowadays, Ar nDraiocht Fein, has based much of its symbolism and ritual practice on Georges Dumezil's theories about the tripartite structure of ancient Indo-European society—theories that ADF members lifted straight out of the scholarly literature in the 1980s. One of my fellow Mount Haemus scholars has pointed out elsewhere that the belief in a Neolithic matriarchal golden age, presented in the last two decades or so by some American Pagan writers as a radical new revelation suppressed by mainstream scholars, was in fact a widely held theory among mainstream scholars until the 1970s.[28] Other examples abound; in fact, it's hard to find any idea current in the modern Pagan scene that can't be traced back to some scholarly source.

All this casts an intriguing light on conventional ideas of relations between the world of academic scholarship and the realms of alternative spiritual traditions where modern Druidry has so often made its home. Many professional archeologists and historians have tended to portray these two as irreconcilable opposites. Stuart Piggott's scathing remarks on the Druid Revival groups of the mid-twentieth century—"bodies of self-styled Druids who today represent the fag-end of the myth ... at once misleading and rather pathetic"[29]—are part and parcel

---

[27] Calder, 1917.
[28] See Hutton, 1998.
[29] Piggott, 1975, p. 181.

of a rhetorical stance that contrasts the cool scientific accuracy of professional scholars with the vagaries of white-robed Druidical crackpots. Yet the scholars who like to draw this distinction have done more than anyone else to provide the raw material for modern Druidry; the very book by Piggott that includes the comments just quoted is on the recommended reading list of nearly every Druid order in the English-speaking world. Perhaps Piggott's contemptuous words might best be compared to the traditional disdain of the scientist engaged in pure research for the engineer who finds practical applications for the scientist's discoveries.

The light this casts on the origins of our modern Druid traditions, though, is not the only lesson that Owen Morgan's phallic Druidry has to offer today's Druids. However obscure he may have become, Morgan's ideas have had a surprisingly wide influence. Many of the oddities of early twentieth-century occultism seem a little less odd when illuminated by *The Light of Britannia*. When one of Aleister Crowley's instructional texts adjures the reader to visualize a "solar-phallic hippopotamus,"[30] those familiar with Morgan's work will recognize in this apparition a familiar symbol, rather than the product of a bad case of delirium tremens. On a broader scale, Morgan's work is quite possibly the first systematic adumbration in the modern West of a duotheistic fertility religion, with one god who comprises all other gods, and one goddess who contains all other goddesses—a pattern that, most of a century after Morgan's time, came to dominate the modern Pagan revival as the fundamental theology of Wicca.

Nor are echoes of Morgan and his kindred writers entirely absent from the writings of Ross Nichols, whose founding of the Order of Bards, Ovates and Druids we are gathered to celebrate today. The exuberant etymologies Morgan may have learned from the author of *Fanny Hill* bear comparison with some of the unbridled linguistic interpretations Nichols placed in the pages of *The Book of Druidry* (1990).[31] The symbolism of Sun and sex appears in many forms in his analysis of ancient sites in the same book, and takes center stage in his programmatic and too little studied work *The Cosmic Shape* (1946), which calls for a new religious consciousness rooted in the cycles of nature as a counterpoise to the negative impacts of an industrial society out of touch with the fundamental realities of human existence.

---

[30] Crowley, 1976, p. 270.
[31] Nichols, 1990, pp. 123 and 130–132.

Such concerns were by no means foreign to Owen Morgan and the Druids of Pontypridd, just as they mattered deeply to many of those who helped build the modern Druid tradition over the last three centuries. They remain, of course, profoundly relevant today, at a time when the trajectory of industrial society has brought it up against unyielding natural limits, with consequences we cannot yet begin to predict. We may find Morgan's choice of symbolism and language a source of amusement, but his attempt to build a Druid tradition, using the best scholarship available to him, to bring the people of his time literally back to earth deserves both our respect and our sympathetic understanding.

And the same point is true, finally, of the Druid Revival as a whole. The false beards and formalities of a bygone era have encouraged many modern Druids to distance themselves from older Druid traditions, and of course the contemptuous dismissal of those same older traditions by academics such as Piggott have given modern Druids another reason to hold the Druid Revival at arm's length. In doing so, however, we risk losing touch with our own history, and with the hard-won experience of other Druids who contended with the challenges of practicing a nature-centered spirituality in an industrial culture. If "real Druids" are by definition those who lived before the coming of Christianity, and every attempt to revive Druidism between St. Patrick and the 1970s is dismissed or ignored, it becomes too easy to turn modern Druidry into a religious reenactment club whose members go about pretending to be pre-Christian Celts, instead of honestly confronting the hard realities and bright potentials of the present age. If we recognize instead that Owen Morgan, like William Stukeley, Iolo Morgawg, Ross Nichols, and everyone here today, are part of a single historical process—the astonishing history of the rebirth of Druid spirituality in the modern West—the last three centuries take on a different meaning; we have a history of our own, a history in which we have a place, and from which we can learn.

## *References*

Bonwick, J. (1883). *Irish Druids and Old Irish Religions*. New York: Dorset Press, 1983.
Calder, G. (1917). *The Auraicept na n-Eces*. Dublin: Four Courts Press.
Crowley, A. (1976). *Magick in Theory and Practice*. New York: Dover.

Godwin, J. (1994). *The Theosophical Enlightenment*. Albany, NY: State University of New York Press.
Hutton, R. (1998). The discovery of the modern goddess. In: J. Pearson, R. H. Roberts, & G. Samuel (Eds.), *Nature Religion Today: Paganism in the Modern World*. Edinburgh, UK: University of Edinburgh Press.
Marcus, S. (1964). *The Other Victorians*. New York: Basic Books.
Morgan, O. (1887). *The Light in Britannia*. Cardiff, UK: Daniel Owen.
Nichols, R. (1946). *The Cosmic Shape*. London: The Forge Press.
Nichols, R. (1990). *The Book of Druidry*. London: Aquarian.
Piggott, S. (1975). *The Druids*. London: Thames & Hudson.
Raoult, M. (1983). *Les Druides: les Sociétés Initiatiques Celtiques Contemporaines*. Monaco: Editions du Rocher.
Showalter, E. (1990). *Sexual Anarchy: Gender and Culture at the Fin de Siècle*. London: Penguin.
Sigel, L. Z. (2002). *Governing Pleasures: Pornography and Social Change in England, 1815–1914*. New Brunswick, NJ: Rutgers University Press.
Tolkien, J. R. R. (1966). *On Fairy-Stories*. In: *The Tolkien Reader*. New York: Ballantine.

# William Blake and the Druid Revival

*Ten years after my Mount Haemus Award paper was presented, I was back in the U.K. for OBOD's fiftieth anniversary celebration, and the William Blake Society asked me to present a paper to its members. The meeting took place at the King's Arms, the London pub where the Ancient Order of Druids was founded in 1781, and the audience—like the Druids just mentioned—dealt with any dryness in the proceedings in the time-honored way, with mugs of good brown ale. It was a pleasant evening, but the paper vanished thereafter into my filing cabinet; this is its first publication.*

Some poets and painters are more colorful, more dramatic, more eccentric than others, and the same rule also applies to eras of history. It so happens that William Blake and his time are both fine examples of that principle in action. I don't imagine I need to convince anyone in tonight's audience of just how brilliant, and just how strange, Blake himself was, but I'm not at all sure how many people nowadays remember that his lifespan embraced, and very nearly defined, one of the most exotic and creative periods in the history of the British imagination.

Even the most cursory glance over the eccentric cultural landscape of late eighteenth- and early nineteenth-century Great Britain could fill a fair-sized book. Tonight, I want to focus on just one small corner of that landscape, the portion marked out with oak and mistletoe, standing stones and white-robed patriarchs brandishing golden sickles: the world of early modern Druidry. It so happens that the first solidly documented modern Druid organizations were founded during Blake's lifetime; it also happens that poetic and scholarly books by these latter-day Druids, not to mention images, ideas, and manufactured mythologies from the same source, had a significant influence on Blake's thinking and his creative works.

Now of course the claim that William Blake was rather more directly involved in the Druid scene of his era has been frequently made, and sometimes that claim has been expanded to a degree that the evidence won't support. Those of tonight's audience who are old enough to have witnessed another of the colorful and eccentric eras I just mentioned, and read the *International Times* in its hemp-scented heyday, may recall an article on "Blake and the Druids" by IT staff writer Joy Farren back in 1971, which fielded a polite but firm response from Ross Nichols, Chosen Chief of the Order of Bards, Ovates and Druids. Farren had cast doubt on the claim that Blake was the Chosen Chief of the Ancient Druid Order from 1799 to 1837, and Nichols insisted that Blake had indeed held that position.

It's only fair to Nichols to point out that he was repeating a claim that had been passed down to him, not making something up out of whole cloth. He lived at the tag-end of an era in which every esoteric spiritual tradition had to have a distinguished lineage going back to ancient roots. Everyone expected it; if you couldn't claim some such pedigree, no matter how valuable your teachings might happen to be, no one was interested; and so the founders of newly minted traditions got very good at retrospective recruitment. The process that installed William Blake as the Chosen Chief of a Druid order also made Bonnie Prince Charlie the founder of the Martinist tradition and the heretic pharaoh Akhenaten an important figure in the history of the Rosicrucians. So Blake was at least in very good company.

This enthusiasm for posthumous recruitment of the distinguished dead also extended, of course, to the ancient Druids themselves, and the resulting muddying of the historical waters has been thorough enough that it's probably necessary to draw a few of what Blake called bounding lines to bring clarity to a chaotic situation. The Druids of our time, of Ross Nichols's time, and of Blake's time are not descended from the ancient Druids. We know that much for certain. We don't know actually know that much else about the ancient Druids, though that hasn't prevented people from filling up elaborate books on the subject.

We know that they were an intellectual class among the ancient Celtic peoples of Ireland, Britain, and Gaul, and maybe other Celtic regions as well. We know that they had a very mixed reputation among the ancient Greeks and Romans, some of whom saw them as wise philosophers contemplating nature in forest sanctuaries, and some of whom saw them as deranged cultists spattered with the blood of human sacrifices. We know that they were persecuted by the Roman empire and then by the Christian Church, and that the last ancient Druids known to history were active in what's now Scotland in the sixth century, where they tried and failed to stop the conversion of the northern Picts by St. Columba.

End of story—or it would have been, except for cultural shifts more than 1000 years later. In the seventeenth century, most of the nations of Europe this side of the Alps were emerging from a long period in which history meant ancient Greece, ancient Rome, and the Bible. In the wake of the Renaissance, people in the U.K. and elsewhere wanted to know about their own history, the history of their land and their ancestors; here in the U.K., and of course in other places as well, they also started paying attention to all these standing stones and earthworks, and wanted to know about their history as well; so British scholars went digging in old books, and among the things they found there were the ancient Druids.

I've long suspected that if some really thorough Greek or Roman account of the Druids had come down to those seventeenth-century scholars, that would have been that: one more dry bundle of facts to add to the heap of history. Fortunately for today's Druids, what those scholars got was a scattershot collection of references, amounting to less than twenty pages in English translation; what's more, half of the references contradict the other half, so there's almost nothing you can say for sure about the ancient Druids—or, more to the point, almost nothing you can't say, should you have a mind to do so.

That's a commonplace of cultural history: the more opaque any particular corner of the past happens to be, the more effectively it can be pressed into service as a screen onto which the dreams and nightmares of the present can be projected. That's what happened to the Druids. By the time the eighteenth century was well under way, Druids were showing up all over British popular culture. The two classical stereotypes I mentioned a moment ago, the wise philosophers and the demented cultists, were both trotted out repeatedly in the prose and poetry of the day, but you also saw Druids as patriotic mascots of Britishness, Druids as proto-Romantic poetic visionaries, Druids as Welsh nationalist icons—well, the list goes on.

Druids were thus a hot cultural property; like many another hot cultural property, they inspired imitation, and since nobody was quite sure what they stood for, it was only a matter of time before somebody co-opted them for a contemporary cause. The year 1740 saw the first and one of the most successful of those acts of co-optation, at the hands of the Reverend William Stukeley. Stukeley was an antiquarian of the old school, the kind of gentleman who liked to make day trips to ruins in the company of friends, complete with picnic baskets and drafting gear; he was also an Anglican vicar of a very learned and broadminded type; and he came to believe that ancient Druids had built Stonehenge and Avebury as temples dedicated to the same god he worshipped.

That much was common enough. Stukeley took it further than anyone else before him, though, putting extensive discussions on Druidical theology into his books on Stonehenge and Avebury, and meeting for Druid ceremonies with a circle of friends at his home in Bloomsbury. That I know of, he and his friends comprised the first known attempt to revive Druidry as a living tradition in the modern world—but it was far from the last.

The next great wave of Druidry was not long in coming, and it came from a different quarter: the realm of friendly societies, which was also in its first great seedtime in the eighteenth century. The year 1772 saw the founding of the Druidical Society of Anglesey, the first documented Druid friendly society; it turned out to be short-lived, and closed its doors in 1844.

A considerably more significant organization was founded in 1781, in this very tavern. That was the Ancient Order of Druids, AOD for short. Documentary evidence from the founding hasn't survived, but according to later accounts, it was organized by a London carpenter named Henry Hurle and a circle of his friends, partly for conviviality and partly for charitable purposes—a very common set of mixed motives among friendly societies then and now. The AOD is still in existence, with lodges in Great Britain and a number of other countries, and several Druid orders that spun off from the AOD are also still going concerns today.

Before we go any further, though, it's probably necessary to raise a point that routinely trips up newcomers to the Druid Revival. How many people here remember the running joke in Monty Python's *Life of Brian* about the People's Front of Judea, the Judean People's Front, the Judean Popular Front, and so on? The Druids got there first. The Ancient Order of Druids, the Ancient and Archaeological Order of Druids, and the Ancient Druid Order are three completely separate organizations. The Ancient Order of Druids in America, which sounds as though it has something to do with the Ancient Order of Druids, actually descends from the Ancient and Archaeological Order of Druids, while the United Ancient Order of Druids divided from the Ancient Order of Druids. Got it? There'll be an exam at the end of the lecture.

The Ancient Order of Druids, like the other Druid friendly societies, was part of a remarkable social movement in Great Britain and elsewhere. Friendly societies, or fraternal orders as they're also called, were among the most distinctive features of the eighteenth- and nineteenth-century English-speaking world: part social club, part charitable foundation, part initiatory order with one or more ornate dramatic ceremonies of initiation, which usually had reference to something ancient and impressive—the Druids were an obvious target. The AOD's initiation ritual had to do with the origins and career of an ancient Druid named Togodubeline.

Togodubeline? Well, yes; that's what you get when you take the first part of the name of Togodumnus, who was an ancient Briton mentioned by Julius Caesar, and the second part of the name of Cymbeline, who of course was made famous by Shakespeare. If this sounds as though the founders of the AOD had a somewhat lighthearted attitude toward their traditional lore, well, yes, it does sound that way—but it's only fair to note, first, that the AOD has accomplished quite a bit of good in the world over the last two and a half centuries, and second, that the name of their legendary founder would not look particularly out of place in a Blake manuscript—Urizen, Theotormon, Togudubeline, it does seem to fit.

Nor was that all. On top of the wave of Druid friendly societies just sketched out came a third wave, the Bardic Druidism launched by that force of nature, Edward Williams, under his Bardic name Iolo Morganwg. Iolo, as we might as well call him, was a figure eccentric enough to find a comfortable place even in a milieu as exotic as Blake's. Poet, linguist, stonecutter, opium addict, and one of the supreme masters of nineteenth-century literary forgery, Iolo came bursting onto the scene in 1794 with a volume evasively titled *Poems, Lyrical and Pastoral*.

That volume did indeed have poems in it, and some were indeed lyrical and others pastoral, but it wound up with a long appendix proclaiming Iolo the heir to an ancient Bardic tradition passed on in secret from Druid times in the mountains of southern Wales and passing on some scraps of allegedly ancient Bardic teaching. Those of you who remember the career of Gerald Gardner, the founder of modern Wicca, will have no difficulty recognizing the type.

In the 1790s and the first decade or so of the nineteenth century, Iolo spent a lot of time in London, and celebrated Bardic rituals on Primrose Hill, "in the face of the Sun, the Eye of Light," as the saying was. That saying was invented by Iolo; so were the ceremonies; so was just about everything else connected with his revived Bardism; but the Welsh expat community here in London adopted them with enthusiasm, they were soon grafted onto the traditional Welsh Bardic assemblies, the *eisteddfodau*, and if you happen to visit Wales this September, I think it is, you can take in those same ceremonies at the National Eisteddfod, complete with gorgeous Victorian costumes. The same ceremonies were transmitted to Bardic organizations in Cornwall and Brittany, where they're still practiced today.

All these currents went on to cross and mingle and give rise to the wild confusion of the contemporary Druid scene, but since that happened after Blake's time, we can let that pass for now. What's important for our present purposes is that Druids were a hot topic all through Blake's lifetime; while he was writing his poetry, engraving his books, and having friendly conversations with an assortment of visionary entities, there were people who called themselves Druids and practiced one or another kind of Druid ritual right here in London and elsewhere throughout the British Isles.

Thus it's not surprising that Druids appeared in Blake's poetry and thought—it would be more surprising if they were absent. That fact, mind you, doesn't prove that Blake was a Druid, much less the head of a Druid order. It's relevant here that the Ancient Druid Order, the order that Blake supposedly headed, didn't exist in Blake's time; it was founded by a Universalist minister and nature-cure promoter named George Watson Reid around the turn of the last century [i.e., c. 1900], and recruited a long list of respectable forebears from before that time, in the manner and for the reasons I discussed earlier.

The Ancient Order of Druids did exist in Blake's time, but their list of presiding officers is public knowledge, and Blake isn't on it. It's always possible to argue that he might have been the chief of some other Druid order, one that didn't happen to leave any documentary evidence behind it. I suspect we've all seen claims of that sort in a variety of recent fields, and since it's rarely possible to prove a negative, that sort of thing makes a good evasive move. It seems almost rude to point out that using the same logic, I could probably also prove that Blake was the secret son and heir of Bonnie Prince Charlie and composed his works in close cooperation with alien intelligences from Mars. Still, there's another point worth noting, which is that when Blake mentions Druids in his poetry and prose, the spin he puts on them is not complimentary.

Blake being Blake, that doesn't mean they were pasteboard villains of the sort that populate so much commonplace thinking today. Behind Blake's mature work is a distinctive historical vision that sees all religions starting off with the Everlasting Gospel of the visionary and prophetic imagination and degenerating from there, vegetating the divine vision, replacing immediate inward experience with form and law; the Emanation gives way to the Spectre, until what began, wheel within wheel, in harmony revolving and in peace, ends in horror and human sacrifice. To Blake, Druidism was the very first human religion—this is an idea he borrowed from contemporary authors in Great Britain, for whom that was just one more expression of national pride: "All things begin and end on Albion's ancient, Druid, rocky shore." Thus Blake explains in *Jerusalem*, in his prose essay "To the Jews," that Abraham, Heber, Shem, and Noah were all Druids, and so Druidism was the first religion to trace out the trajectory I've just described, from the Everlasting Gospel to Albion lying on his rock in deathly Druidical sleep.

The Druids didn't take on that role in Blake's thought all at once. In his *Descriptive Catalogue* of 1809, in fact, Blake wrote a number of imitation Welsh triads, and at that point he seems to have thought of the Druids—or at least of Iolo Morganwg's Bardic inventions—as having more in common with the Everlasting Gospel of poetic vision than with the dark Satanic mills of Urizen. This honeymoon, if it was one, didn't last long; by the time Blake was making his final additions to *The Four Zoas*, Druidism had begun to take on what would be its enduring role in his work. In the last two chapters of *Jerusalem*, Druidism appears as a monstrous cult of law and blood, the endpoint of the process by which imagination and love are replaced by dogma and reason.

Blake's negative gloss wasn't limited to Druids themselves, either. It also extended to what were already, in his time, the core symbols of the Druid Revival. Let's take the most obvious one first—the oak tree. Druids and oaks were all but inseparable in the imagination of that age; it's indicative, to cite only one detail, that the first English book on the planting and culture of oak trees, dating from 1743, was titled *The Modern Druid*. Many eighteenth-century scholars held that the word "druid" itself came from the word for "oak," *drus* in Greek.

So it's worth checking out what Blake has to say about oaks. In his early works—the unfinished *King Edward III* and *Songs of Innocence*—the oak has roughly the same meaning it has in other English poetry of the same period, which is to say, it's just one more part of the scenery. With the first of the Prophetic Books, though, oaks get the symbolism they have straight through until the end of Blake's career, and it's not a favorable one. In *Tiriel*, for example, Har and Heva, the representatives of degraded poetry and painting, sit beneath an oak; and the oak appears as a symbol of the purely material world in *America, The Book of Ahania*, and so on through his mature work. "So Enitharmon cried upon her terrible earthy bed, while the broad oak wreath'd its roots round her, forcing his dark way thro' caves of death into Existence." That's from *The Four Zoas*, and it's a typical example.

By the time we get to *Jerusalem*, the oak is among the primary symbols Blake uses to represent the sin of vegetating the divine vision, and oak groves break out over the body of Albion like some kind of rash after Albion rejects Jesus the Imagination and sinks into his deathly sleep in Ulro. "If we are wrathful," say the four Zoas, "Albion will destroy Jerusalem with rooty groves; if we are merciful, ourselves must suffer destruction on his oaks. Why should we enter into our Spectres to behold our own corruptions? O God of Albion, descend! Deliver Jerusalem from the Oaken Groves!"

As this suggests, the oak has the nasty reputation it does in Blake's work because of its connection with the Druids. That linkage doesn't have to be left to speculation; in *The Ghost of Abel*, Satan himself swears "By the Rock & Oak of the Druid," and in the essay on the *Vision of the Last Judgment*, Satan puts in an appearance wearing an archdruid's crown of oak leaves.

"Why did you take Vengeance, O ye sons of the mighty Albion, planting these oaken groves, erecting these dragon temples?" The dragon or serpent is another of the symbols closely associated with the

Druids in late eighteenth- and early nineteenth-century scholarship and literature. William Stukeley, whom I discussed earlier in this talk, identified Avebury as the center of a Dracontium, a Dragon Temple, and ancient Roman chitchat about Druids carrying serpents' eggs made of glass became recycled in various contexts as the revival of Druidry got under way in Blake's time. We know for a fact that Blake was familiar with Stukeley's speculations about Avebury, since the image along the bottom of the last page of *Jerusalem* shows Stukeley's Dragon Temple spread out across the visionary landscape.

Serpents and dragons, here again, have specific meanings in Blake's imagery, and those meanings aren't favorable. Serpents represent degeneration—in *Tiriel*, again, Har and Heva, degenerated poetry and painting, turn into serpents creeping dolefully over the ground—and the dragon form of Urizen is among the most splendid and terrible images in all of Blake's works: "Arise, O stony form of death! O dragon of the deeps! Lie down before my feet, O dragon! Let Urizen arise." And arise he does. So we have Albion's sons as Druids offering up the human sacrifices of war and oppression, worshipping in oaken groves that vegetate the divine vision, and raising dragon temples to the greater glory of Nobodaddy. Not exactly the way you'd expect the chief of a Druid order to portray the practitioners and symbols of his tradition.

It's when we ask why Blake had such an antipathy to the Druids that the history of the Druid Revival becomes a key worth having. Among Blake's biggest bugbears, among the chief opponents with whom he carried on his lifelong mental fight, was natural religion: the idea, very common in his time though rather less so in ours, that it was possible to figure out the truths of religion by applying human reason to the world of nature. One of his early works was quite simply titled *There Is No Natural Religion*, and that insistence remained central to his thought straight through his career: Urizen, your reason, is incapable of seeing God, who can only be approached through the visionary imagination.

Central to the religious dimensions of the Druid Revival, in turn, was precisely the view that Blake condemned. The Rev. William Stukeley, whom we've discussed more than once already in this talk, makes a suitable poster child for that aspect of Druidry. In his book on Avebury—the same book whose illustrations provided Blake with the dragon temple of Urizen on the last page of *Jerusalem*—Stukeley spends quite a few chapters explaining Druid theology, which is basically High Church Anglicanism *avant la lettre*. According to Stukeley, the ancient

Druids weren't inconvenienced in the least by the mere fact that the religion whose theology they were copying hadn't gotten around to being founded yet; by the exercise of pure reason and the contemplation of the mysteries of nature, they were able to figure out nearly every detail of Anglican theology millennia in advance, right down to the doctrine of the Trinity.

It probably needs to be said here that there's some reason to wonder just how seriously Stukeley meant this display of natural theology. Ever since the eighteenth-century revival of Druidry, the tradition has displayed a very distinctive sense of humor, which hinges on saying absurd things with a straight face so as to have fun with those who take themselves too seriously. Stukeley was a pioneer there as in so much else of modern Druidry; his book on Stonehenge includes a chapter speculating that the stones might have been raised by a tribe of intelligent elephants who traveled to Salisbury Plain from Africa for the purpose.

It's a joke with a purpose, because the arguments Stukeley deploys to make the case for his imaginary megalithic pachyderms are all borrowed from previous scholars who tried to insist that Stonehenge must have been built by someone other than the ancient Britons. Still, it's absolutely typical that he never lets on that it's a joke, and there are still earnest scholars scratching their heads and wondering, what exactly did he mean by that business about the elephants? In the same way, Stukeley may have been grinning from ear to ear as he penned the chapters where he proved that Druids were good Trinitarians, having reasoned their way to unanimity over an issue that Christians in Stukeley's own time were busy fighting over.

If that was a joke, though, it went right over William Blake's head. It went over the heads of a great many people, for that matter, including a great many Druids, and helped to make a sort of green Deism one of the most common flavors of nineteenth-century Druid belief. It thus guaranteed a furious response from Blake, for whom natural religion was the negation of the divine vision. Nature, Natural Morality, and Natural Religion were for him the tangled net holding humanity trapped in Ulro, wandering blindly in the dark oaken groves of Entuthon-Benython.

Obviously the Druids disagreed. From the perspective of the Druid Revival, the ability of the individual human being to reason his or her own way to religious truths on the basis of personal contemplation of nature, without having to depend on any human authority whatsoever, was a source of freedom and vision, not of slavery and blindness. To Blake, Druidism was the archetypal priestly hierarchy; and yet the Druids of his time, and since his time as well, have had quite a noticeable shortage of priestly hierarchies, legalistic dogmas, and the other things against which Blake hurled his thunders. It's hardly the first time that a visionary has been so intent on the objects of his vision that he's lost track of relevant details down here on the rather less incandescent plane of matter.

The irony here, and it's a rich one, is that while Blake denounced the Druids in heated language, the Druids saw no reason to return the favor. In the letter to the *International Times* I cited toward the beginning of this talk, Ross Nichols comments that "within today's Order of Bards, Ovates and Druids may be practiced a large part of the teaching central to 'The Four Zoas' "—and he was quite correct. Blake's work has many dimensions—as the sustained creation of a coherent imaginary world, it bears comparison with the writings of J. R. R. Tolkien; as a contribution to English epic poetry, it can stand next to Milton's great poems; but as the evocation of a complete body of mystical symbolism, rooted in tradition but reflecting the unique historical experience of England and the English-speaking peoples, it stands alone.

Recognizing this, Druids over the two centuries separating Blake's time from ours did the sensible thing and borrowed heavily, if selectively, from Blake's work. You won't find evil oak groves pinning Albion down to the material plane in contemporary Druid teachings, to be sure, but the symbolism and meaning of the four Zoas, the complementary relation between Emanation and Spectre, the centrality of the visionary imagination, the quest for the same fourfold vision Blake sought and found in his supreme delight—you'll find those aplenty, along with a great deal of appreciation for Blake's distrust for those dark Satanic mills that were spewing coal smoke in his time and fracking fumes in ours.

"There is a place where contrarities are equally true," where Jesus the Imagination swaps stories with Satan in his archdruid's oak leaf crown, where prophet and priest—and Druid, for that matter—can sit down and explore the common ground uniting their different but complementary quests for the four-gated city of Golgonooza. I like to think that there, in soft Beulah's night, William Blake and the eighteenth- and nineteenth-century Druids he excoriated have likewise had the chance to talk over their differences and find the many places where they agreed with one another, and in particular about the struggle of the visionary imagination against the mind-forg'd manacles of a blind materialism—a struggle that has at least as much relevance today as it had in Blake's own time.

# The myth of Einigan

*In 2014, as my tenure as Grand Archdruid of AODA was winding down, Archdruid of Air Dana Lynn Driscoll launched an annual journal of Druid studies, titled* Trilithon. *She asked me to contribute an essay, and I jumped at the chance. This was the paper that resulted, delving into one of the more controversial ends of Druid history—the validity of material from the writings of Iolo Morganwg.*

Every spiritual tradition has its founders; every spiritual tradition also has its black sheep. It so happens that in the case of the Druid Revival, one figure falls into both those categories. Edward Williams (1747–1826), better known during and after his time by his Bardic nom de plume Iolo Morganwg, has the curious distinction of being simultaneously one of the most influential and one of the most despised figures in the history of modern Druidry. His writings remain central to most Druid orders and traditions that date from before the modern Neopagan movement, while most of the Druid orders and traditions that have emerged from contemporary Neopaganism reject Iolo and all his works as mere frauds spun from the raw fibers of eighteenth-century Romanticism.

There's ample justification for a suspicious attitude, at least, toward Iolo's claim to have received Bardic traditions dating back to Celtic antiquity. At the same time, the hardening of attitudes that turned that suspicion into dogmatic rejection may not be justified. As I will show, at least one of the myths that Iolo handed down as an inheritance from antiquity may actually deserve that label, for it contains details Iolo himself could not have identified as relics of the distant past.

## The origins of the myth

Iolo's lifetime spanned a crucial period in the emergence of the Druid Revival. It was during his time that the first known modern Druid orders appeared and began to attract public notice. Furthermore, he himself contributed greatly to that rise, as the creator of ceremonies and traditions that had an immense impact on the Druid movement then and later.

Until recently, though, these contributions were overshadowed by Iolo's reputation as one of the most glittering stars in the firmament of Romantic literary forgery. There seems to be no doubt that most if not all of the verses and triads Iolo presented as authentic relics of medieval Welsh tradition came from his own busy pen (Constantine, 2007). Some of his creations were not identified as such until the 1950s, and it may well have been a reaction against the resulting embarrassment that led to the blanket condemnation of Iolo by modern scholars.

That condemnation was echoed, and with added heat, in many corners of the modern Druid community. The oversupply of grandmother stories and equally dubious attempts to claim historical legitimacy in the mid-twentieth-century Neopagan scene sparked an inevitable reaction, and Iolo's insistence that his invented Bardic lore dated from time immemorial made him an easy target for that reaction. It didn't help that some of the Druid orders that used his work most heavily also claimed a direct descent from the ancient Druids they didn't have. Even after the academic community got over its irritation with Iolo and began taking a less one-sided view of his work (see for example, Jenkins, 2005), many contemporary Druid writers continue to treat Iolo as a fraud pure and simple.

Forgery, though, is a complex thing. Iolo's contemporary and fellow forger James McPherson, to name only one example, wrote a series of long poems, credited them to the legendary figure of Ossian (Oisín in modern Gaelic spelling), and published them as the traditional epic verse of his Highland Scots ancestors. The Ossianic poems were unquestionably McPherson's invention, but the tales of the Fianna on which those poems were based were part of a rich oral and written tradition in Scotland as well as Ireland that is attested long before McPherson's time. Had those tales survived instead only in fragmentary oral form in a few remote corners of the Highlands, the tales as well as the poems might have been dismissed as McPherson's inventions.

The possibility that a similar process might have provided some of the raw material for Iolo's creations has rarely been considered. Still, there is at least one narrative in his published work that is all but impossible to explain if Iolo invented the story out of whole cloth. Nor can that narrative be dismissed as a bricolage of ancient fragments. Rather, it shows the distinctive traces of descent from one of the core mythic patterns of Indo-European antiquity—traces that Iolo, with the resources available in his time, could not have recognized as such.

## The myth in Barddas

The narrative in question is the creation myth of Iolo's Bardism, the story of Einigan the Giant and the three rays of light. Originally published in *Barddas*, the posthumous collection of Iolo's papers on Bardic and Druidic teachings, that myth went on to play a central role in many of the later Druid Revival traditions. Here's the clearest of the several versions of the myth included in the published text of *Barddas*:

> *Einigan the Giant beheld three pillars of light, having in them all demonstrable sciences that ever were, or ever will be. And he took three rods of the quicken tree, and placed on them the forms and signs of all sciences, so as to be remembered, and exhibited them. But those who saw them misunderstood, and falsely apprehended them, and taught illusive sciences, regarding the rods as a God, whereas they only bore His Name. When Einigan saw this, he was greatly annoyed, and in the intensity of his grief he broke the three rods, nor were others found that contained accurate sciences. He was so distressed on this account that from the intensity he burst asunder, and with his parting breath he prayed God that there should be accurate sciences among men in the flesh, and there should be a correct understanding for the proper discernment thereof. And at the end of a year and a day, after the decease of Einigan, Menw, son of the Three Shouts, beheld three rods growing from the mouth of Einigan, which exhibited the sciences of the Ten Letters, and the mode which all the sciences of languages and*

> speech were arranged by them, and in language and speech all distinguishable sciences. He then took the rods, and taught from them the sciences—all, except the Name of God, which he made a secret, lest the Name should be falsely discerned, and hence rose the Secret of the Bardism of the Bards of the Isle of Britain. (Williams ab Ithel, 2004, pp. 49–50).

There are several other versions of the same story in *Barddas*. Figuring out their relationship to one another is a serious challenge, because *Barddas* itself is a compilation, assembled after Iolo's death, of various manuscripts of his on the subject of his Bardic mysteries. This raises steep difficulties in the way of any attempt to trace the origins of the stories and lore included in *Barddas*. In most cases, even when there's reason to suspect that a given passage dates from before Iolo's time, there's no easy way to ascertain which of the versions is older, or closer to the putative original. As we'll see, that challenge is commonly faced by students of comparative mythology, and it's precisely by way of comparative mythology that some light can be cast on the myth's origins.

The story of Einigan as given in the various texts, while it's a creation myth, is also a myth concerning the discovery of letters. The three pillars of light—/ | \ in Iolo's as well as later Druid usage—are also the three original letters, spelling out the secret name of God. They are also three vocalizations or voices and three notes of music, as well as the shadow cast by the Sun from a post at morning, noon, and evening.

This last meaning had a long afterlife in the Druid Revival, and a great many accounts of nineteenth-century Druidry make astronomical symbolism central to the three pillars of light (see, for example, Morgan, 1890). An oral tradition current in several older Druid Revival organizations equates the head of Einigan and the three rowan staves growing from it with the vault of the heavens and rays cast by three positions of the Sun; whether this bit of symbolism dates back to Iolo or not is impossible to answer at this point, as the "Secret of the Bards of the Island of Britain" Iolo referenced so often in *Barddas* and elsewhere, remains secret to this day, part of the inheritance of the Gorsedd y Beirdd—the Welsh Gorsedd of Bards, part of the National Eisteddfod of Wales—and of its daughter gorseddau in Cornwall and Brittany.

The central character of the story, Einigan, is himself something of a mystery. In most of his appearances in *Barddas*, he is the first of all created beings, but one genealogical passage makes him the son of Huon and the great-great-great-grandson of Noah (Williams ab Ithel, 2004, p. 11); a version of the story in Iolo's unpublished papers makes him Menw's son (Constantine, 2007, p. 141), and two versions in *Barddas* make Menw rather than Einigan the witness of the three rays of light (Williams ab Ithel, 2004, pp. 17, 47). I have been able to find no trace of Einigan before Iolo's time, as his other appearances in Welsh literature can all be traced back to Iolo's deft forgeries. Eiddin son of Einigen, for example, is listed as the perpetrator of one of the Three Accursed Deeds of the Island of Britain, but this triad and the whole Third Series to which it belongs are among Iolo's many fabrications.

The name is a puzzle all its own, not least because it appears in several forms in *Barddas*: Einiged, Einiget, Einigan, Einigair, and Einiger. Current French and Breton Druid sources interpret the name as the modern Welsh form of a Gaulish name, Oinogenos, a plausible name (from Proto-Celtic *oino* "one" and *genos* "born") meaning "firstborn" or "single born."[32] Names of the same structure appear elsewhere in insular Celtic tradition; the name of the Irish god Aenghus, for example, has the same first element—the meaning of the second part of the name is still disputed—and appears in Adomnán's seventh-century *Life of St. Columba* as Oinogusius (Anderson & Anderson, 1991). Whether or not this is the source of the name, though, remains wholly uncertain, and would not explain the multiple names cited by Iolo.

## *The myth in Indo-European tradition*

If we turn from the name to the details of the story, though, we land abruptly in territory familiar to all students of Indo-European mythology. Among the reconstructions of Proto-Indo-European myth, the best known is probably the story of creation. This has two characters, *Mannus (Man)[33] and *Yemos (Twin), who are the first human beings. *Mannus kills and dismembers *Yemos, and makes the world out of the fragments of his body—his bones become the rocks, his skull the sky, his hair the grass,

---

[32] Ironically, Oinogenos or Oinogenes is also an attested Greek name, meaning "wine-born," and in ancient times implied having been conceived during a drunken bender (Harris, 2000).

[33] In historical linguistics, an asterisk in front of a word indicates that the word does not appear in any original source and has to be reconstructed by working back from later words descended from it.

and so on. *Yemos then becomes the king of the dead, while *Mannus becomes the forefather of living human beings (Lincoln, 1975).

This narrative can't be found in intact form in any of the cultures descended from the Proto-Indo-Europeans. What appear instead are fragments of the story, and these can be found both in Indo-European cultures and in the cultures of neighboring peoples: evidence, if any were needed, that a colorful story travels easily. Those of my readers who grew up with the D'Aulaires' colorful children's book *Norse Gods and Giants* will recall the story of the giant Ymir, who was killed and dismembered by the brother gods Odin, Vili, and Ve, and whose parts then became the raw material for the world (Orchard, 2011). Yama in Hindu myth is the first man, who died and became the king of the dead. The Vendidad, part of the Zoroastrian sacred scriptures, similarly features a king named Yima Xsaeta, who became the ruler of an underground city that closely resembles the legendary realm of the dead (Darmestetter, 1880).

The *Shah-namah* of Firdausi, the great epic poem of Persia, includes the story of the great king Jamshid—the name is an exact equivalent of Yima Xsaeta in a later version of the same language—who was sawn in half by the evil Zahhak. The legendary history of Rome, remarkably enough, includes a close copy of the old myth in the tale of the twin brothers Romulus and Remus; Remus's death at Romulus's hands brings about the foundation of Rome rather than the creation of the world, but it's far from uncommon for cosmological myths to be redefined in later eras as foundation legends and the like.

The same myth also found its way into non-Indo-European cultures in the Middle East. (This is far from surprising, as some of the major powers of the ancient Near East, notably the Hittites and the Mitanni, spoke Indo-European languages.) In Babylonia, the hero-god Marduk slays and dismembers the primal being Tiamat and creates the world from the pieces of her body; in the Levant, the Ugaritic texts include an account of Baal's slaying and dismembering of Yam, the ruler of the sea, and it's been argued on a variety of grounds that Psalm 74:13–15 contains an echo of the same mythic narrative, with the Jewish god Elohim slaying and dismembering the sea (in Hebrew as in Ugaritic, Yam). Finally, the Egyptian myth of Osiris, who was killed and dismembered by his brother Set and then became the king of the dead, is arguably another expression of the same mythic pattern. Table 1 sets out these mythological parallels in a convenient form.

THE MYTH OF EINIGAN    37

Table 1. Mythological parallels

| Tradition | Killer | Action | Relation | Victim | Description | Fate | Kingship | Cosmic result |
|---|---|---|---|---|---|---|---|---|
| Indo-European | *Mannus | killed | his brother | *Yemos | the first man | who was dismembered | became king of the dead | and his body became the cosmos |
| Roman | Romulus | killed | his brother | Remus | — | — | — | Rome was founded |
| Norse | Odin, Vili, and Ve | killed | | Ymir | the first being | who was dismembered | — | and his body became the cosmos |
| Hindu | Manu | killed | | Yama | the first man | who was sawn apart | became king of the dead | — |
| Avestan | — | — | | Yima Xsaeta | the first king | who was dismembered | became king underground | — |
| Iranian | Zahhak | killed | | Jamshid | — | — | — | — |
| Babylonian | Marduk | killed | | Tiamat | the first being | who was dismembered | — | and her body became the cosmos |
| Egyptian | Set | killed | his brother | Osiris | the first king | who was dismembered | became king of the dead | — |
| Ugaritic | Baal | killed | | Yam | (the sea) | who was dismembered | — | — |
| Hebrew | Elohim | killed | | Yam | (the sea) | who was dismembered | — | — |
| Welsh | Menw | — | | Einigen | the first being | who burst asunder | — | and his head became the heavens |

The myth of Einigan fits neatly into this family of narratives. It is no more complete than any of the other versions, and like many medieval and modern mythic narratives in the Christian West, it has been reworked to some extent to fit such standard biblical tropes as hostility to idolatry and the sacred and secret character of the divine name. Its most interesting borrowing from Christian sources, though, appears to derive from the medieval legend of the skull of Adam.

This is found in the *Golden Legend* of Jacobus de Voragine (1230–1298) and a great many other medieval Christian sources. According to de Voragine's version, Seth, son of Adam, visited Paradise and was allowed to take with him three seeds from the Tree of Life. When Adam died, Seth planted the three seeds in his skull, and they sprouted and grew into three trees. The trees were eventually cut down and passed through various vicissitudes before becoming the wood of the cross on which Jesus was crucified. While most of the Christian legend is unrelated to the story of Einigan, the image of three trees growing from the skull of the first man is distinctive enough that some influence, at least, is likely.

This sort of mythological bricolage is a commonplace of comparative mythology, and occurs in several other daughter myths of the story of *Mannus and *Yemos. Einigan's role as the first created being and his dismemberment both reflect the death and destiny of *Yemos, however, as does the identity between his skull and the heavens, if this belongs to the original narrative. The texts in *Barddas* do not identify Menw as Einigan's brother, but the two are coeval; Menw is described as "son of the Three Shouts" (ap Teirwaedd in the original), and the Three Shouts are another form of the three pillars of light, voices, letters, and so on, by which Einigan and the world came into being. Had the story of Einigan and Menw appeared in any less controversial source, it would doubtless have been taken up long ago by comparative mythologists and added to the list of daughter myths of the story of *Mannus and *Yemos.

### *The origins of an origin myth*

The obvious question, given Iolo's known proclivities, is whether he could have invented a creation story that echoed the Indo-European pattern well enough to pass for a descendant of original myth. Such things have certainly happened since his time. To name only one instance, the invented mythology of J. R. R. Tolkien includes a typically deft example, in the struggle between the gods Manwe and Melkor that provides the principal plot engine for *The Silmarillion*. Tolkien's professional training as a philologist included close attention to exactly the patterns of Indo-European mythology discussed here, among many others, and it's surely no accident that the victor of the two should have a name closely related to *Mannus, or that the loser should have become the ruler of the underground and distinctly infernal kingdom of Angband, "the Hells of Iron" in Elvish (Tolkien, 1977).

Any such hypothesis about Iolo's possible invention of the Einigan myth, though, runs into a serious difficulty: The reconstruction of Indo-European myth that revealed the parallels just listed had not even begun at the time of Iolo's death in 1826, and was still in its infant stages when *Barddas* finally saw print in 1862. It was in 1786 that Sir William Jones first proposed that Latin, Greek, and Sanskrit, and possibly the ancient Celtic, Germanic, and Iranian languages as well, might all be descended from a common source; the first thorough exploration of the linguistic dimensions of the hypothesis was Franz Bopp's *Comparative Grammar* of 1843; not until the work of linguistic reconstruction was well advanced could comparative mythology get beyond the basics and begin tracing mythic patterns such as the *Mannus/*Yemos myth; and the myth itself was not finally reconstructed from surviving fragments until 1975 (Lincoln, 1975).

Until that work was done, in turn, faking a creation myth that would fit an Indo-European pattern not yet reconstructed would have been a stunningly difficult challenge. It might be objected that myths of the dismemberment of a primal being were common enough that Iolo could simply have decided to include one, but any such suggestion runs up against a further difficulty: the presence of a name descended from *Mannus in Iolo's myth.

None of the daughter myths that evolved from the Indo-European original, as it happens, put descendants of the names *Mannus and *Yemos in their original positions. The Hindu tradition preserves the name of Manu as the first king and progenitor of humanity, but his role in the death of Yama is nowhere attested; a German myth recorded by the Roman writer Tacitus names Mannus as the forefather of the human race, but lacks the dismemberment motif; a few other mythologies of Indo-European origin echo the name, but their relationship to the Indo-European creation myth was not recognized until long after Iolo's death. Most of the daughter myths, in a pattern long familiar to students of comparative mythology, assign the deed of *Mannus to some more recent or more popular hero or god, while the name of the victim has more commonly survived.

The myth of Einigan, like the other daughter myths referenced above, no longer identifies *Mannus/Menw as the sacrificer and dismemberer of *Yemos/Einigan. The two are still clearly connected by the narrative, however, as they are in very few other sources—and in no source available to Iolo during his lifetime. Here again, had the narrative of Einigan and Menw appeared first in a less controversial source, this detail would have guaranteed it a significant spot among the surviving traces of the original Indo-European myth.

Though Iolo Morganwg's gifts as a poet, a scholar of medieval Welsh, and a forger were by no means minor, his surviving work does not support the claim that he was among the most gifted comparative mythologists in history. Yet something like this would have been required to allow him to successfully reconstruct an archaic Indo-European myth, create a plausible Welsh descendant of that myth, and muddle it together with scraps of medieval legend in a highly convincing manner, a century and a half before anyone else could have done so. The most likely hypothesis instead is that he stumbled across some fragment of genuinely ancient lore in his studies of medieval and early modern Welsh poetry and culture, and added it to the mass of inventions and borrowings that became his system of Bardic lore.

The casual dismissal of Iolo as a simple forger and fraud thus clearly requires some degree of revision. That conclusion by no means justifies a swing to the opposite extreme, since much of what appears in Iolo's *oeuvre* was unquestionably his own creation. Rather, the points I've tried to raise here suggest that a much more nuanced understanding of Iolo's achievement is needed—an approach that considers the ingredients of his Bardic system individually, on their own terms, and uses the full range of scholarly tools to sort out possible scraps of older lore from Iolo's inventions and interpretations.

Within the modern Druid community, by contrast, a more straightforward approach may be helpful. The spiritual and personal validity of a myth does not depend on its historical origins; rather, it depends on the myth's resonance with personal and collective experience, and with the teachings and values of traditions that consider the myth a sacred narrative. Taken on its own terms, as a teaching story, as a theme for meditation, or in any of the other ways myths are used in living spiritual traditions, the myth of Einigan has plenty to offer. The possibility that it might reflect mythic patterns dating back to Indo-European antiquity has no effect on its value in these terms—though it does bring a certain additional interest to the tale.

## References

Anderson, A. O., & Anderson, M. O. (Ed. & Trans.) (1991). *Adomnán's Life of St. Columba.* Oxford: Oxford University Press.

Constantine, M.-A. (2007). *The Truth against the World: Iolo Morganwg and Romantic Forgery.* Cardiff, UK: University of Wales Press.

Darmestetter, J. (Trans.) (1880). *The Vendidad.* In: M. Muller (Ed.), *The Sacred Books of the East, vol. 4, The Zend-Avesta, Part 1.* Oxford: Oxford University Press.

Harris, W. V. (2000). A Julio-Claudian business family? *Zeitschrift für Papyrologie und Epigraphik, 130*: 263–264.

Jenkins, G. H. (Ed.) (2005). *A Rattleskull Genius: The Many Faces of Iolo Morganwg.* Cardiff, UK: University of Wales Press.

Lincoln, B. (1975). The Indo-European creation myth. *History of Religions, 15*(2): 121–145.

Morgan, O. (1890). *The Light of Britannia.* Cardiff, UK: Daniel Owen.

Orchard, A. (Trans.) (2011). *The Elder Edda: A Book of Viking Lore.* New York: Penguin Classics.

Tolkien, J. R. R. (1977). *The Silmarillion.* New York: Ballantine.

Williams ab Ithel, J. (Ed.) (2004). *The Barddas of Iolo Morganwg.* Boston, MA: Weiser.

# The Coelbren of the Bards

*A practical introduction*

*My second article for* Trilithon, *this followed on my discovery of the symbolic meanings of Iolo Morganwg's Coelbren alphabet in an old Welsh grammar—a discovery that led promptly to my book* The Coelbren Alphabet *(Llewellyn, 2017).*

That astonishing figure Edward Williams (1747–1826), better known then and now by his Bardic nom de plume Iolo Morganwg, bequeathed a diverse and contentious legacy to the Druid Revival. Like many other innovative figures in the history of alternative spirituality, he found it advisable to wrap his creations in the borrowed garments of a spurious antiquity, and did this so skillfully that some of his inventions were not recognized as such until well over a century after his death (Constantine, 2007). At the same time, historians have gradually been forced to admit that Iolo was far from the mere forger that the fulminations of an earlier era of scholarship liked to portray (Jenkins, 2005), and there is evidence that Iolo's Bardic synthesis incorporated, in and among his inventions, scraps of genuinely ancient and medieval lore that are not attested elsewhere (Greer, 2014).

Among the elements of Iolo's legacy most often condemned by scholars as blatant forgery is the Bardic alphabet he called the Coelbren y Beirdd, the Coelbren of the Bards. The website of the National Museum of Wales, as of this writing, even labels it a "false alphabet" (National Museum of Wales, 2014). That latter comment is typical of the modern scholarly treatment of Iolo, in that it takes its condemnation a good deal further than the facts permit.

The Coelbren, to begin with, is certainly not a false alphabet. If that phrase means anything, it would be something that looks like an alphabet but isn't actually one. The Coelbren, by contrast, is an actual alphabet, that is, a series of signs denoting individual phonemes that can be used for writing a language. If it was created by Iolo Morganwg, as seems likely, that simply puts it in the already substantial category of writing systems with a known inventor; no one calls Japanese *kana* false writing, for example, because it was created by the Buddhist monk Kukai in the ninth century CE, nor is the Cherokee script dismissed as a false syllabary because it was invented by Sequoyah in 1824. The Coelbren deserves the same status, for it is not merely a theoretical alphabet; in Welsh Bardic and nationalist circles through most of the nineteenth century, it was routinely used for poems, inscriptions on gravestones and other monuments, and an assortment of other writings.

Now of course the point the National Museum of Wales website attempts to make, however clumsily, is that Iolo's claims about the origin and antiquity of the Coelbren are rejected by nearly all scholars these days. That consensus deserves to be taken seriously. I know, for example, of no inscriptions in the Coelbren that definitely date from before Iolo's time; the first significant discussion of the Coelbren in print which I have been able to locate dates to 1848 (Williams, 1848, pp. 618–623), after Iolo's death, and references from before that time that clearly deal with an alphabet all appear to come from Iolo's busy pen. It remains possible that he salvaged his Bardic alphabet out of one of the old Welsh documents he is known to have studied, but until and unless hard evidence surfaces showing that the Coelbren was in use before Iolo's time, the most likely explanation for the Coelbren's origin is the one currently accepted by scholars: that is, that Iolo created it.

As already noted, though, that consensus doesn't deprive the Coelbren of its potential value or interest. An entire category of writing systems known to linguists and epigraphers, often termed ethnographic scripts (Senner, 1989, pp. 10–21), are the creation of individuals. In a remarkable number of cases, the inventors of ethnographic scripts are visionaries who belong to a native society struggling for survival against a politically and economically dominant foreign power. That Iolo and many of his fellow Welsh nationalists saw the position of Wales relative to the Anglophone culture of Great Britain in exactly these terms is an interesting parallel, if nothing more.

More broadly, in a study of another controversial body of writing, the Don Juan tales of Carlos Castaneda, Richard W. de Mille (1980) has pointed out that there's a significant difference between authenticity and validity. Authenticity has to do with whether a given set of teachings has the origins its author claims for it; validity has to do with whether a given set of teachings yields the results it claims for itself, by providing a workable philosophy of life, for example, or by facilitating desired psychological and spiritual changes in those who practice its disciplines. A great many writings on spirituality from before the modern era are, by modern standards, inauthentic—that is, they were not written when, where, and by whom the title page claims—but valid—that is, those who put their teachings into practice reliably achieve the results they describe. Castaneda's Don Juan stories, de Mille argues, fall into that same well-tenanted category, and a strong case can be made that those parts of Iolo Morganwg's Bardism that were his own invention deserve the same classification.

It's in this spirit that this essay approaches the Coelbren of the Bards. The Coelbren is part of the heritage of the Druid Revival. The questions surrounding its origin and early history, though these are worth study in their own right, have no bearing on whether it may be used by today's Druids, who are after all among the inheritors of the Druid Revival to which Iolo contributed so richly. Those of today's Druids who, as I do, find the Coelbren of interest are thus wholly justified in taking up the study of this remarkable Bardic alphabet, as a product of our own history and as a symbolic alphabet of the sort used by so many other spiritual traditions—a role for which, as I hope to show, the Coelbren is very well suited indeed.

## The traditional history of the Coelbren

The great majority of invented alphabets are presented by their makers as finished products set out once and for all. There are, however, exceptions, and the Coelbren of the Bards is among them.[34] As it appears in Iolo's manuscripts and the collections of Bardic lore derived from them (Williams, 1848; Williams ab Ithel, 1856; Williams ab Ithel, 2004), the Coelbren alphabet is the product of a complex history extending over many centuries, involving innovations and adaptations by a variety of legendary and historical figures. Whether or not that history is a product of the creative imagination, it provides the best available introduction to the Coelbren and its uses.

According to Iolo's account (Williams ab Ithel, 2004, pp. 39, 47–53), the Coelbren had its origin at the beginning of the world, for the three rays of light that brought the world into being in the Bardic creation myth were also the original letters of the Coelbren. According to that myth, Einigan Gawr (Einigan the Giant), the first created being, carved the wisdom he obtained from the three rays of light in letters onto three staves of rowan. This established a pattern that would be followed throughout the history of the Coelbren of the Bards.

The Coelbren is in fact well designed to be scratched or cut onto wooden or stone surfaces, rather than written on paper; it shares this mode of use, interestingly enough, with the two other historically attested indigenous scripts of northwestern Europe, the Germanic and Norse runes and the Irish Ogham alphabet. The letters of the Coelbren are composed entirely from the vertical and diagonal lines that represent the original three rays of light, / | \. This has symbolic importance, but it's also highly practical for an alphabet meant to be carved into wood: the Coelbren lacks curves, which are difficult to make quickly and cleanly with a knife, and horizontal lines, which would tend to split wood along the length of the sticks that were used, in Iolo's account, as writing surfaces for Coelbren in its earliest days. It may be worth noting that the Germanic runes were also composed entirely of vertical and diagonal lines, with no horizontals (Williams, 2004, p. 267).

The number of letters in the Coelbren varied over the course of the history described in Iolo's documents. While the three rays of light were the first Coelbren, the first practical form consisted of ten letters, which were equivalent to ABCEDILROS or APCETILROS. This may seem inadequate for a writing system, and in many other languages it

---

[34] Another is the Tengwar script invented by J. R. R. Tolkien for the Elves of Middle-earth, for which he created a detailed history, full of the same sort of changes to which other writing systems have historically been subject (Tolkien, 1965, pp. 492–500).

would be. Welsh, however, shares with its sister languages of the Celtic family a great deal of fluidity in consonant sounds.

In Welsh, the sounds represented by the letters P, B, Ff (equivalent to English F), F (equivalent to V), and M are, if not quite interchangeable, then closely related, and they can flow into one another under certain circumstances without changing the meaning of the words in which they appear. Depending on its place and grammatical function in a sentence, for example, the name of the god Bran can be pronounced Vran or Mran, and the name of the hero Pryderi can turn into Bryderi, Mhryderi, and Phryderi. The same flexibility connects T, D, Th, Dd, and N—in Welsh, Dd sounds like the "th" in "these clothes"—and C, G, Ch, Gh, and Ng. In the original ten-letter Coelbren, one letter did duty for each of these three clusters of related sounds.

The ten-letter Coelbren, called Abcedilros after the letters composing it, was attributed in Bardic legend to Menw the Old, who discovered the rowan staves carved by Einigan. A slightly later version of the alphabet added M and N as independent letters, and was called Mabcednilros. The exact forms of the primitive Coelbren of ten and twelve letters were among the secrets of the Bards, according to Iolo, and they may have that status even today; the Gorsedd Cymru, the premier organization of Welsh bards, still uses the rituals and symbolism Iolo created for them, and the primitive Coelbren may well remain among the secrets of that body.

Iolo's history of the Coelbren continues from there to the days of Dyfnwal Moelmud and his son Beli the Great, two legendary figures from late pre-Roman Britain. One of these rulers—different accounts in *Barddas* disagree about which one—established a new Coelbren of

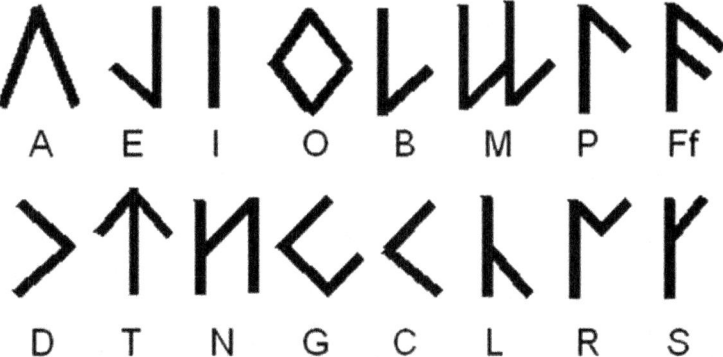

sixteen letters, which was not a Bardic secret, but came into general use in Britain. There are several versions of the Coelbren of sixteen letters in Iolo's papers; the most common runs as follows.

According to the traditional lore, the Coelbren was almost forgotten after the Roman conquest of Britain, when writing with ink on parchment became standard and Latin letters were in common use. After the Roman legions departed and parchment became an expensive luxury, the Coelbren was again needed, and the bards Talhaiarn and Taliesin revived the Bardic alphabet and added two new letters—again, the documents disagree as to which those were, but the best candidates are H and W.

Later, Ithel the Tawny added two more, probably U and Y. According to Iolo's documents, the twenty letters that resulted were said to express the complete set of primary sounds in Welsh.

Finally, in the time of King Hywel the Good (reigned 920–950), Geraint the Blue Bard added four more letters representing compound sounds common in Welsh: Ch, Dd, F (pronounced V), and Ll.

After Geraint's time, many other compound letters were proposed by Bardic grammarians, and came to be included in scholarly documents in the Bardic tradition, but by all accounts they were not used in practice.

## The practicalities of the Coelbren

As already mentioned, the letters of the Coelbren alphabet were written on wooden sticks with a knife. According to the tradition, this was the original medium of writing among the ancient Celts. As noted earlier, this parallels the use of runes and Ogham, the two historically attested indigenous scripts of northwestern Europe; it also has a more distant parallel in ancient Chinese, which was normally written on lengths of wood or split bamboo until the invention of paper in the second century BCE (Bagley, 2004, pp. 216–217). The traditional account goes on to say that writing with ink on parchment was introduced to Britain just before the Roman conquest, as already noted, but the older form of writing came back into use whenever parchment became too expensive or difficult to obtain, notably during the revolt of Owain Glyndwr in the fifteenth century, when the English embargoed sales of writing materials to Wales.

The Bardic literature includes a great deal of detailed information about how the wooden sticks were prepared and used. Long straight branches of the appropriate size were harvested from trees in winter, before the sap rose. Hazel was the easiest wood to use for writing purposes, oak was the most enduring, and willow, alder, birch, plum, hawthorn, and apple were also common sources for writing materials. The bards preferred rowan, however, because the wood resists rot, and has the traditional power to drive away evil spirits and enchantments.

To prepare the wood, clean straight branches were cut into rods the length of a cubit (around eighteen inches); each rod was then divided into four lengthwise, producing four long thin billets, and these were allowed to dry. The wood was then planed with a sharp knife so that each billet had a square cross section and four flat sides, each about half an inch wide, and the corners were trimmed down by a tenth of an inch, so that cuts made on one side wouldn't cross onto another. The ebill, as the billet of wood was called, was then ready for use.

Cutting the letters into an ebill requires the same skill and attention as any other kind of calligraphy. "And on this stave or ebill the letters are cut with a knife," according to *Barddas* (Williams ab Ithel, 2004, p. 145), "in small grooves the thickness of a leaf or small straw in depth, and as wide as a slender stalk of hay. Let every groove be cut fair and clear in its cutting." When it was desired to make writing more legible than ordinary knife-cut grooves could manage, a plant-based dye such as woad was rubbed across the face of the ebill before letters were carved into it, so that the letters stood out white against a colored surface. Once the text had been written on it, the ebill could be warmed, smeared with beeswax, and lightly roasted by the fireside to make the wax penetrate the wood, as a further protection against decay.

A single ebill could hold four lines of poetry or an equivalent amount of prose; each side was marked with a number on one end so that readers could tell the order in which to read the sides. If a text required more than one ebill, they could be pierced at both ends with an iron auger heated in the fire, and strung together on two strong cords, or inserted into a wooden frame that was lashed together at top and bottom. A frame of this sort, called a peithynen, normally held ten ebillion, or forty writing surfaces, enough for a substantial poem or a short tale; some frames are said to have held up to thirty ebillion.

No peithynen survives from before Iolo's time, though it's only fair to note that neither the climate nor the history of Wales are well suited to the preservation of fragile wooden objects tarred with the memories of a troubled past. For most of a century after Iolo's death, though, peithynenau were a common sight at Bardic events in Wales and elsewhere. For that matter, the same National Museum of Wales website mentioned earlier in this essay has a photo of a peithynen bearing a poem commemorating Iolo Morganwg.

Ebillion carved with a knife were said to be the most common medium for the Bardic alphabet, but certain other media were used as well. In the time of Llyr Llediaith, the father of Bran the Blessed of *Mabinogion* fame, the bards were said to have devised a system in which heated iron stamps were used to burn the Coelbren letters into wood; if this story has any historical validity, that process would count as one of the earliest forms of printing. There were also small ebillion, the size of a finger, which were used by the bards to communicate their secret teachings; there were wooden cubes like dice, which had a letter carved onto each face, so that four of these cubes comprised the alphabet of 24 letters; there were also small pieces of wood with individual letters on them. The Bardic literature claims that these latter two were used by bards for secret communication; there is at least one other possible use for them, which will be discussed below.

The same symbols could also be scratched onto stone with a sharp steel point. In this context they were called Coelfain rather than Coelbren (with *maen*, stone, in place of *pren*, wood). Stones bearing individual letters or the "marks of mystery," whatever those may have been, filled the same roles as the small ebillion and individually lettered pieces of wood mentioned above. On a larger scale, the laws of King Hywel the Good were said to have been originally written on pieces of slate that lined the walls of his royal hall, and King Arthur was said to have had the laws of the Round Table and the praiseworthy deeds of its knights written on plates of tin and brass at his three principal courts, at Caerleon, Celliwig, and Penrhyn.

## The symbolism of the Coelbren

One curious detail of the Coelbren lore in Welsh Bardic literature of the nineteenth century is that it includes a dimension more commonly found in ancient alphabets than in modern ones, invented or otherwise: a symbolic meaning assigned to each letter. Those readers who are familiar with the Norse or Germanic runes, the Irish Ogham alphabet, or for that matter the Hebrew alphabet in its Kabbalistic applications, will be familiar with the way a letter in any of these scripts serves as an anchor for a cluster of images and meanings.

Each of the sixteen ancient letters of the Coelbren similarly has its own distinct meaning, but there's an important difference. In the runes, the Ogham, the Hebrew alphabet, and most other examples of letter-symbolism, each letter has a name that is a meaningful word, and the symbolic meanings of each letter are linked to the letter-name. The Coelbren have letter-names: the vowels sound their own names, and the names of the consonants consist of the letter followed by I, such as bi, ci, di, and so on.[35] Some of these have symbolic meaning, but the core meanings of the letters are instead linked to the quality of the sound represented by each letter and the way that the mouth and tongue are held and moved to make that sound.

There are, as it happens, other writing systems that derive their symbolic meanings in the same way. *Kotodama*, the Japanese system of esoteric phonology and script symbolism, takes its meaning from sound values instead of letter-names (Gleason, 1995), and certain schools of central European occultism worked out similar systems

---

[35] In practice, according to John Williams ab Ithel, the I is pronounced as an obscure vowel sound like the E before R in such English words as "butcher" and "baker" (Williams ab Ithel, 1856, p. 14).

using the sounds of the German language (Bardon, 1971; Lomer, 1997). Still, it's an uncommon approach to letter symbolism, and rendered even more remarkable by the way that the Bardic lore draws the meaning of each letter from a sort of vocal gesturing which, they suggested, preceded verbal language at some very ancient point in the emergence of humanity.

The idea that language descends from some form of natural gesture is an old one, dating back at least as far as Plato's *Cratylus*, and was part of the common parlance of scholarship in the eighteenth century, playing an important part in the writings of Giambattista Vico among others (Vico, 1948). In linguistics today, by contrast, this way of thinking about the origins of language—usually termed "sound symbolism" (Hinton, Nichols, & Ohala, 1998)—is generally rejected, in favor of the claim that the relationship of words to their meanings is entirely arbitrary (e.g., Saussure, 1966).

The example of the Coelbren serves as a reminder, though, that whether or not sound symbolism played any role in the origin of language, it has certainly been put to work after the fact in a range of cultural contexts. Just as *kotodama* has had a significant role in shaping aspects of Japanese thought and practice concerning language, the sound symbolism of the Coelbren may well have helped shape nineteenth-century Welsh poetry, and of course it also has potential applications in the work of Druids today.

The traditional meanings of the sixteen ancient Coelbren letters are as follows. I have based the paragraphs below on the commentary in John Williams ab Ithel's *Dosparth Edeyrn Davod Aur* (1856, pp. 13–20).

## A

This power is uttered by opening the lips, and the interior part of the mouth, moderately and evenly, and breathing firmly, freely, and steadily from the larynx, while the tongue rests in its natural situation, at the bottom of the mouth. By this oral gesture, and this open, uninterrupted sound, men may be conceived naturally and spontaneously to have expressed the ideas of a tendency forwards—positive continuance in a uniform state, whether of motion, of action, or of rest. Its Bardic name is A, which in Welsh means "and," suggesting continuation.

## E

Let this power be uttered immediately after, or alternately with, an open A, and it will be found that all the organs of speech retain the same position, except that your tongue is now bent forcibly toward the root of the palate, as if it were intended by nature to arrest or check the egress and free passage of breath. It is therefore diametrically opposite to A. Instead of representing uniform and free continuance of motion or agency, a direct and positive state or tendency, it seems naturally to express a sudden check, motion, or act interrupted or broken, an indirect, distorted, or negative state or tendency. Its Bardic name is E, which in Welsh is a prefix that reverses what comes after it; for example, *ang* is "narrow, confined," but *eang* is "open, spacious."

## I

In uttering this tone or sound, the tongue is thrust forwards till it rests on the lower teeth, at the same time as it closes the whole interior of the mouth, except a confined and a direct passage for breath along the middle of the palate. By this oral gesture and the sound it produces might be naturally described the application or direction of a thing to its proper object or place: a being or becoming appropriate or internal, or that which approaches, or is applicable, subordinate, or inherent. Its Bardic name is I, which means "to" or "into" in Welsh.

## O

In uttering this power alternately with the preceding, the organs of speech entirely reverse their position. The tongue which, in pronouncing I, advanced to the teeth, almost closed up the mouth, and confined the breath to a direct and narrow passage is now retracted; it retires from the palate, and leaves the way open. The lips at the same time are forcibly projected outwards, with a large and circular opening. The whole mouth is thus adjusted, as nature itself would dispose it, for the act of vomiting, or casting forth. By this gesture and its correspondent sound, an idea diametrically opposed to that of I would be spontaneously expressed—a casting, yielding, or putting forth—an emanation or projection from a certain thing, instead of application, direction, or relation to a particular object. Its Bardic name is O, which in Welsh means "from" or "out of."

## B

This articulation is formed by an easy and natural opening of the mouth, without any forcible impulse of breath, or protrusion of the lips or any other vocal organ.[36] It may therefore be naturally applied to express the idea of simple perception—the being of any thing in a quiescent state or condition, and hence receive the following appropriations—being, to be, thing, or what is, condition or state of being. Its Bardic name is Bi, which in Welsh means "will be."

## C

This letter is pronounced by fixing the root of the tongue firmly against the root of the palate, so as entirely to fill and close up the interior part of the mouth, until breath forces its way with strong impulse. Such an oral gesture and its correspondent sound naturally attend every effort to hold or contain a large mass with both arms, and also to catch, reach, or touch a distant object. This term, therefore, is not limited to the expression of one simple idea, but naturally describes a holding, containing, or comprehending—a reaching, touching, or catching—attaining to, or apprehending. Its Bardic name is Ci, which in Welsh means "dog," in reference to a dog's aptitude to catch and hold. (This is pronounced "kee," not "see"—C in Welsh is always pronounced like K, never like S.)

## D

The articulation of this letter is formed and uttered by closing the edges of the tongue to the upper gums throughout their whole extent, and suddenly laying it open. We may, therefore, consider this power as descriptive naturally of expanding, spreading, unfolding, laying open, distribution, or division. Its Bardic name is Di, an old term for deity, also for day—what unfolds, lays open.

---

[36] This is less true in American English than in Welsh, as most American speakers tend to aspirate B—that is, let out a puff of air when saying the "B" sound.

## G

In hugging a substance with the arms, and as it were forcibly adhering to it, we acquire additional power by placing the tongue in the same position as that in which the letter C is pronounced, but as this action is of a less protrusive nature than that of catching or holding, breath is not propelled with new force, and the sound of G is produced. It may then be considered to have a natural aptitude to describe the ideas of appetite, a grasp, adhesion, mutual attachment, compensation. Its Bardic name is Gi, which means a sinew or tendon—the cause of connection and cohesion in the joints. (G in Welsh is always pronounced hard, as in "give," rather than soft, as in "genius.")

## L

This power, whether expressed as in English words, or aspirated, as in the Welsh Ll, is formed by fixing the tip of the tongue against the upper gums, while both sides of it hang open, suffering the air to be poured out and equally dispersed through all the extremities of the mouth. Such an act of the vocal organs naturally accompanies the act of throwing open the hand and the arms, to describe solution, effusion, evanescence, open space, gliding, softness, smoothness, lightness. Its Bardic name is Li, which conveys the ideas above specified, as in the Welsh word *lli*, "flood, stream."

## M

If it were attempted to describe naturally, by means of the organs of speech, that one substance was entirely shut up, enclosed, and comprehended in another, the lips would close together, the cheeks would swell moderately into the imitation of capacity, and breath would endeavor to attract notice by sounding the power of M through the nostrils. M is therefore a natural expression of comprehending, embracing, or surrounding. Its Bardic name is Mi, that which is in, or identical to, myself.

## N

When we put forth the hand, or extend the finger, to discriminate a simple or minute object, the eye is naturally directed the same way; we look steadfastly at that which we wish another to observe. The tongue at that same instant spontaneously mimics the action of the hand and the eye, by thrusting forth its point in the same direction till it rests against the upper gums. The breath, being denied a passage through the mouth, tends toward the same spot, through the nostrils, with the sound of N. This sound is then a natural interjection for "Look!" or "Lo there!" and is naturally answered by M, "I observe or comprehend." We may thus regard the power N as a natural expression of an object, subject, thing produced or new, discriminated or simplified—the self-same, simple, and small. Its Bardic name is Ni, which primarily means a particular thing.

## P

A person desirous of communicating the idea of pushing would place his body in an inclining posture, his hands would be protruded, his lips pressed together and forced outwards, as in the very act of the impulse described, and the puffing sound of P would be uttered. The most obvious gesture also to convey the idea of plumpness, protuberance, or convexity, is to swell and puff out the cheeks, till the articulation is produced. P may therefore be regarded as naturally descriptive of springing, putting forth, pushing, penetrating, prominence, convexity. Its name in the Bardic alphabet is Pi, which signifies the magpie. It is the root of the Welsh words *pic*, "dart," *pig*, "beak," and *pid*, "point."

## Ff

In uttering this sound, the organs of speech are not put into complete contact at the point of articulation, as in the case of P. Some portion of breath escapes, and vibrates in the interstice. It accordingly expresses ideas of agency or cause, of like nature with, but less powerful than the preceding. Its Bardic name is Ffi, which signifies the act of casting off or putting forth.

## R

This sound is produced by fixing the sides of the tongue firmly against those of the palate, and forcing out the breath in front, so as to cause a rough and strong vibration between the tip of the tongue and the upper gums. Its mechanical production is a direct contrast to that of L. By this energetic power the first linguists would naturally describe force, prevalence, or superiority; a motion or action performed by main strength—rubbing, tearing, pervading, breaking. Its Bardic name is Ri, which implies a king, a chief, a ruler. Taken too far, it implies the Welsh word *rhy*, which means "too much, excess."

S

When someone designs naturally to point out some particular object so as not to attract general observation, the point of the tongue drops downwards and rests against the lower teeth. The upper teeth close over it, as it were, to conceal the unavowed design, and the low, insinuating, hissing sound of S is produced. This power is therefore naturally descriptive of secret discernment, insinuation, a private marking, and distinguishing. Its Bardic name is Si (pronounced "she"), which appears in such Welsh words as *siarad*, "talk," and *sibrwd*, "whisper, murmur."

T

In tugging or drawing a line forcibly, the tongue is applied firmly and spontaneously to the forepart of the palate or upper gums, and forces out a vehement articulation of T. This power therefore naturally describes tension, drawing, or straining, in whatever manner; extension, stretching, or drawing out; intension, or drawing tight or close; drawing a line or bound around anything—confining, straitening, limiting, circumscribing. Its Bardic name is Ti, which occurs in Welsh words such as *tid*, "chain," and *tidaw*, "to tether, tie, or confine."

## The uses of the Coelbren

Barring a prolonged paper shortage, it's unlikely that the Coelbren of the Bards will ever again be necessary as a writing system for everyday use. The potential value of a symbolic alphabet, however, is not limited to such quotidian tasks. Many systems of esoteric spirituality rely on symbolic scripts of one form or another for a variety of theoretical and practical purposes; the use of the Hebrew alphabet in the Cabala and the runes in Norse and Germanic spirituality will be familiar to many readers. The Coelbren of the Bards, with its sound symbolism and its close links to the traditions of the Druid Revival, can serve similar purposes in today's Druidry.

It might be noted that the modern Druid tradition already has one symbolic alphabet, the Ogham letters of medieval Irish tradition. The bards of nineteenth-century Wales were familiar with the Ogham and its symbolism, and one source from that period suggested that the tree-symbolism in Taliesin's poem "Cad Goddeu" was a reference to the Irish alphabet (Williams ab Ithel, 1856, pp. 19–20). Both scripts, along with others such as the Alphabet of Nemnivius (Williams ab Ithel, 1856, pp. 10–11), seem to have had a place in Druid Revival symbolism in the nineteenth century.

There is, after all, no law restricting a spiritual tradition to only one symbolic alphabet. Many branches of Japanese esoteric spirituality, for example, use both *kotodama*—the system of occult phonology mentioned earlier, which is based on the 50-character *kana* syllabary—and the Siddham script introduced from Indian sources as part of Buddhist lore; each of these fills a different role in the broader context of Japanese esotericism. The Ogham and Coelbren have very different styles of symbolism; the Ogham derives its meaning from the phenomena of the natural world, the Coelbren from basic conceptual categories represented in sound symbolism. A case can be made that the two are thus complementary, and both have their place in modern Druidry.

Mention a symbolic alphabet in alternative-spirituality circles these days, and the first thought that comes to many minds is whether it can be used as an oracle for divination. Not only can the Coelbren be used in this manner, there's some reason to believe that it was so used. The word *coel*, which forms the first half of Coelbren and Coelfain, means "belief, trust, confidence" in modern Welsh, but its meaning in the medieval Welsh that Iolo and his fellow bards studied so closely was something rather more specific: "omen." The Coelbren are, strictly speaking, "omen sticks," and the Coelfain are "omen stones."

Thus it's at least possible that nineteenth-century Welsh Bardic circles used stones or pieces of wood marked with the Bardic alphabet to cast divinatory reading, along something like the same lines as a modern rune reading. The meanings of the sixteen ancient letters given above provide a good starting point for work with the divinatory Coelbren, and the meanings of the eight remaining of the twenty-four letters of the modern Coelbren can be worked out from first principles following the examples given above.[37] In much the same way, the Coelbren can be applied to other forms of practice appropriate to contemporary Druid spirituality, given the necessary investment of time and effort. I hope to contribute to this process, and welcome other efforts along these lines.

## *References*

Bagley, R. W. (2004). Anyang writing and the origin of the Chinese writing system. In: Houston, S. D., *The First Writing: Script Invention as History and Process* (pp. 190–249). Cambridge: Cambridge University Press.

Bardon, F. (1971). *The Key to the True Quabbalah*. Wuppertal, Germany: Dieter Rüggeberg.

Constantine, M. A. (2007). *The Truth against the World: Iolo Morganwg and Romantic Forgery*. Cardiff, UK: University of Wales Press.

de Mille, R. W. (1980). *The Don Juan Papers: Further Castaneda Controversies*. Santa Barbara, CA: Ross-Erikson.

de Saussure, F. (1966). *Course in General Linguistics*. W. Baskin (Trans.). New York: McGraw-Hill.

Gleason, W. (1995). *The Spiritual Foundations of Aikido*. Rochester, VT: Destiny.

Greer, J. M. (2014). The Myth of Einigan. *Trilithon, 1*: pp. 19–26.

Hinton, L., Nichols, J., & Ohala, J. J. (Eds.) (1998). *Sound Symbolism*. New York: Harcourt Brace College.

Jenkins, G. H. (Ed.) (2005). *A Rattleskull Genius: The Many Faces of Iolo Morganwg*. Cardiff, UK: University of Wales Press.

Lomer, G. (1997). *Seven Hermetic Letters*. G. Hanswille & F. Gallo (Trans.). Salt Lake City, UT: Merkur.

National Museum of Wales (2014). Coelbren y Beirdd—The Bardic Alphabet. http://museumwales.ac.uk/en/888/ (accessed 22 December 2014).

Senner, W. (1989). Introduction. In: W. Senner (Ed.), *The Origins of Writing* (pp. 1–26). Lincoln, NB: University of Nebraska Press.

Tolkien, J. R. R. (1965). *The Return of the King*. New York: Ballantine.

Vico, G. (1948). *The New Science of Giambattista Vico*. T. G. Bergin & M. H. Fisch (Trans.). Ithaca, NY: Cornell University Press.

Williams, H. (2004). Reasons for runes. In: Houston, S. D., *The First Writing: Script Invention as History and Process* (pp. 262–273). Cambridge: Cambridge University Press.

Williams, T. (Ed.) (1848). *The Iolo Manuscripts*. Llandovery, UK: William Rees.

---

[37] A book-length work along these lines is in preparation as of this writing. [It was published in 2017 as *The Coelbren Alphabet*.]

Williams ab Ithel, J. (Ed. & Trans.) (1856). *Dosparth Edeyrn Davod Aur, or, The Ancient Welsh Grammar*. London: Longman.

Williams ab Ithel, J. (Ed. & Trans.) (2004). *The Barddas of Iolo Morganwg*. York Beach, ME: Weiser.

# The fourth quaternio

*Jungian symbolism in the sphere of protection*

*Another essay for* Trilithon, *this paper focuses on the early history of the Ancient Order of Druids in America, examining the work of an earlier Grand Archdruid and finding traces of Jungian symbolism in one of the core rituals of the AODA tradition. In the process of writing it, I began an intensive exploration of Jung's work that continues at present.*

Alternative spiritual traditions tend to leave faint tracks in the sands of history. Plenty of organizations that once counted members in the thousands or tens of thousands have vanished with next to no trace, taking their histories and teachings with them. Had the Ancient Order of Druids in America (AODA) not managed an improbable revival in the first decade of the present century, that same fate would almost certainly have happened to its history and teachings—and as it is, an enormous amount has been lost despite that last-minute reprieve.

When I became the order's seventh Grand Archdruid in 2003, very little AODA material survived outside the memories of a handful of elderly initiates. Archdruid Emeritus Betty Jean McCloud Reeves's history of the order,[38] written not long before her passing, was one of the few sources of historical data we had, and many of the details have proved difficult or impossible to confirm. It took me ten years of research, for example, to find solid documentary evidence that Dr. Juliet Ashley, the third Grand Archdruid of AODA and the creator of most of its current rituals and teachings, actually existed.[39] Again, this sort of thing is far from unusual in the history of alternative spirituality, but it makes life interesting for those of us who are absorbed in chasing down the facts of our order's past.

Where direct evidence is unavailable, though, indirect evidence can sometimes fill in a gap here and there. It so happens that one claim about Ashley told me by several of AODA's elderly members in the early days of my involvement has a certain amount of indirect evidence to back it up—and investigating that claim led straight to a source that casts unexpected light on one of the basic practices of the AODA tradition.

## A Jungian connection?

According to two of the order's past archdruids, the late Betty Reeves ("Mother Betty" to all her associates in the order) and John Gilbert, Dr. Juliet Ashley made her living as a hypnotist, lay psychotherapist, and teacher of alternative spirituality, and in the years following the Second World War served as the presiding officer of a series of interlinked initiatory orders, including AODA. Some years before, in the late 1930s, she traveled to Europe, where among other things she is supposed to have studied with the famous psychologist Dr. Carl Jung.

I have not yet been able to determine whether this actually happened, for the inquiries I've made so far have not turned up any record of Ashley among Jung's known American students. It's entirely possible, of course, that Ashley studied in a less formal manner; she could, for example, have visited Zurich, where Jung taught and practiced, and taken in a lecture or two by Jung himself or one of his students, but it's also possible that the entire story was an invention of hers, or of some of her students. It would not be the first time, or the hundred and first,

---

[38] Available online at http://aoda.org/AODA_History.html.
[39] The evidence finally surfaced in a book of new age philosophy written by a friend of hers. See Keyes, Elizabeth, *Living Can Be Fun* (Denver, CO: Gentle Living, 1968), p. 89.

that a teacher of alternative spirituality cooked up a colorful story to give his or her students more faith in the teachings they were receiving.

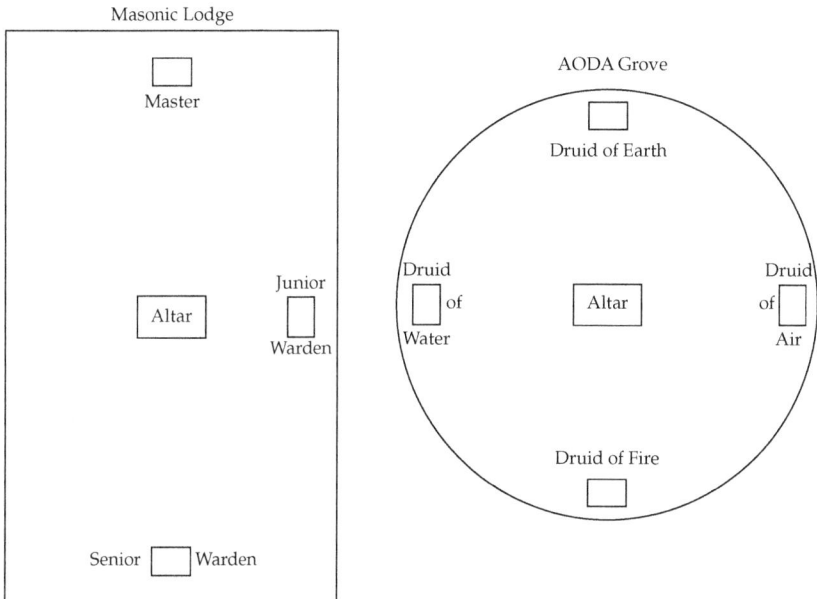

That Ashley had at least some knowledge of Jungian psychology, though, seemed likely even before I began serious research into the possibility. In their original form, the AODA initiation rituals were closely modeled on those of Freemasonry, with three main officers—in a Masonic lodge, these are the Master, the Senior Warden, and the Junior Warden, and sit in the east, west, and south of the lodge respectively— and three degrees of initiation. Jungian theory, however, considers most threefold patterns to be unbalanced, and considers fourfold symmetry to be a sign of psychological wholeness. Jung's essay on mandala symbolism is thus full of circles divided into four equal parts, or with four equidistant points marked around the circumference. Ashley's revision of the AODA rituals thus transformed the Druidical grove into a Jungian mandala, with four officers equally spaced around a circle and four elemental symbols placed on the central altar, and added a preliminary Candidate initiation to bring the number of rituals up to four. It's hard to dismiss the possibility that this revision could have been influenced by a study of Jung's work.

Possibility is not proof, however, and there were other sources from which Ashley might have gotten the idea of a fourfold circle as the basic template for AODA grove work. To make a stronger case for a direct connection between the AODA tradition and Jung's psychology, something far more distinctively Jungian would have to be located in the teachings of the order. As it happens, though, exactly such a telltale clue can be found in one of the core AODA practices—the Sphere of Protection.

The version of the Sphere of Protection practiced by AODA members at present was created by past archdruid John Gilbert in the early 1970s, as part of his doctor of divinity studies with Universal Seminary, a divinity school then connected with AODA by way of the Universal Gnostic Church. The original version created by Juliet Ashley, however, survives in the AODA initiation rituals, especially the Candidate ceremony, and the Grove opening and closing ceremonies. A comparison with these shows that Gilbert's revisions did not change the basic spatial structure of the Sphere of Protection, which is the detail relevant to this paper.

The Sphere of Protection differs from more commonly used protective rituals such as the Lesser Ritual of the Pentagram in that it includes the third dimension.[40] When casting the Sphere, the practitioner invokes the powers of air to the east, fire to the south, water to the west, and earth to the north, as done in most rituals of the same kind. Once this is done, though, the practitioner also invokes Spirit Above, Spirit Below, and Spirit Within to provide a vertical axis.

The result is as shown in diagram 2.

The Sphere of Protection is not unique to AODA; it is (or was until recently) practiced as a significant part of the training program of all the magical traditions that were headed by Juliet Ashley in the 1950s and 1960s. This is all the more striking in that its spatial structure closely duplicates that of an important theme in Carl Jung's later work—the system of quaternios in his late work *Aion: Researches into the Phenomenology of the Self*.

---

[40] For a detailed account of the Sphere of Protection as currently used by AODA, see Greer, John Michael, *The Druid Magic Handbook* (York Beach, ME: Weiser, 2007).

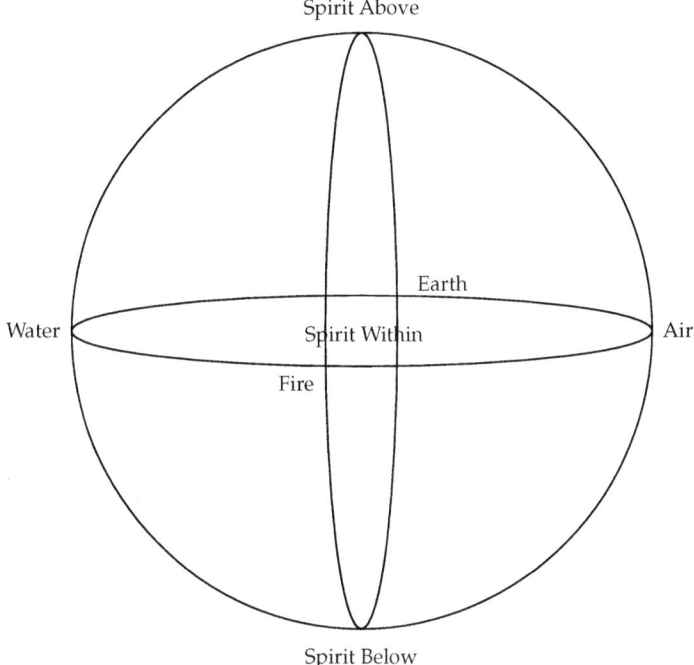

*The four quaternios*

Some grasp of the basic concepts of Jungian psychology will be necessary to make sense of what follows. To summarize an intricate theory all too briefly, Jung proposed that the conscious personality—in his terminology, the ego—is only one portion of the whole psyche, and far from the most important part at that. In addition to the ego, the psyche contains the shadow, which consists of everything in the psyche that the ego refuses to accept; the anima (in a man's psyche) or animus (in a woman's psyche), which sums up the psychological potentials of the opposite gender; and the Self, which is the latent center of the entire psyche, equivalent to the Higher Self of many schools of mysticism. Surrounding all these are many other archetypes, basic structures of consciousness in the psyche, which are the inner reflections of human instincts and thus form a psychological framework shared by all human beings irrespective of culture or race.

The goal of Jungian therapy is the process of individuation, by which the ego comes to terms with the existence of these other forces in the psyche and enters into healthy relationships with them, so that the ego as the part of the psyche that deals with the outside world can draw on the resources of the whole psyche, and conversely the whole psyche can seek the fulfillment of its needs through the ego. Broadly speaking, the process of individuation Jung outlines in the pages of *Aion* proceeds in the order just sketched out: first the ego grapples with the shadow, then it interacts with the anima or animus, then it enters into relationship with the Self and the whole world of archetypes reflected in the Self.[41]

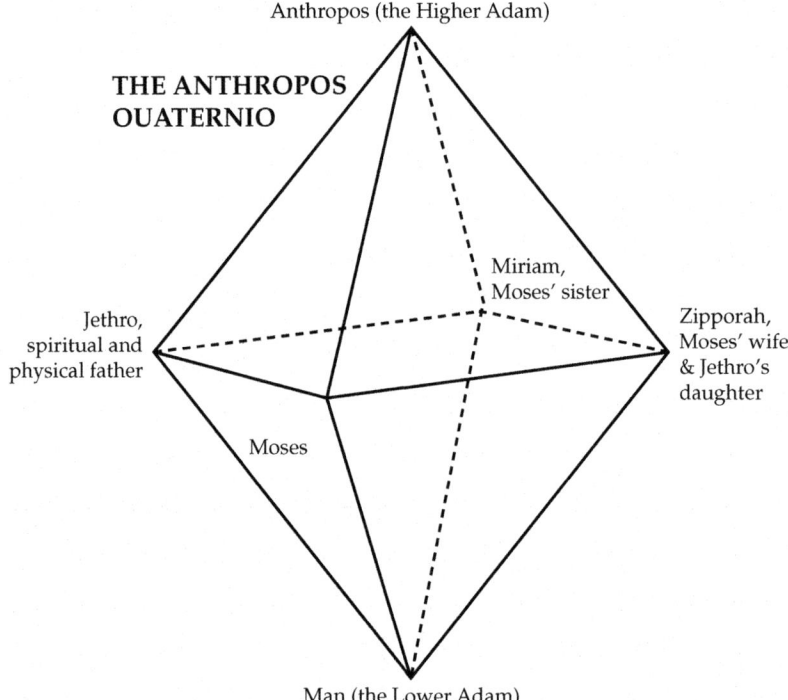

---

[41] See Jung, Carl, *Aion: Researches into the Phenomenology of the Self*, trans. R. F. C. Hull (Princeton, NJ: Princeton University Press, 1969), pp. 222–265. I have also drawn extensively on Stein, Leslie, *Becoming Whole: Jung's Equation for Realizing God* (New York: Helios Press, 2012) in the discussion that follows.

Each step along this route shares a common archetypal structure, which Jung diagrams geometrically as a quaternio—that is, a set of four archetypal images that unfold together from a common origin and then coalesce again into a common result. The first of these, which Jung called the Anthropos quaternio, is typical of the ego before it begins the process of individuation. Jung's discussion of this and the next stage in *Aion* relies extensively on symbolism borrowed by the ancient Gnostics from the Old Testament, and this isn't especially relevant to the present theme. The point that deserves attention here is that the Anthropos quaternio shows how the unseen self (here the Anthropos, or Higher Adam) expresses itself in consciousness as a set of archetypes: the wise old man (Jethro the Midianite priest), the virgin priestess (Miriam, sister of Moses), the lover and wife (Zipporah, daughter of Jethro), and the ego itself, seen through the rose-colored lenses usual among those who have not yet encountered the shadow.[42]

All of these archetypes are projected onto people in the outside world: the individual's father, or some other older male role model, may be identified with the wise old man, the lover and wife with some actual woman the individual desires, and so on. At this stage the ego has not yet realized that its value judgments and interpretations are subjective, and insists on seeing them as objective qualities of the world around it. Thus the apparent fourfold pattern draws together into a unity, whom Jung identified with the mythic figure of Adam.

The next stage, the Shadow quaternio, takes these same archetypes and transforms them into their hostile and negative equivalents. Here again, the symbolism Jung used comes from ancient Gnostic sources commenting on stories from the Old Testament, and can be passed over for the present. What happens in this phase is that each of the archetypal characters displays its unpleasant side: the wise old man suddenly becomes a tyrannical and superstitious old fool, say, the lover and wife becomes the unfaithful femme fatale or the nagging harridan, and so on. The person who has this experience can run away from it by abandoning his or her existing relationships and projecting the positive side of the archetypes onto someone else; some people spend their

---

[42] Though Jung doesn't actually discuss this point, his model is specifically relevant to the heterosexual male psyche; a corresponding model of the heterosexual female psyche would reverse the gender signs, with a wise old woman and so forth. Other gender polarities have their own archetypal patterns.

entire lives this way, running from one failed relationship to the next, because it never occurs to them that both the desirable and unwanted qualities they see in the other person are projections out of their own psychological structure.

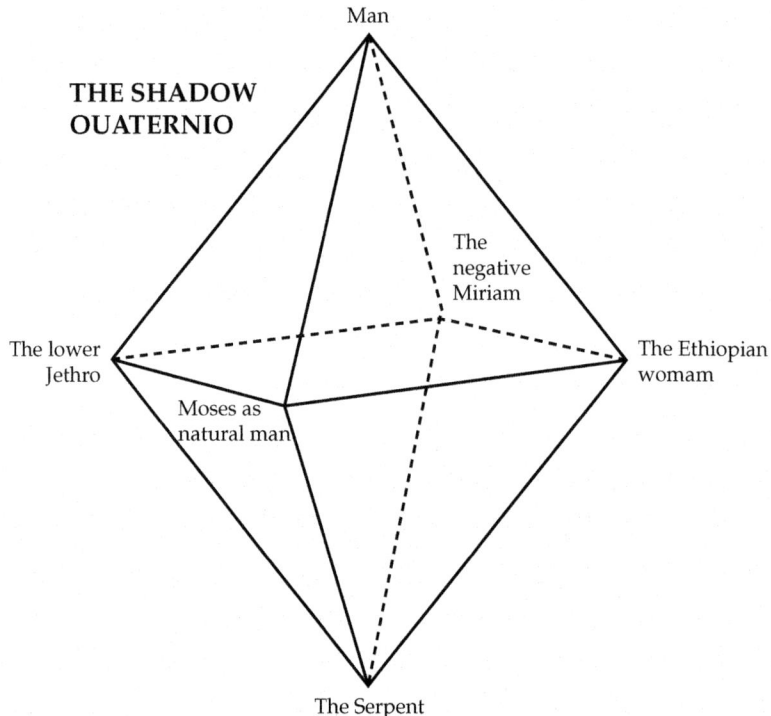

The alternative is to recognize that these archetypal qualities don't actually belong to the people onto whom they're projected. The elderly friend, for example, was neither as wise nor as foolish as he appeared when seen through the distorting glasses of a projected archetype, and so on. Once this realization occurs, the quaternio draws together once again into a unity: the serpent of the myth of Genesis, the emblem of projection and deceit.

The third quaternio, the Paradise quaternio, then unfolds. The four archetypal forces are recognized at this stage as processes rather than persons, a transformation which makes it much easier to keep from projecting them onto other people. At this stage a relationship with an actual person, uncontaminated with archetypal projections, for the first time

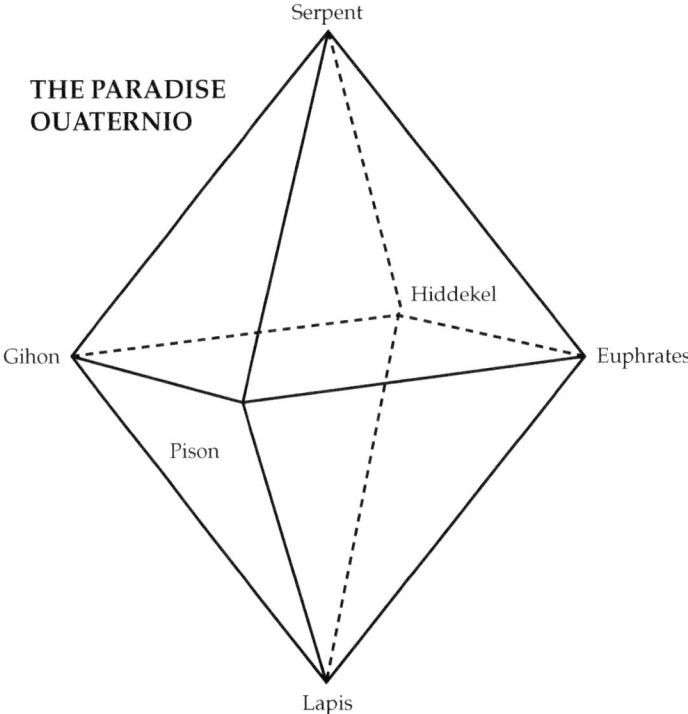

becomes a possibility. The symbolism of Paradise, with its implied reference to Adam and Eve, is obviously relevant here, and the four archetypes of the quaternio thus take their names from the four rivers of Paradise in Jewish legend.

This is the stage in which the anima or animus, the contra-sexual archetype, has to be encountered and brought into a balanced relationship with the ego. Jung suggested that the traditional idea of the poet as inspired by a muse, a feminine spiritual power who embodied the poet's creativity, is a precise reflection of the experience of interacting with the anima, and proposed that an equivalent process accounts for the idea, just as common in religious traditions, of a spiritual marriage between a female mystic and a male deity. More broadly, this stage marks the point in the process of individuation when the ego can begin to relate to the archetypes as inner realities rather than outward projections. As this process unfolds, the quaternio draws together yet again into a unity: the Lapis, the alchemical stone, which is an emblem of the Self.

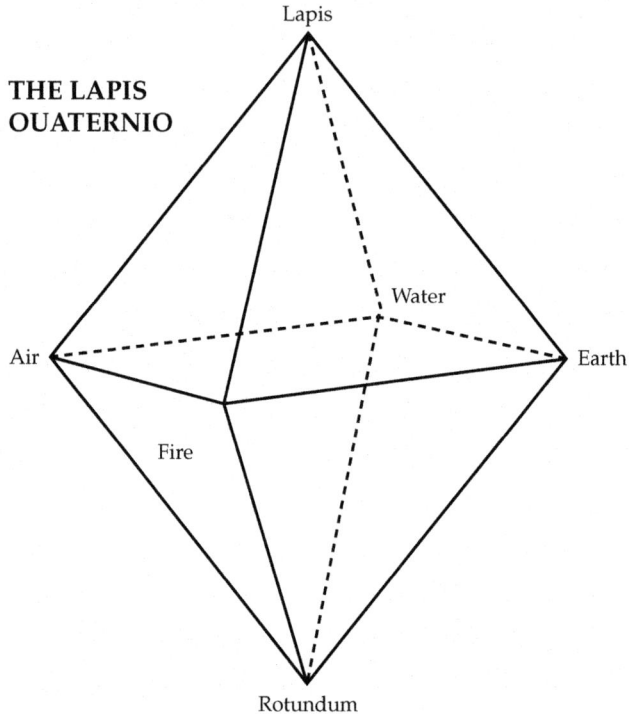

**THE LAPIS QUATERNIO**

The fourth quaternio, the Lapis quaternio, then unfolds from the Lapis. Jung identified its four powers as the traditional elements of alchemy, fire, air, water, and earth, the ingredients of the alchemical stone. At this stage of the individuation process, the ego finds its proper place as an element of the psyche, and the four elements then draw together a final time to become the Rotundum, the fully individuated Self. The Lapis quaternio, though, has another significance for those who know their way around the traditions of the Ancient Order of Druids in America or its sister orders: It is mirrored almost precisely in the spatial structure of the Sphere of Protection, as may be seen readily by comparing Diagram 2 to Diagram 6.

## *The sphere of protection*

What this implies, in turn, is that Juliet Ashley may have intended the original form of the Sphere of Protection as a way of helping to catalyze the process of individuation in initiates of the orders she led.

That suggestion makes sense in terms of Jungian psychology; Jung's patients, after all, were encouraged to use painting and other arts to give concrete form to the contents of their inner lives. Jung himself insisted that such exercises only had the desired effect when they happened spontaneously,[43] but magical traditions emphatically contradict his claim. What, after all, is a talisman, if not a mandala symbol deliberately created for the purpose of bringing about specific changes in someone's inner or outer life?

In exactly the same way, the deliberate and regularly repeated enactment of the Lapis quaternio using the performing art of magical ritual could quite conceivably have been intended to help constellate, as Jung liked to say, the desired endpoint of the individuation process. Whether this was an appropriate activity in terms of orthodox Jungian therapy is of course beside the question, for no one to my knowledge has ever claimed that Juliet Ashley was an orthodox Jungian or, for that matter, orthodox in any other sense. She had her own distinctive approach to spirituality and the quest for psychological wholeness, and within that approach, a borrowing from Jung's theory of individuation makes perfect sense.

At least two consequences follow from the likelihood that the Sphere of Protection was at least partly influenced by the fourth, or Lapis, quaternio that Jung described in *Aion*. The first, obviously enough, is that it might well be worth exploring other aspects of AODA tradition with an eye for other borrowings from Jung, or from important writers of the first generation or so of Jungian theorists such as Marie-Louise von Franz. Exactly what such an exploration might turn up is anyone's guess, but if other connections can be identified, the result would be a clearer sense of AODA's descent from the psychological and spiritual traditions of the twentieth century, and thus a clarification of its history.

A second consequence relates to the present and future of AODA rather than its past. If the Sphere of Protection was in fact modeled on Jung's Lapis quaternio, as part of a general revision of the order's work inspired by Jung, the entire body of Jungian psychology becomes a resource for further expansions and developments of the still somewhat

---

[43] See Jung, Carl, "Concerning Mandala Symbolism," in *The Archetypes and the Collective Unconscious*, trans. R. F. C. Hull (Princeton, NJ: Princeton University Press, 1969), pp. 355–384.

fragmentary body of theory and practice AODA offers its initiates. In order to reach a destination, it helps a great deal to know where one is going; if the goal (or at least one potential goal) of initiation and spiritual practice in the AODA tradition is understood as individuation, in something like the sense Jung gave the word, a very broad field for the development of rituals, practices, and instructional materials would be opened up by that understanding.

# RELIGION AND OCCULTISM

# The god from the house of bread

*In 2008 I was invited to submit an essay for an anthology titled* Jesus Through Pagan Eyes, *which was published the following year. Looking back over the essay I wrote, I find the idea solid but the development less thorough than it should have been; if I were to rewrite it today, it would rely much less on Owen Morgan and much more on Carl Jung, on the one hand, and Ross Nichols's powerful but largely forgotten manifesto* The Cosmic Shape *on the other. Still, one of the advantages of hindsight is the freedom to see what should have happened.*

"I do not know much about gods," wrote T. S. Eliot in his poem "The Dry Salvages," "but I think that the river is a strong brown god."[44] He was a devout Anglican, but Eliot lived at a time when classical education and a self-confidence long since vanished from today's Christianity still gave Christian thinkers and creative minds room to allow Pagan religious metaphors free play in their work.

The same ease that allowed him and his Christian contemporaries to move at will between Pagan and Christian religious visions was just as common in the nascent Pagan scene of the time. Eliot's contemporary

---

[44] T. S. Eliot, *Four Quartets* (New York: Harcourt Brace Jovanovich, 1943), p. 35.

Dion Fortune, whose writings played a central role in the birth of modern Pagan spirituality, also wrote a work of Christian devotional literature—*Mystical Meditations on the Collects*[45]—without sensing, or being accused of, the least inconsistency. To Fortune, and in a different sense to Eliot as well, Christianity and Paganism were simply different ways of talking about spiritual realities and relationships that could not be reduced to a single symbolic formula.

Those times are unhappily long past. During the second half of the twentieth century, most Christian denominations in the Western world responded to the reemergence of Pagan religion by reviving centuries-old stereotypes of devil worship or, at best, restricting their efforts at interreligious dialogue to a narrow circle of "world religions" hedged in by definitions that exclude today's reborn Pagan faiths. Today it's almost impossible to imagine an Anglican poet anywhere this side of heresy wielding Pagan religious metaphors with Eliot's aplomb. The same narrowing of options can be found on the other side of the newly raised barrier, for that matter; Pagan writers nowadays are far more likely to pen extended diatribes about the misbehavior of Christian churches in the past than to explore, as Dion Fortune did, the interpenetration of Pagan and Christian religious experience.

It's anyone's guess when, or whether, this sorry state of affairs will end. Still, there are exceptions to the generalizations just made. Some Christians have made serious efforts to grasp the nature of Pagan religious consciousness, just as some Pagans have tried to understand Christianity as a valid religious expression that doesn't happen to be theirs. There are also those who feel called to a faith that blends Pagan and Christian traditions, and despite the hostility such ventures too often receive, their number is growing. From such initiatives, with luck and the blessing of the gods, a wider context of mutual tolerance and acceptance may someday arise.

My own background places me in a complex relationship to this hope. I am a Pagan even in the strictest Christian sense of the word; that is, I have not been baptized, nor have I ever belonged to a Christian church of any kind. I grew up in a comfortably secular milieu in one of the least religious parts of the United States; among the families on the block where I lived for much of my childhood, for example, only one went to church on Sundays.

---

[45] Dion Fortune, *Mystical Meditations on the Collects* (London: Aquarian Press, 1988).

When Christianity finally came to my attention, it was by way of the strident evangelical revival that swept over America in the late 1970s, and that movement's passion for dwelling on assorted motes in other people's eyes and ignoring the beams of intolerance, hypocrisy, and political opportunism in its own did not exactly encourage me to take Christianity seriously as a spiritual option. Instead, like much of my generation, I explored other paths—atheism, Asian religions, a handful of the new religious movements—before finding my spiritual home; in my case this was on the far end of the religious spectrum, in that branch of the alternative spiritual scene that embraces the name and draws on the inspiration of the ancient Druids.

The modern Druid movement has a complex and quirky history of its own, reaching back to the eighteenth century, when it evolved out of a collision between liberal Anglicanism, nature worship, and fragments of Celtic tradition.[46] It inherits from its origins a distrust of dogmatism that has made it a haven for eccentrics and a nightmare for would-be systematizers. Even so simple a question as the number of deities Druids worship—one, two, many, none—finds nearly as many answers as there are Druids. At the core of most visions of the contemporary Druid way, though, lies a sense that living nature is the least murky expression of the divine accessible to human beings. We may not agree about much else, but the shorthand creed drafted by one Druid tradition wins almost universal assent: "Nature is good."[47]

This apparent platitude has depths that may not appear to a casual glance. It's not a statement of fact, since nature routinely violates most conventional human ideas of goodness. Rather, it's the first postulate in a system of values. By taking living nature as our basic measure of the good, the qualities expressed by nature—wholeness, flow, spontaneity, elegance, and the like—become core values that can be expressed in the life of each Druid. Equally, the central role of nature in Druid thought makes symbols and imagery derived from nature equally central in contemporary Druid myth, ritual, and practice.

This may appear worlds apart from Christianity in its modern forms. In the hands of an almost forgotten tradition of nineteenth-century

---

[46] See John Michael Greer, *The Druidry Handbook* (Newburyport, MA: Weiser, 2006), pp. 9–43, for a history of the Druid Revival.
[47] This is the basic creed of the Reformed Druids of North America (RDNA). See David Frangquist, "Outline of the Foundation of Fundamentals," in Michael Scharding, ed., *A Reformed Druid Anthology* (Drynemetum Press, 2004), pp. 33–34.

Pagan thought, however, it forms an unexpected bridge crossing the chasm that now separates the religious visions of Paganism and Christianity.

Very few of today's Pagans, and even fewer contemporary Christians, have ever heard of the redoubtable Welsh author and Druid Owen Morgan. In his day, though, Morgan—Archdruid Morien of Pontypridd, to use his religious title—was a prominent figure on the far end of British spirituality, with a substantial following in Great Britain and the United States.[48] Those who like to imagine the Victorian era as a glacial landscape of conformity and sexual repression should stay far away from Morgan's writings, and especially his 1887 textbook of Druid philosophy and theology, *The Light in Britannia*, which argued that Christianity was a Pagan fertility cult.[49]

Morgan himself did not put the matter quite so baldly. He argued, rather, that the core of all true religion was the worship of the life force; that the most prominent emblems of the life force—in the macrocosm, Sun and Earth; in the microcosm, the male and female genitals; in both, the activities that give rise to new life—were the foundation of all religious symbolism, in Pagan as well as Christian traditions; and that Christianity was simply a restatement of the old Pagan gnosis of fertility and new life. He considered himself a good Christian as well as a Druid, and saw nothing inappropriate in attending church regularly; for him, after all, the church was a stone representation of the vagina of the Earth goddess, its portal facing east to welcome the virile and penetrating rays of the rising Sun: the Bride of Christ, in another symbolism, eagerly awaiting her heavenly bridegroom.

Ideas such as these were far from unique to Morgan, or for that matter to the Druidry of his time. Behind his book lay more than a century of pioneering explorations of the origins of human religion, and the rise of two major schools of thought—one arguing for an astrological and seasonal origin to religion and myth, the other tracing all religion and myth back to what was primly called "the worship of the generative powers"—that many alternative thinkers of his time were trying to reconcile.[50] Some of these had already taken the final, daring step of

---

[48] James Bonwick, *Irish Druids and Old Irish Religions* (repr. New York: Dorset Press, 1983), pp. 3–5.
[49] Morien (Owen Morgan), *The Light in Britannia* (Cardiff, UK: Daniel Owen, 1887).
[50] See Joscelyn Godwin, *The Theosophical Enlightenment* (Albany, NY: State University of New York Press, 1994) for a readable history of these schools of thought.

including Christianity in their syntheses, though none ever quite managed to equal Morgan's flair or his genius for deadpan humor. Despite this, Morgan's own cultural impact has gone surprisingly unnoticed. You can read any number of histories of the rise of modern Neopaganism, for example, and never learn that *The Light in Britannia* was the first modern expression of a fertility religion that places a single god, a single goddess, and their sexual relationship at the center of its spiritual vision—a pattern that became popular after its publication, and eventually took definitive form with Gerald Gardner's invention of Wicca.

The broader tradition of seasonal and sexual religious interpretation has had a little more visibility in recent times, not least because it helped shape important works of scholarship such as James Frazer's *The Golden Bough* and iconic cultural works such as T. S. Eliot's *The Waste Land*. Still, such interpretations have been unfashionable in scholarly circles for some decades now. This is unfortunate, for however overblown some of the old analyses may have been—and Morgan's were among the most colorful, it must be admitted—they capture a crucial factor in ancient Pagan religions that is also amply present in the origins of Christianity.

The "strong brown god" in Eliot's "The Dry Salvages," mentioned at the beginning of this essay, offers a useful starting place. To any Pagan in ancient times, Eliot's recognition was so obvious that it scarcely required mentioning. Of course rivers were deities—gods to the ancient Greeks, for example, and goddesses to the ancient Celts. Other natural phenomena were equally full of divinity. An ancient Greek who wanted to comment on wet weather would as likely as not say "Zeus is raining."

Whatever else Zeus was in classical Greek religion, in other words—and Pagan gods and goddesses were richly complex beings, impossible to pin down with simple definitions—he was always, in part, the sky as a conscious and potent divine being. Poseidon was similarly the ocean, Demeter the fertile earth, Aphrodite sexuality in all its forms, Pan the raw unhuman presence of wilderness, and so on. Even through the elegant literary constructions of late classical myth, it's not difficult to see each god and goddess as a distinct force of nature with its own power to shape the weaving of the fabric of human life.[51]

---

[51] For a useful exploration of these issues, see Philippe Borgeaud, *The Cult of Pan in Ancient Greece*, trans. Kathleen Atlass and James Redfield (Chicago, IL: University of Chicago Press, 1988), and Jon D. Mikalson, *Athenian Popular Religion* (Chapel Hill, NC: University of North Carolina Press, 1983).

The same principle applies in a different way to a class of beings the Greeks carefully distinguished from the gods—the heroes or demigods, who were born of loves between a god or goddess and a mortal. Each of these embodied one of the realms where the human and natural worlds fused into unity. The twelve labors of Heracles, for instance, echo precisely the seasonal movement of the Sun through the signs of the Zodiac as reflected in the agricultural cycle—compare Heracles's labors to the tasks of the Greek farmer as outlined, say, in Hesiod's *Works and Days*, and it's not too hard to make sense of the myth. Heracles, half god and half human, is the divine spirit of farming as what we would now call an ecosystem, half natural and half human, contending with its seasonal opponents, bringing treasures from the underworld, and then dying in the flames of the burning stubble to be reborn. The Greeks called Heracles "son of god" and "savior," and since their daily bread depended on him, this was entirely appropriate.

Another god whose cult thrived in the late classical world had the same titles, of course, and the parallels linking the myth of Jesus with the seasonal cycle of agriculture are at least as precise as those that can be traced in the myth of Heracles. Just as Heracles had his twelve labors, for instance, Jesus had his twelve disciples, whose connection with the signs of the zodiac has been a commonplace of Christian symbolism for many centuries.

Yet the mythic narratives that surround Jesus have the greater richness one would expect from the classical Levant, where fertility deities who die and rise again had been a commonplace of Pagan religious thought for thousands of years before the rise of ancient Greece. It's for this reason that Jesus is paired throughout his myth with his alter ego John the Baptist. The two mirror each other seasonally; Jesus is born at the winter solstice and dies in the spring, the harvest time in the eastern Mediterranean, suspended above the earth like the ripe grain on the stalk; John is born at the summer solstice and dies in the autumn, the planting time, beheaded in a prison beneath the earth, like the seed that goes to its burial behind the plowshare's iron blade. "He must increase," John says of Jesus, "while I must decrease."[52]

Evidence for this interpretation of Christian myth is abundant in the Bible and other early Christian sources. Jesus's traditional birthplace is in Bethlehem, for example, a town whose name literally means "house

---

[52] John 3:30.

of bread" in Hebrew, and the central act of traditional Christian ritual centers on eating the bread that is Jesus's body and drinking the wine that is his blood. (John has no similar ritual attributed to him, since one does not eat the seed corn or the rootstock of the grapevine.) "I have come that they might have life," Jesus says in the Bible, "and that they might have it more abundantly;"[53] any other fertility deity could have said as much, and it's only the intellectual distance that separates us from the context of early Christianity that makes so many people nowadays think that the "life" Jesus spoke of is a spiritual abstraction.

Christianity, it must be remembered, had its birth in the bustling spiritual marketplace of the classical Mediterranean world, where religious metaphors of this sort were commonplaces of contemporary thought. The mystery religions, which offered salvation to those who sought union with a god or a goddess through rituals of initiation and communion, were among the most powerful religious forces of the time, and nearly all of them focused on exactly this kind of agricultural symbolism. Thus it's hardly a leap to suggest, as so many scholars of myth have suggested, that the precise parallels between Christianity and the other mystery religions, and the rich agricultural symbolism of Christianity itself, show that the original Christian faith may well have been something not far from what Owen Morgan claimed it to be: a mystery cult venerating the life force in nature, expressed through a rich mythic symbolism, that became associated through a complex historical process with the events of the life and death of an otherwise obscure Jewish religious reformer.

The relationship between the mythic role assigned to Jesus and the sparse historical traces left by his life is a challenging issue for many modern versions of Christianity. Some theologies refuse to draw any distinction between myth and history—if the Bible says that Jesus rose into heaven, according to these interpretations, then that's what happened, and if television reporters had been there, they could have filmed it for the eleven o'clock news. Others draw a distinction between the "Jesus of history" and the "Christ of faith," though data on the former is so sparse that it can be, and has been, redefined to fit any of a dizzying assortment of modern agendas. Still others have come to reject the idea that a historical Jesus existed in the first place.

---

[53] John 10:10.

If Christianity was originally a mystery cult focused on the life force, though, these confusions evaporate. Whatever historical reality might have formed the kernel around which the Jesus myth emerged—and in all probability no one will ever know what that reality was—the spiritual meaning of the myth is not dependent on that reality. In Morgan's sense, there is no question as to the factual nature of the resurrection of Jesus, since it takes place in every sunrise and in the sprouting of every seed. The historical figure around which the myth coalesced is simply not that important; there was doubtless some dimly remembered historical figure at the root of the myth of Heracles, too.

The claim that Christianity's dying and resurrected god was a historical person who lived in the very recent past, rather than a wholly mythic figure, played an important role historically in giving the newborn Christian church an edge over its competitors. When the fall of Rome dragged the classical world to ruin, however, the elegant mythic metaphors that had made Christianity the most successful of the Pagan mystery religions were reinterpreted in blindly literal terms. Later on, in the Reformation and afterward, these metaphors lost the last of their original meaning, and were transformed into bloodless ideologies completely detached from the seasonal and vegetative context that once gave them their power.

Nowadays, the obscure historical figure around whose life the original core of mythic narratives clustered lies in the distant past, and attempts to force a literal meaning out of those narratives have long since crossed over into absurdity. The widespread modern notion of the Rapture, in which believing Christians will soon be beamed up to heaven by some miraculous equivalent of *Star Trek*'s transporter beams, is a troubling case in point. It's a lightly disguised fantasy of mass suicide—when someone tells their children that Grandma has gone to heaven to be with Jesus, most people understand what that means—and its popularity suggests that the conflict between overly literal interpretations of Christianity's exuberant seasonal myths and the awkward solidity of a world that refuses to fit those interpretations may finally have become too great for many Christians to bear.

Efforts to reconnect Christianity with its origins as a mystery religion of life and fertility have been going on for more than two centuries now, and might have succeeded in revitalizing the old myths and rituals, except for one detail: Nearly all these attempts aimed at discrediting Christianity as just another Pagan fertility cult, and therefore unworthy of respect.[54] It took a believer in a different Pagan fertility cult, Owen Morgan, to realize that the equation could be worked the other way. He saw, as a handful of visionaries since his time have seen, that the ancient worship of the life force is a potent and valid spiritual option in its own right, and that Christian ritual and symbols can readily carry this primal constellation of meanings.

It is only fair to say that many other interpretations of Christianity are possible; many people will find some other way of approach to the Christian faith more relevant to their own spiritual lives, and many others will find no need to approach the Christian faith at all. Central to the old Paganism was the realization that different people are called to worship different deities, and the corresponding sense that each person has the right and the duty to pursue his or her own religious path within a context of respect and toleration for the deities of others. Still, for those who feel drawn to the rituals and symbolism of Christianity, the vision of Jesus as an image of the ever-returning life force, and of Christianity as a mystery cult that need not conflict with a wider reverence for the divine presence in the world, may offer unexpected possibilities.

---

[54] See the discussion in Godwin, op. cit.

# The hidden church of the Golden Dawn

*An essay contributed to the occult journal* Hermetic Virtues *and published there in 2012, this paper sketched out the unexpected parallels between the grade system of the Golden Dawn and the traditional major and minor orders of sacramental Christianity. While it attracted next to no notice, I remain convinced that the subject deserves more attention.*

Among the puzzles of Golden Dawn history is the source of the order's grade structure, or more precisely the origin of the changes the Golden Dawn's founders made to the system of grades they inherited. That older system, which seems to have been invented by the founders of the Orden des Gold- und Rosenkreutz (Order of the Golden and Rosy Cross) in eighteenth-century Germany, comprised the nine grades in Table 1. It has been used by many Rosicrucian orders since that time, notably the Societas Rosicruciana in Anglia (Rosicrucian Society in England, SRIA), to which William Wynn Westcott and Samuel Mathers belonged before they founded the Hermetic Order of the Golden Dawn.

The parallels between this grade system and that of the later Golden Dawn are obvious, but the differences deserve attention as well. The addition of a new grade, Ipsissimus, at the top of the structure is

Table 1. Grades of the Gold- und Rosenkreutz

| Number | Title | Name |
|---|---|---|
| 1,9 | Magus | Luxianus Renaldus de Perfectis |
| 2,8 | Magister | Pedemontanus de Rebus |
| 3,7 | Adeptus Exemptus | Janua de Aure Campis |
| 4,6 | Adeptus Major | Sphaere Fontus de Sales |
| 5,5 | Adeptus Minor | Hodus Camlionis |
| 6,4 | Philosophus | Pharus Illuminans |
| 7,3 | Practicus | Monoceros de Astris |
| 8,2 | Theoricus | Poraius de Rejectis |
| 9,1 | Junior | Pereclinus de Faustis |

a straightforward modification to fit the Golden Dawn's assignment of grades to the Tree of Life. The renaming of the grade of Junior as Zelator is equally uncomplicated, but then there are two new grades, Neophyte before Zelator and Portal between Philosophus and Adeptus Minor, both of which disrupt the assignment of grades to sephiroth just mentioned—there is, after all, no sephirah below Malkuth on the Tree, and none between Netzach and Tiphareth. The somewhat uneasy fit between the grades of the order and the Tree of Life has been explained in various ways, but none so far presented seem convincing.

The possibility this essay will explore is that the restructuring of the older Rosicrucian grade was done to bring the structure of Golden Dawn initiation in line with another ancient system of spiritual training—a system that was a subject of great interest in the British occult scene of the early centuries of the second millennium, and was revived by several occult organizations in the decades immediately after the original Golden Dawn collapsed. Definite proof of the connection seems to be lacking, but some elements of the Golden Dawn system are difficult to explain in any other way, and if the connection exists, it opens up an intriguing range of options for Golden Dawn practitioners today.

A personal reminiscence may help clarify the connection I intend to trace. In September 2004 I was consecrated as a Gnostic bishop by three bishops of the Universal Gnostic Church (UGC). This was not something I had sought or expected to receive, and it came about in an unlikely way.

The previous year, I was elected the seventh Grand Archdruid of the Ancient Order of Druids in America (AODA), a Druid order originally founded in 1912. Since the time of Matthew Shaw, the fifth Grand Archdruid of AODA and one of the founding bishops of the UGC, there had been a close connection between these organizations, and archdruids of AODA were consecrated as bishops of the UGC as a matter of course. The surviving members of AODA's "old guard" felt that the consecration was a vital part of the empowerments communicated to each Grand Archdruid, and I accepted it on that basis, despite my own misgivings, the lack of familiarity I then had with the traditions of Gnostic Christianity, and the fact that I had not been baptized and knew that for this reason, according to a substantial body of tradition, I was not qualified for consecration at all.[55]

The experience of suddenly being tossed into an unfamiliar spiritual tradition at its uppermost end is not one I recommend. Still, the research and practice that followed had at least one benefit, in that it put me in a position to take a close look at the entire body of tradition of Gnostic Christianity from what was essentially an outsider's perspective, without the familiarity that so often obscures connections and resemblances with other traditions. It was from this perspective that I considered the system of ordination that has long been standard in the sacramental Christian churches, Gnostic and otherwise.

That system is divided into two parts, the minor orders and major orders. As shown in Table 2, there are five minor orders, a transitional

Table 2. Holy orders of the Christian church

| Minor orders | Transitional order | Major orders |
| --- | --- | --- |
| Cleric | Subdeacon | Deacon |
| Doorkeeper | | Priest |
| Reader | | Bishop |
| Exorcist | | |
| Acolyte | | |

---

[55] It is probably worth noting that having received consecration in the manner just described, I work as a Gnostic bishop solely in a Druid context and do not, for example, claim the right to perform the Christian sacraments.

order formally classed with the major orders, and three major orders. In the modern Christian mainstream, at least in the Western world, the minor orders are conferred on seminary students who are seeking the priesthood, and treated very nearly as an afterthought; in ancient times, the minor orders were generally held by ordinary members of the community serving in their off hours, while the transitional and major orders alone pertained to the full-time priesthood; in contemporary Gnostic churches, beginning in the early twentieth century, the sequence serves as a process of initiation and inner transformation, and most church members pass through each step in order as they advance in the way of Gnosis.

Those readers who paid close attention to the foregoing paragraph may have noticed that this process of initiation has a great deal in common with the grade structure of the Hermetic Order of the Golden Dawn. The similarities go well beyond the outline just sketched; exact parallels also exist between each order and grade in sequence.[56] They can be outlined as follows:

## Minor orders/Outer Order grades

The minor orders require only the most basic kinds of study and practice, impose very modest requirements on those who receive them, and grant the right to take equally modest roles in the work of the church. In the Golden Dawn, similarly, the outer order grades could be earned with relatively little work, involved obligations that were not especially burdensome, and conferred the right to take on minor roles in the order's rituals.[57]

## Cleric/Neophyte

Both these are preparatory stages in which the aspirant accepts the essential obligations of the path and begins the study of its teachings and practices.

---

[56] The descriptions of the duties of the minor and major orders given here are drawn from C. W. Leadbeater's *The Science of the Sacraments*, which is used as a textbook by many contemporary esoteric Christian groups.

[57] Many contemporary Golden Dawn orders require much more of Outer Order initiates; the reference here is to the practice of the original order.

### Doorkeeper/Zelator

The doorkeeper cares for the material fabric and physical properties of the church, and has charge of the door to the church. The Zelator grade is assigned to Malkuth, the sephirah of physical matter, and the element of Earth, and qualifies the initiate to serve as Kerux in a Golden Dawn temple—the officer who has charge of the door to the temple.

### Reader/Theoricus

The reader or lector traditionally had the task of reading lessons from the scriptures when the various sacraments are performed, and normally studies theology during this stage of his or her training. The Theoricus grade is assigned to Yesod and the element of Air, which corresponds to mind; the title of the grade suggests, as well, an involvement with theoretical "book learning."

### Exorcist/Practicus

The order of exorcist in most contemporary churches is purely a formality, but in ancient times those who received this order were empowered to cast out demonic forces, to heal by laying on of hands, and to have charge of the water used in religious services. The grade of Practicus is assigned to the element of Water and to the sephirah Hod, which is the sphere of healing, and to which is attributed the archangel Michael, who casts out demons.

### Acolyte/Philosophus

The acolyte is traditionally responsible for the candles and lamps used in church, carries the candlestick in processions, and is qualified to serve at the altar during the sacrament of communion. The grade of Philosophus is assigned to the sephirah Netzach, which is assigned to Fire; the Philosophus is also qualified to serve as Hegemon in a Golden Dawn temple, the officer who sits closest to the altar.

### Major orders/Inner Order grades

In contrast to the minor orders, the major orders require a serious commitment to study and practice, impose extensive and lifelong duties on those who receive them, and grant access to the most central dimensions of the religious life of the church. Similarly, the Inner Order grades of the Golden Dawn require the initiate to engage in a great deal of study and practice, involve very extensive obligations, and confer the right to take an active role in every aspect of the order's work.

### Subdeacon/Portal

Both of these are transitional and probationary stages, during which the aspirant is prepared for advancement to the major orders or higher grades.

### Deacon/Adeptus Minor

The first of the major orders in the strict sense, the order of deacon is an apprenticeship for the priesthood, and commits the deacon to an intensive course of study in the theory and practice of the sacraments. The Adeptus Minor grade is the first of the grades above the Veil of the Sanctuary, and likewise commits the initiate to an intensive course of study in the theory and practice of the Magic of Light.

### Priest/Adeptus Major

The priest has the power to perform the central sacrament of the church, the eucharist or rite of communion in which bread and wine are changed into the body and blood of the Christ and offered in sacrifice. The grade of Adeptus Major received little development in the original Hermetic Order of the Golden Dawn, but is assigned to Geburah, the sephirah of transformation and of bloodshed.

### Bishop/Adeptus Exemptus

The bishop embodies the entire tradition of the church, and alone has the right to ordain candidates to any of the minor or major orders and to confer the sacrament of confirmation. In contemporary Gnostic churches, as in the early days of Christianity, bishops are not subject to a hierarchy, but function as independent teachers and exponents of the Gnosis. The Adeptus Exemptus grade received even less development in the original Hermetic Order of the Golden Dawn than did that of Adeptus Major, but it is assigned to Chesed and thus to Jupiter, the planet that among other things rules religious institutions.

These parallels are precise enough that it's vanishingly unlikely they are the results of chance. Nor is it enough to suggest that both derive from the Cabalistic Tree of Life; the Tree of Life as we know it was first created in the twelfth century,[58] while the system of holy orders was established well before that time. Relying on the Tree of Life for an explanation of the structure of both systems also begs an explanation of the mismatch between the orders or grades and the sephiroth, as explained above. The only hypothesis that seems to fit the facts is that the Golden Dawn system of grades was deliberately modeled on the holy orders of Christian tradition.

That by itself might simply suggest that the founders of the Golden Dawn were familiar with the sequence of holy orders and saw advantages to using a similar pattern. Still, there is another parallel between the Golden Dawn system and the Christian tradition that has rarely been given the importance it deserves. In the sacramental traditions of Christianity, the most important working is the eucharist or communion ceremony, in which in one sense or another—the sense in question varies considerably from one branch of the tradition to another—bread and wine are transformed into the body and blood of the Christ. At the core of this working are the words of institution, a recitation of the words spoken by Jesus of Nazareth at the Last Supper:

"Who the day before he suffered took bread into his holy and venerable hands, and with his eyes lifted up to heaven unto thee, God, his almighty father, giving thanks to thee, blessed, brake, and gave it to his disciples, saying: Take and eat ye all of this, for *this is my body*;

"In like manner after he had supped, taking also this excellent chalice into his holy and venerable hands, again giving thanks to thee, he blessed it and gave it to his disciples saying: Take and drink ye all of this, for *this is my blood*. As oft as ye shall do these things, ye shall do them in remembrance of me."[59]

The Golden Dawn also has a eucharist, the Mystic Repast, which is performed whenever a Golden Dawn temple is closed in the

---

[58] See Gershom Scholem, *The Origins of the Kabbalah*.
[59] The wording here is given in Leadbeater's *The Science of the Sacraments*, pp. 204, 207, and 226; different churches use slightly different phrasing, though the content is essentially the same.

Neophyte Grade. It also has its own words of institution, which may be found in the Order's paper Z-1, "The Enterer of the Threshold":

> For Osiris on-Nophris who is found perfect before the gods, hath said:
> "These are the elements of my body,
> Perfected through suffering, glorified through trial.
> For the scent of the dying rose is as the repressed sigh of my suffering:
> And the flame-red fire as the energy of mine undaunted will:
> And the cup of wine is the pouring out of the blood of my heart:
> Sacrificed unto regeneration, unto the newer life;
> And the bread and salt are as the foundations of my body,
> Which I destroy that they may be renewed.
> For I am Osiris Triumphant, even Osiris on-Nophris, the justified:
> I am he who is clothed with the body of flesh,
> Yet in whom is the spirit of the great gods:
> I am the lord of life, triumphant over death.
> He who partaketh with me shall arise with me:
> I am the manifestor in matter of those whose abode is the invisible:
> I am purified: I stand upon the universe:
> I am its reconciler with the eternal gods:
> I am the perfector of matter:
> And without me, the universe is not."[60]

These words appear without commentary in "The Enterer of the Threshold" paper, after a brief discussion of the placement of the elemental symbols on the altar in the Neophyte grade. No explanation is given for them, though I have seen a good many Golden Dawn temples use them to consecrate the elements of the Mystic Repast. They clearly form the core invocation for a eucharist of Osiris, in which four substances—rose, flame, wine, and bread with salt—become the body of Osiris.

Thus the Golden Dawn tradition embodies a system of initiations that closely parallels the holy orders of the Christian church, a ritual that closely parallels the central rite of the Christian church, and an

---

[60] Israel Regardie, *The Golden Dawn*, vol. 3, p. 87.

invocation that closely parallels the core words of that rite. My hypothesis is that these parallels are not accidental: that one of the things the original Golden Dawn was meant to become, as it matured, was a church or something like one, in which a eucharist of Osiris would be the central ritual and the grade structure of the order would provide the course of training for priests and priestesses.

If this hypothesis is correct, ordination to the priesthood would have been conferred at the grade of Adeptus Major, while the Adeptus Exemptus grade would confer the equivalent of consecration as a bishop. If such plans existed, however, they do not seem to have survived the explosions that wrecked the original Golden Dawn during and after the revolt of 1900; published versions of the Adeptus Major and Adeptus Exemptus grades that came into use in the Stella Matutina later on, certainly, show no trace of the priestly functions suggested here.[61]

It may not be coincidental, though, that alternative priesthoods working new versions of the Christian eucharist appeared in the British occult scene not long after the Alpha et Omega, the fragment of the original order that remained loyal to Mathers, finally came apart. One of these was the Liberal Catholic Church, organized by Theosophists in 1917, which practiced sacraments closely modeled on the traditional Christian rites, but with a transformed theology and a greatly expanded esoteric dimension. Another was the Guild of the Master Jesus, a Christian sacramental branch of Dion Fortune's Fraternity (later Society) of the Inner Light, which evolved its own distinctive eucharistic ritual and system of spiritual exercises on the basis of Fortune's own esoteric teachings.

Both of these took the system of minor orders, which had become little more than a formality in the Catholic and Anglican churches, and redefined them as a sequence of initiatory grades. This could have been inspired by rumors of what had been discussed in the innermost circles of the Golden Dawn, though it's equally possible that they were independent movements in the same direction, guided by the same widely felt need for a sacramental religion with a magical and initiatory dimension, free from the fossilized hierarchies and dogmatic rigidity that burdened

---

[61] Patrick J. Zalewski, *Secret Inner Order Rituals of the Golden Dawn*, gives one version of these.

the mainstream churches then as now. That need is still powerfully felt, and the rise of the independent sacramental movement—a fascinating mix of independent priests, bishops, and local churches who have by and large discarded the hierarchical and dogmatic dimensions of institutional Christianity to focus on the experiential and sacramental core of the tradition—is one current measure of that fact.[62]

These later movements all embraced the heritage of Christianity in one way or another. The hidden church of the Golden Dawn may have included a Rosicrucian Christian dimension, but the material that survives focuses on a different option, more radical but also less problematic at a time when the opportunity to receive consecration as a bishop outside the established churches was a great deal less common than it is today. By centering its sacraments on Osiris and the gods of Egypt rather than Christ and the god of Judeo-Christian tradition, the founders of the Golden Dawn may simply have hoped to provide an option for the practice of sacramental religion for those who were excluded by the Christian churches of the time. In the process, though, they outlined a possibility that may well be relevant and appealing to students of the tradition today.

As a point of history, the hypothesis that the Golden Dawn system was meant to include the dimension suggested here may never be settled conclusively. Still, the Golden Dawn is a living tradition, not merely an oddity of Edwardian culture, and the hypothesis traced out in this essay is at least as relevant to the present as to the past. The hidden church of the Golden Dawn is little more than a vague possibility at present, and one that will require a great deal of work to bring into manifestation. Still, for those orders that seek a more public side of their work, and those adepts who experience their initiations as a call to a priesthood or priestesshood—and in my experience, both of these are fairly common—the option of a public ministry, celebrating the eucharist of Osiris and other magical sacraments for the benefit of a wider community, may be worth exploring.

---

[62] See John P. Plummer, *The Many Paths of the Independent Sacramental Movement*, for a good summary of this movement by an author sympathetic to its magical possibilities.

## References

Fortune, D., et al. (c. 1930). *Guild of the Master Jesus Instructional Papers* (unpublished manuscripts).

Leadbeater, C. W. (1920). *The Science of the Sacraments.* Wheaton, IL: Theosophical Publishing House.

Plummer, J. P. (2006). *The Many Paths of the Independent Sacramental Movement.* Berkeley, CA: Apocryphile.

Regardie, I. (1984). *The Golden Dawn.* St. Paul, MN: Llewellyn.

Scholem, G. (1987). *Origins of the Kabbalah.* Princeton, NJ: Princeton University Press.

Zalewski, P. J. (1988). *Secret Inner Order Rituals of the Golden Dawn.* Phoenix, AZ: Falcon.

# The place of mingled powers

### Spiritual beings in the magical lodge

> *In 2015 I was invited to submit a paper for an anthology on spirits in magical practice,* Liber Spirituum. *It seemed worthwhile to talk about magical lodges again, using the way that lodge magic relates to spirits as a focus.*

Magic is in large part a solitary practice, but mages, like other human beings, are social primates. Group workings of various kinds thus have a long-established place in magical lore. The world's magical traditions, diverse as they are, have an equal diversity of structures for group work, and a fair sample of that diversity is on display in the contemporary occult scene.

The modern magical tradition has made a notable contribution to that diversity. By "modern magic"—as distinct from older systems such as classical, medieval, and Renaissance magic on the one hand, and post-modern magical systems such as chaos magic on the other—I mean the tradition that took shape in the wake of Éliphas Lévi's *Dogme et Rituel de* *la Haute Magie*⁶³ (*Doctrine and Ritual of High Magic*, 1854) in Europe, the Americas, and Australasia, and kept its place as the predominant form of occultism on those continents until it was elbowed aside by the rise of popular Neopaganism in the late twentieth century. When operative mages in that tradition worked together, they normally did so in the context of a magical lodge.

Even today, when the tradition just described is only one of many options for the operative mage, lodge methods are still part of the common practice in a great many corners of the magical scene. Those methods are not always well understood even by those who practice them, and one aspect of the magical lodge particularly prone to confusions just now is the role of spiritual beings in magical lodge work. That's a crucial dimension of the system, for human beings are not the only participants in a properly functioning magical lodge. When a magical lodge functions as it should, it becomes a place of mingled powers where the Seen and the Unseen work together at common tasks.

## *The magical lodge*

The magical lodge itself is a complex phenomenon with a long history. I hope my readers will not be too bitterly disappointed, though, if I mention that the history in question didn't originate in the mystery temples of the Nile, the lamaseries of the Himalayas, the Sun temples of lost Atlantis, or any of the other exotic and untraceable homelands to which occultists of an earlier day assigned it. The Neopagan habit of backdating freshly minted traditions to the distant past via untraceable "grandmother stories" is nothing new; a century ago, magical lodges and occult traditions did the same thing with even more panache, manufacturing origin stories going back millennia in which Egypt, Atlantis, Lemuria, and the like routinely played an important part.⁶⁴ All this is great entertainment, but it has little if anything to do with history.

The historical origins of the magical lodge are more prosaic, though not without interest. In Europe during the Middle Ages, religious organizations of laymen called confraternities were a common form of

---

⁶³ Badly put into English by A. E. Waite and retitled *Transcendental Magic*—Waite could never settle for a good title when he could think of a boring one instead. See Lévi, 1972; a less pompous and tendentious translation of this occult classic is badly needed. [This need was met by me and Mark Mikituk a few years later.]

⁶⁴ See, as one example out of many, Fortune, 1987, pp. 23–29.

social organization. The confraternities early on evolved a distinctive way of managing their regular meetings, with a presiding officer sitting on the side of the room opposite the door, a second officer near the door whose duties included controlling access to the meeting and maintaining discipline, and the members sitting on the two remaining sides of the room, facing one another across the floor. As confraternities developed their own initiation rituals and other ceremonial activities, the open floor became a blank slate onto which any desired pattern might be drawn—in many cases, quite literally, with chalk, charcoal, and red clay serving as writing media that could be scrubbed away after the ceremony was done.

This same set of practices passed over into the craft guilds of the High Middle Ages, most of which started out as religious confraternities focused upon reverence to patron saints. Among the guilds that absorbed the confraternity system and added to it were the stonemasons. Because their work required them to travel to job sites far from home and identify themselves as trained craftsmen to the master mason in charge, the stonemasons developed passwords and signs of recognition; their initiation rituals were more complex than average, and their involvement with church building brought them into contact with the rich medieval lore of symbolism and sacred geometry, much of which found its way into the stonemasons' rituals and traditions.

Those borrowings were probably responsible for the survival of the stonemasons' guild when the Middle Ages gave way to what historians awkwardly call the Early Modern period, and the medieval economic system of local guilds serving local markets was swept aside by the first wave of mercantile capitalism. Beginning in Scotland in the seventeenth century, and spreading from there, educated gentlemen began to join stonemasons' lodges as "accepted members"—"honorary members" would be the equivalent modern term—and their influence gradually transformed what had been a medieval craft guild into the modern institution of Freemasonry.

It's almost impossible to overstate the influence of Freemasonry on modern Western occultism. For more than two centuries, from around 1750 to the cultural convulsions of the 1960s, if you were a male occultist in Europe or North America, you were probably also a Freemason—and if you happened to be female, your chances of belonging either to a Masonic auxiliary or to one of the irregular branches of Masonry that admit women to membership were not small. By that channel among others, the practices and habits that Freemasonry inherited from its medieval ancestry were picked up enthusiastically by occultists and imported wholesale into most branches of Western occultism.

At first, though, that inheritance was used purely as an educational and instructional framework. The earliest occult lodges in the eighteenth century borrowed the toolkit of lodge ritual and organization more or less intact from Freemasonry; their rituals included plenty of occult symbolism but the actual practice of operative magic was carried on by initiates on their own time. It was in the second half of the nineteenth century, after Éliphas Lévi popularized ritual magic, that lodge workings in occult orders started to make room for magical practices in the initiation rituals themselves. The Hermetic Order of the Golden Dawn was the most famous of the magical lodge organizations that resulted from that creative fusion, but it was far from the only example.

## *The magical mesocosm*

Enthusiastic adaptation of lodge rituals and forms to new purposes had many products alongside the magical lodges. An astonishing range of organizations, from labor unions and insurance cooperatives to ethnic societies and youth groups, borrowed the lodge template either from Freemasonry or from a handful of less famous organizations descended from medieval guilds and confraternities, such as the Odd Fellows.[65] The sheer popularity of the lodge system in popular culture added to its attractiveness to occultists and operative mages, but there were other excellent reasons why the vast majority of occult traditions in the Western world ended up using that particular toolkit and no other.

One of those reasons is far more significant than is often recognized: Magical lodges are usually part-time phenomena. Most magical lodges don't have the financial resources to buy or lease their own buildings, and even those that do rarely have meetings more than once a week. The constant flow of ritual and practice that takes place in a monastery or a temple is a very rare thing in Western occultism. That imposed two

---

[65] My collection of old lodge rituals includes, among others, one from the Daughters of Norway, which was an ethnic-heritage organization; one from the Ladies Auxiliary of the Amalgamated Transit Workers Union, which was exactly what the name suggests; and one from the Woodmen of the World, which was an insurance cooperative. All of these, and many more, use the standard lodge system, complete with initiation rituals.

requirements for magical lodges. First, they had to use a generic space for their purposes; second, they had to be able to turn that generic space into fully charged and activated sacred space in short order whenever they wanted to do an initiation or any other kind of ritual working.

Those requirements had a profound impact on the structure of initiation, because people realized very quickly that the same processes that allow you to turn an empty lodge room into a magically charged sacred space in a single ritual working will also allow you to turn an ordinary candidate into a magically empowered initiate in a single ritual working. Thus you'll find that in the great majority of initiation rituals in our Western tradition, the opening ritual for each degree has very close structural similarities to the initiation ritual of that degree.

This led the occult lodge tradition into very deep waters. The Hermetic doctrine of macrocosm and microcosm, the mirroring of the universe in the individual human being and vice versa, is of course one of the standard concepts of Western occultism. What the participants in magical lodges realized, though, is that those are two terms of a three-term relationship. Between the macrocosm and the microcosm, the universe and the individual, stands the mesocosm—literally, the middle universe—which reflects both the macrocosm and the microcosm. That's what a magical lodge becomes when it's opened with the proper ceremony. It's a mirror of the macrocosm, representing the entire universe in miniature. It's also a mirror of the microcosm, representing every aspect of the individual in expanded form.

The advantage there is the advantage that always comes in magic when you move from a twofold to a threefold relationship. Put any two things in relationship with one another and they polarize; they become a pair of opposites; and that opposition, that polarization, fixes the volatile and locks both ends of the binary into place. If you want to build on that foundation, you have to bring in a third factor: It's with the triad, Binah the Great Mother, that the abstract becomes manifest and creation happens. In the same way, macrocosm and microcosm can polarize one another, but there's always the risk of fixation, of "stuckness." Bring in the mesocosm and things start to move; having fixed the volatile, you volatilize the fixed, and transmutation becomes possible on many different levels.

This happens in any form of magical work. One of the great discoveries that came out of the evolution of the occult lodge tradition in the eighteenth and nineteenth centuries is precisely that occultists had been working with mesocosms all along. Consider the medieval sorcerer in his magic circle, sword in one hand and grimoire in the other, conjuring demons by the mighty names of God. The magic circle is a mesocosm; it represents the entire universe in symbolic form, with its four quarters, the divine names and the working tools of the art representing the powers of the cosmos, and chaos and old night pressing close around the periphery; it also represents the sorcerer himself, the four quarters and innate powers of his own body, mind, and spirit.

Among other things, this is one way to understand how magic works. The macrocosm reflects the microcosm, and vice versa, but when you create a mesocosm between them, the static condition of reflection becomes a flowing process that allows magical changes to occur. You start with the mesocosm reflecting the macrocosm and microcosm, but then the macrocosm and the microcosm reflect the mesocosm; when you change things in the mesocosm, corresponding changes reflect outward to the macrocosm, and inward to the microcosm. If you constellate an influence through a ritual in your magical mesocosm, that same influence reflects in both directions and constellates itself in your inner and outer life. As between, so above, and so below.

## *The outer lodge*

The first step in any magical lodge working is thus the preparation of the space, the formulation of the mesocosm on outer and inner levels alike. Since magical lodges are part-time phenomena, this has to be done every time the lodge is opened; the lodge can't simply be consecrated once and for all, and left at that. Fortunately, the standard methods of magical lodge work provide effective tools to do what needs to be done.

The vast majority of magical lodge rituals are designed to be performed in a completely generic space. Those readers who have been inside a lodge hall of any kind, no matter what organization it serves, already know the design, as shown in Diagram 1 below. The basic structure is a rectangular space with chairs along the sides, a seat for the presiding officer on one end, a seat for the secondary officer on the other, a door and an officer to guard it, and an altar that can be put at the center of the space.

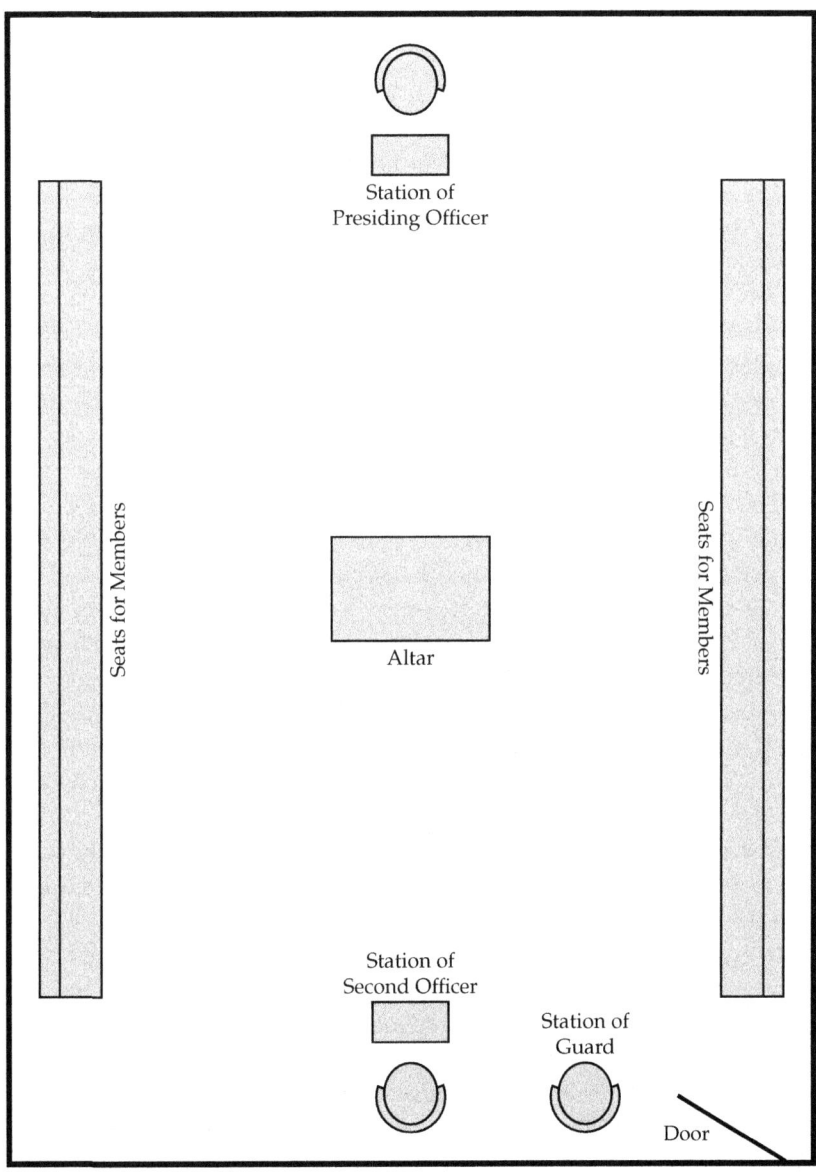

The basic structure, in turn, is subject to almost limitless variations. Additional officers can be added, and assigned to stations anywhere in the lodge hall. Additional furnishings can be brought in, and distributed with equal freedom. A floor cloth or carpet marked with appropriate emblems can be used to divide the lodge space into symbolic regions. Veils can be set up across the hall, dividing it more dramatically. At the furthest end of ritual complexity are those lodges in which a smaller enclosed space—a chamber, a vault, the tomb of Hermes or Merlin or Christian Rosycross—is set up somewhere in the lodge hall and becomes the focus of the ritual work.

In the great majority of cases, though, the only variations to the space are those that can be set up and taken down in a half hour or so. Unless the lodge has enough resources to afford a building of its own, and these are very much an exception, the whole kit and caboodle is designed to be packed away in a closet between lodge meetings. Setting up the lodge furnishings thus serves as an effective prelude to setting up the lodge on a more magical level.

The procedure here is just as standardized as the basic lodge architecture itself. The presiding officer makes sure that the doors are closed and everyone present is already an initiate, and a banishing ritual may be performed; a litany recounts the symbolism of the degree and the names and duties of the officers; an invocation calls on whatever spiritual force presides over the working; and then the lodge is formally declared open. Ritual designers have plugged almost every conceivable variation into this framework, but it still works out to the same process. First, the mesocosm is set apart from the world around it; second, the symbolic patterns and stations are established and reinforced in the collective consciousness of the lodge and in the minds and wills of each person present; third, a spiritual influence is called down into the waiting receptacle; finally, by an act of will, the mesocosm is made complete and the work begins.

In an ordinary non-magical lodge, this is done in an entirely exoteric way, without any conscious magical technique involved. That has certain advantages, since in a fraternal lodge the effect of the ritual doesn't depend on the magical prowess of the initiators, and of course it also happens that people who've been doing lodge ritual for long enough end up practicing magic without ever quite realizing that that's what they're doing. I've been astonished more than once by the head of magical steam that some old men and women without a trace of occult training can build up when they're working a lodge ritual they love, and doing it for the three thousandth time. In an occult lodge, though, the same thing is done consciously, and whatever set of inner tools a given tradition provides can be brought to bear on the process of charging the hall.

The mesocosm concept mentioned earlier is crucial in this process. The lodge as mesocosm represents the universe, and it also represents the candidate in an initiation, as well as every other individual in the lodge. The presiding officer of the lodge represents the divine power presiding over the universe, and also represents the higher self or guardian angel of the individual, the reflection of the divine in the sphere of the self. Each of the other officers of the lodge represents a power of the cosmos and a factor in the individual psyche. Each piece of lodge furnishing represents an aspect of the universe and of the self. When the officers take on their roles consciously and mediate the energies they represent, the work has noticeably more impact, and the more skilled they are at handling magical energies, the more pyrotechnic the results can be.

## The inner lodge

The lodge space itself also undergoes transformation in this process, from a blank slate to a map of the cosmos and the self. Every traditional initiation ritual divides up the lodge hall into areas corresponding to different aspects of the universe, which are also different aspects of the individual. For example, the lodge may be divided up into five zones— the four material elements in the four quarters and the element of spirit in the center. It might be divided into two zones of darkness and light, with the place of balance at the central altar. The whole Cabalistic Tree of Life, or some part thereof, may be mapped onto it; alternatively, some other map of the symbolic cosmos can be used in the same way. As the opening ritual proceeds, each section of the lodge room is charged with the appropriate influence; the officers begin mediating the appropriate forces, and the mesocosm is readied for work.

All this is done whenever a magical lodge opens. It can also be done with equal effectiveness by an individual mage working in the privacy of his or her own home. This was another of the discoveries that came out of the fusion of the lodge tradition with magical practice in eighteenth- and nineteenth-century Europe. Since the same magical mesocosm can be constructed in a solitary ritual as in a magical lodge meeting, magical lodges learned to teach their initiates simplified versions of the opening and closing ritual as a basic magical practice; among the many effects of this habit is that the initiates in question became intimately familiar with the magical work required to open and close the lodge, and thus generally did a better job in practice.

The furthest extension of this sort of thinking was pioneered by the Hermetic Order of the Golden Dawn in the 1890s, though it's been borrowed by a variety of other magical lodges since that time. Just as the opening and closing ceremony can be converted into an opening and closing ritual for solitary use, rituals of initiation and other group rituals can also be converted into solitary rituals for practical and spiritual magic.

The rituals the Golden Dawn derived from its Neophyte grade ceremony are the most famous examples of this conversion process.[66] Those rituals have fielded a certain amount of criticism over the years on the grounds that there are simpler ways to get the same results. This is true only if "the same results" are limited to the practical goals of the ceremonies. In the Golden Dawn curriculum, the "Z-2 rituals" also serve as ways to train adepti to fulfill certain key functions in Golden Dawn temple ceremonies. Many other magical lodges rely on a similar kind of multitasking in their training systems, using bits of lodge ritual as elements of individual work for training purposes even when a simpler approach might seem more practical.

The opening ceremony, though, is the most commonly reworked element of magical lodge practice, and for good reason. This is the ceremony that defines the magical space in which a lodge will accomplish its work, and the powers and potencies that will assist the lodge in its labors are called into operation. In a great many magical lodge systems, these powers include gods, angels, and spiritual beings of various kinds: the nonhuman inhabitants of the magical mesocosm.

## Spiritual beings

In this essay as elsewhere, I treat spiritual beings as real, conscious, intelligent entities who have an existence independent of the human mind. I'm aware that this is a controversial stance in some parts of the magical community just now. A substantial number of mages these days prefer a cosmology in which human beings are the only real, conscious, intelligent entities around, and gods, angels, spirits, and the like are purely imaginary forms called into being by the human mind and will. That's certainly one way of understanding the cosmos; philosophically speaking, it's impossible either to prove or to disprove the objective

---

[66] Regardie, 1984, vol. 3, pp. 152–276.

existence of spiritual beings—but the two options are not interchangeable. Important issues ride on the distinction.

It so happens that for wholly personal reasons, I find a universe chockfull of real, conscious, intelligent spiritual beings with whom I can interact far more interesting and appealing than a universe that's simply an echo chamber for my ego. If, as many chaos magicians like to claim, the universe is whatever we will it to be, then it's as reasonable for me to will a universe crammed with spirits as it would be for someone else to will one in which spirits have no independent existence. By almost any other theory—and in particular, by the standard occult theory that underlies modern magic—things are considerably more straightforward: According to that latter theory, spiritual beings exist, and much of the work of the operative mage takes place in interaction with them.

All this is relevant to the work of the magical lodge, because most magical lodge systems derive from occult traditions that affirm the reality of spiritual beings, and nearly all such systems include direct or indirect interactions with such beings as part of the work done in a magical lodge. It would certainly be possible to construct an effective magical lodge ritual in which impersonal spiritual influences play the critical roles in the work, and I wouldn't be surprised to learn that such rituals exist, but that isn't the standard approach in magical lodges working in the modern magical tradition.

There are any number of ways to classify spiritual beings, and none of them are exact. For our present purposes, it's sufficient to note three very general classifications which are also the three basic roles that spiritual beings fill in most magical lodge workings, and in fraternal lodges as well. For simplicity's sake, we'll call them deities, powers, and creations.

## Deities

In the sense meant here, deities are primary spiritual powers whose influence pervades every aspect of the work of a lodge. In the oldest lodges and proto-lodges that have left detailed ritual texts, the deity who presided over meetings and rituals was the Christian god, and ordinary religious practices such as prayer were used to invoke him in the opening ceremony and at various points during lodge workings. That remains the case in regular Freemasonry, which includes prayers to the god of the Bible in its lodge opening and closing rituals; a great many other fraternal lodges do the same thing. In magical lodges, the options are considerably broader; the god of the Bible is still very much an option, as a glance at Golden Dawn lodge rituals will demonstrate.[67] but he stopped being the only game in town a very long time ago.

Philosophers and theologians of many traditions have kept up a centuries-long debate about what differentiates deities from other classes of spiritual beings, but their quarrels can be left aside for our present purpose. What matters within the four walls of a magical lodge is that the entities I'm describing as deities are not localized in space. Once a deity is invoked in a magical lodge, all the activities of the lodge take place in the deity's presence, and so long as care is taken to maintain a satisfactory relationship, under his or her blessing and protection as well. What is required to keep such a relationship in good order depends, of course, on the deity in question; what will maintain good relations with Jehovah, for example, is not necessarily going to further a working relationship with Bacchus, or vice versa.

When designing a magical lodge, or for that matter choosing to be initiated into one, it's well to be sure that the deity invoked in its workings is of a nature congenial to the work to be done. It's at least as important, though, to be sure the deity is congenial to the initiates of the lodge, and vice versa. There's a certain wry amusement to be gotten from watching a magical lodge go through the motions of invoking a deity whom none of the lodge members reverence and some actively detest, but effective magic rarely comes out of such exercises. Deities are conscious entities, not vending machines, and trying to extract things from them by the equivalent of dropping in a quarter and pushing a button is rarely a good idea.

## Powers

In the sense meant here, powers are spiritual beings whose powers are localized in space in an open magical lodge. The classic example, familiar to most operative mages these days, are the elemental archangels who are invoked in the Lesser Ritual of the Pentagram. Whether or not archangels occupy specific points in space, on the head of a pin or otherwise, may be left to the theologians; all I mean here by "localized" is that,

---

[67] See, for instance, Regardie, 1974, vol. 2, pp. 46–47.

within the space established by the ritual, it's possible to face toward Raphael and away from Gabriel, or vice versa. Different points in or around the lodge hall are assigned to different powers, who are evoked in those locations by one or another of the standard magical means.

Powers called into a magical lodge working can be evoked into various portions of empty space, into specific items of lodge furniture, or into members of the lodge. Various kinds of mediumship have long played a role in magical lodges. In some lodges, for example, it's standard to have a lodge officer who goes into trance in lodge ritual and serves as a mouthpiece for a specific spiritual being, or a series of such beings. In other lodges, officers make contact with specific powers assigned to their offices and stations, and consciously mediate those powers when the lodge is working ritual.

There are risks involved in this latter process. In some branches of the Hermetic Order of the Golden Dawn, officers used to go to great lengths to protect themselves from being obsessed by the powers behind the godforms they mediated in ritual. In other branches of the tradition, to be sure, the danger of obsession and the resulting inflation of the ego do not seem to have been taken seriously enough! After the original Golden Dawn blew itself to pieces in 1900–1903, a good many magical lodges took the hint, and had their officers mediate energies without the added challenge of being overshadowed by a conscious entity. The tool of choice for this work was usually a creation.

These are spiritual beings who are brought into existence by the work of a magical lodge, as distinct from those who exist independently of the lodge and who thus have to be invoked or evoked. Some creations come into existence automatically, as a product of certain phenomena familiar to students of the inner side of human social interaction; others are deliberately constructed by magical means.

## Groupminds

The automatic creation most often used in magical lodge work is the groupmind or collective personality.[68] Any group of human beings united by a shared emotion, even temporarily, generates a groupmind, which feeds the emotional state that creates it back into the psyches of its creators. Mob violence and the behavior of crowds display the

---

[68] See Fortune, 1987a, pp. 21–27, and Fortune, 1987c, pp. 58–62.

groupmind at its most basic level; an operative mage with well developed magical senses can learn a great deal about groupminds by observing the crowds at a football game, a rock concert, or any other venue where people habitually check their minds at the door and surf the waves of emotion.

The same thing in a more controlled and directed fashion plays an important part in the magical lodge tradition and its work. The opening ritual in a magical lodge, or for that matter a fraternal lodge, is among other things a way of calling up shared emotional states among the members of the lodge, and thus building and feeding a groupmind. That process has a feedback component; the shared emotion builds the groupmind, which then elicits more of the shared emotion from the lodge members. This is a very powerful tool, but it can also backfire spectacularly; those readers who have watched a magical working group disintegrate in an unstoppable spiral of pointless bickering have seen that latter effect at work.

## *Artificial spirits*

Two kinds of deliberately constructed creations are commonly used in magical lodge systems. Interestingly, the one that gets most of the discussion is the less common of the two—though a census would be impossible, lodge secrecy being what it is, fewer than half of the traditional magical lodge rituals I know of make use of the type in question. This is what is usually called an "artificial elemental," a constructed spirit assigned a specific station and task in a magical lodge.

The term's a misnomer—artificial beings of this sort can be considerably more or less intelligent than elemental spirits are generally held to be, and need not have any connection at all with whatever set of elements a magical tradition happens to use. "Artificial spirits" would be a more accurate term, or possibly "magical robots"—the latter because, at least to start with, created beings of this kind tend to carry out their assigned functions with mechanical precision.

This is their great strength; their great weakness, and one of the two reasons many magical lodge systems don't use them, is that they only have as much strength as the lodge members put into them. This is not the case with powers, and even more emphatically not the case with deities; both these categories of spiritual being have their own sources of power, while artificial spirits do not. Like battery-powered devices, they need to be recharged at intervals.

The second difficulty with artificial spirits is more complex. In the long run, artificial spirits, groupminds, and most other creations tend to display what might as well be called the "Frankenstein effect"—that is, they start to behave like independent entities with their own wills and concerns, perhaps in harmony with the purposes and intentions of the lodge, perhaps not. It's a neat problem in magical theory whether creations sprout minds of their own, whether independent spiritual beings take over the energetic form in a manner similar to obsession, or whether some other process might be involved.

Whatever explanation turns out to be the right one, though, the fact of the matter remains: Most creations are unstable, and can become problematic in unpredictable ways, while deities and powers are much more reliable to work with. This is the second reason why most traditional magical lodge rituals rely on deities and powers rather than creations, and when creations are unavoidable—for example, the groupmind of the lodge, which comes into being whether it's wanted or not—a deity is invoked to indwell the groupmind and make sure it behaves itself.

One instructive exception to this rule is the second form of creations commonly found in magical lodges: the use of creations by lodge officers as a way of mediating magical energies in ritual. Here the Frankenstein effect is kept in check by a novel use of the principle of obsession: The created forms are obsessed by the lodge officers who wear them, and this functions very effectively to keep the forms from being obsessed by anyone or anything else. The act of mediation does tend to have an impact on the consciousness of the mediating officer, molding it in the direction of whatever influence the form embodies. For this reason, it's standard practice to have the officers of the lodge rotate from one position to another at regular intervals to avoid personality imbalances.

## Interacting with spiritual beings

Operative mages around the world have figured out any number of ways to interact with spiritual beings and involve them in magical workings. In lodge workings based on the modern magical tradition, only two of them have seen much use, and one of those—trance mediumship—is used by a small minority of lodges. In most lodge systems, the work is done by the method that the Golden Dawn papers call "scrying in the spirit vision" and Carl Jung called "active imagination."

There are good practical reasons for this choice of methods. Most other approaches to making contact with spiritual beings would pose real challenges if practiced in a lodge. Conjuring spirits to visible appearance, for example, is a lengthy and cumbersome operation. This also usually requires burning large amounts of dittany of Crete or some other materializing incense, which risks setting off smoke alarms and can cause trouble with the landlord as well.

Conjuring spirits into a mirror or scrying crystal would be less cumbersome, but that would limit contact with the spiritual beings to those members of the lodge who have the particular talent of mirror or crystal scrying, and the need to look back and forth from the mirror or crystal and the lodge room would be a source of distraction. By contrast, the use of the imagination as a vehicle for contact with spiritual beings allows everyone in the lodge to participate in the contact, so long as they have done the necessary training.

Modern popular culture disparages the human imagination—it's telling that in contemporary usage, the word "imaginary" is treated as a synonym for "unreal." As Henri Corbin pointed out in his classic essay "Mundus Imaginalis," however, the imagination can function as a mode of cognition. There is a crucial difference, in Corbin's phrasing, between the imaginal and the merely imaginary.[69] Given systematic training along the lines taught in traditional occult schools, the imagination becomes an organ of perception and action in the *mundus imaginalis*, the realm of images and similitudes that modern magical traditions generally call the astral plane; trained mages can construct forms in that realm, but they can also experience forms that they do not create; they can also participate with spiritual beings in the construction of forms as a means of mutual communication.

## *A practical example*

It's easier to understand how these factors work in practice through an example. I've chosen to use a fictional one, to avoid squabbles over territory. Magical lodge traditions vary widely in the fine details of

---

[69] Corbin, 2006.

technique; the methods described below are among the more common, and provide a convenient overview of some of the available options.

The lodge, let's say, is working a Grail ritual along the lines sketched out by the late Jessie Weston in *From Ritual to Romance*. The cosmology and symbolism on which the lodge is based is Gnostic, or more exactly that curious fusion of Gnostic spirituality and fertility cult found in the Naassene Document and reflected in the rituals that Weston believed formed the original background of the Grail legends.[70]

The deities invoked to preside over the working are the Gnostic Christ, Iesseus Mazareus Iessedekius, who is also Attis and Adonis, and the Moirothea, the mother of the four Gnostic luminaries and of all living things, who is also Cybele and Aphrodite. The powers evoked to govern the four elemental quarters are the four luminaries, Dauiethe in the east ruling air, Harmozel in the south ruling fire, Oroiael in the west governing water, and Eleleth in the north ruling earth.[71]

There are three lodge officers—the Master in the east, the Warder in the west, and the Summoner beside the door—and each of them has a created form as a structure for mediating the energies of the ritual: The Master uses the form of the Fisher King, the Warder of the Grail Bearer, and the Summoner of the Questing Knight. In each degree of initiation, an additional created form is prepared for the initiate. There is also a created form used by every member of the lodge who does not hold an office in any given ritual: This is the image of a Grail Knight in armor.

All the members of the lodge, in the course of their training, have practiced invoking the Christ, the Moirothea, and the four luminaries in daily ritual workings, and have meditated at length on the symbolism and structure of the ritual as well as the teachings that underlie it. The members who sit along the sides of the lodge in any given working aren't there as spectators; they have their own created forms to maintain, and they also build and maintain the imaginal forms through which the officers move, assist the officers in their magical work, and in initiations, put the appropriate created form on the candidate and keep it in place through the working. Their effort is an important ingredient in the success of the working.

Just before the lodge meets, the Master enters the hall, makes sure all the lodge furnishings are in place, and then advances to the west

---

[70] Weston, 1983, pp. 149–163.
[71] I have used the Gospel of the Egyptians as a source here; see Layton, 1987, 105–120.

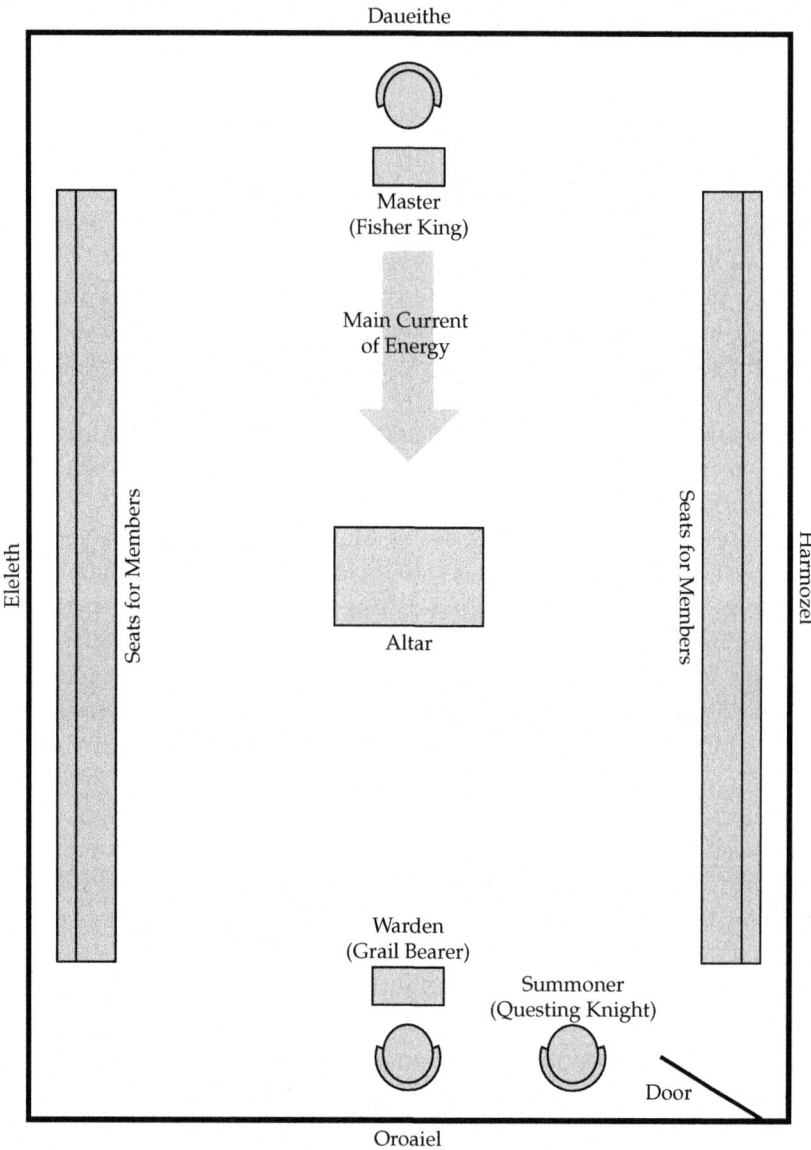

of the altar. His responsibilities include establishing and maintaining a good relationship with the deities and powers that work with the lodge; on the basis of that relationship, using a set of standard ritual forms, he invokes the Christ and the Moirothea, calling on them to be present during the working. He then faces each of the quarters and evokes the four luminaries, again using a standard ritual form, and asks and receives their help in the work of the lodge. He then advances to his station in the east, sits in his chair, takes on the form of the Fisher King, and with the help of the deities and powers, establishes the imaginal forms and energy flows that define the lodge in its inner dimension. (One such pattern, the primary flow of energy between the Master's station and the altar, is shown in the diagram.)

Meanwhile, the other members of the lodge are preparing themselves for the work. When the Master has finished his work, he goes to the door and signals the others to join him. The two remaining officers take their stations, take on their respective forms, and invoke the Christ and the Moirothea. The other lodge members then file into the lodge and take their places along the sides of the hall, where they take on their created forms and add their efforts to the imaginal structures the Master has created.

At this point the opening ceremony begins. The opening ceremony in a magical lodge serves an assortment of different functions,[72] but one of them is the formal invocation of the deities and evocation of the powers who will be adding their influences to the efforts of the lodge members in the working. While the invocation and evocation rituals will be performed by one or more of the lodge officers, all the lodge members participate in the work inwardly. By the end of the opening ritual, the presence and conscious cooperation of the deities and powers should be clearly sensed by everyone present.

The work of the lodge then takes place within the space thus prepared and empowered. If the lodge is performing an initiation, the deities and powers will be called upon to add their powers to the efforts of the lodge members to awaken one or more centers in the subtle body of the initiate, or bring about whatever other transformation might be central to the initiation process. If the lodge is performing a seasonal ritual, the deities and powers will be called on to do much the same thing on a macrocosmic scale. The spiritual beings involved in lodge work, in other words, are not merely abstractions or symbols; they are active presences whose efforts make a clearly perceptible contribution to the success of the lodge work.

When the work of the lodge is done, the closing ceremony is performed. Like the opening, this has multiple functions, but one important

---

[72] See Greer, 1998, pp. 159–182 for a discussion.

element is thanking the spiritual beings who have participated in the work of the lodge, licensing the powers to depart in the traditional manner, and clearing the imaginal structures from the lodge hall, returning it to its former status of blank slate onto which some other set of patterns can be drawn at need. The mingled powers are allowed to return to their proper places, until the magical mesocosm of the lodge is formed again by its incarnate and discarnate participants.

## References

Corbin, H. (2006). Mundus Imaginalis, or the Imaginary and the Imaginal. In: *Swedenborg and Esoteric Islam*. L. Fox (Trans.). West Chester, PA: Swedenborg Foundation.

Fortune, D. (1987a). *Applied Magic*. Wellingborough, UK: Aquarian Press.

Fortune, D. (1987b). *Esoteric Orders and Their Work*. Wellingborough, UK: Aquarian Press.

Fortune, D. (1987c). *Sane Occultism*. Wellingborough, UK: Aquarian Press.

Greer, J. M. (1998). *Inside a Magical Lodge*. St. Paul, MN: Llewellyn.

Layton, B. (1987). *The Gnostic Scriptures*. New York: Doubleday.

Lévi, É. (1972). *Transcendental Magic*. A. E. Waite (Trans.). York Beach, ME: Weiser.

Weston, J. (1983). *From Ritual to Romance*. Gloucester, MA: Peter Smith.

# POLITICS, WAR, AND MAGIC

# Getting beyond the narratives

*An open letter to the activist community*

*This is my response to a book,* Globalize Liberation, *edited by David Solnit and published in 2004. Media activists James John Bell and Patrick Reinsborough sent me a copy and asked for my thoughts about it; the result turned into an essay of some length, which got a certain amount of exposure and discussion online. Looking at the travails of progressive activism since its publication, I find very little that needs revision, except the tone of relative optimism expressed toward the end.*

James asked me for my thoughts on *Globalize Liberation*, and I hope neither of you will mind a lengthy, even labored, response. The book is extremely thought-provoking in its strengths and weaknesses alike, and it's given me an opportunity to rethink many of the assumptions I've had about social change and the potential shape of the future. Since I come to these issues from a somewhat unusual perspective—the perspective of a practicing mage and initiate of several magical orders—I recognize that the ideas *Globalize Liberation* evoked in me are perhaps a little different from those common in the progressive community. Thus I've chosen to explain those ideas here at some length.

James, we've talked extensively about magic, but I don't know how much of that you've shared with Patrick. For that reason, not to mention the off chance you might pass this around to others, I should probably take a moment to explain what I mean by magic and why it's relevant to social change at all. Dion Fortune (Violet Firth Evans), one of the most important magical theorists of the twentieth century, defined magic as "the art and science of causing changes in consciousness in accordance with will." While magic as I understand it is more a craft than an art or a science, the basic principle holds. The medium of magic is consciousness—one's own consciousness, that of other people, and (more controversially, at least within the worldview of modern industrial culture) that of other-than-human entities of various kinds. The tools of magic are will, imagination, and the innate structures of consciousness itself, constellated through formal patterns of symbol and ritual. The goals of magic are defined by the individual magician.

The relevance of all this to social change and society in general was pointed out powerfully by the late Ioan Culianu, one of the few significant modern scholars of magic who was also a competent mage. In his groundbreaking *Eros and Magic in the Renaissance* (1984) Culianu argued that modern advertising is a form of magic, and proposed that modern consumer societies can be seen as "magician states" in which social control is primarily maintained not by violence but by manipulation through magically charged images. It's a crucial insight; when people treat, say, fizzy brown sugar water as a source of their identity and human value, their resemblance to fairy-tale characters under an enchantment isn't accidental. They're quite literally caught up in a spell.

Those who aren't used to magic may find it easier to think of spells as stories. Quite a lot of magic, in fact, can be understood as storytelling. The mage uses symbol and ritual to tell a story, and makes it so spellbinding that the listeners come to believe that it's real—and then make it real by their actions. Magical combat is a struggle between storytellers, in which each mage tries to define a common reality in terms of the story that best serves his or her purposes. The struggle between the global corporate system and the activist community, to build on Culianu's insights, can be seen as a conflict of magicians telling opposing stories.

One obvious danger in magical combat is that of falling under the spell of the other mage's story—but there's also the subtler danger of falling under the spell of one's own story, losing track of the fact that it's a story rather than the raw undefined reality of human experience out of which stories are assembled. When that happens, the self-enchanted mage may not be able to let go of the story, even when it's no longer relevant and another story would be more useful. As the old tale of the Sorcerer's Apprentice points out, if you lose control of the magical forces you summon, you're in trouble. Something of this sort seems to have happened in large parts of the progressive community.

Reading *Globalize Liberation* highlighted for me three stories, or spells, in which many of today's progressives seem to be caught. Let's call them the spell of reification, the spell of corporate triumphalism, and the spell of rescue. (This last has another name that's more revealing, but I'll save that for a bit; I'm sure you know that mages don't bandy about true names too freely.) I'd like to talk about those spells first, and then go on to talk about the more hopeful side of the book: some of the ways in which today's progressive community has begun to master its own magical powers and, with them, the future of the world.

## I. The spell of reification

To my mind, one of the most striking essays in *Globalize Liberation* is Van Jones's piece "Behind Enemy Lines: Inside the World Economic Forum" (pp. 87–96). It's especially valuable because it brings core assumptions of the progressive community up against the very different world of industrial society's ruling elite.

Jones was astonished to find that the vast corporate structures against which he and many other progressives had been campaigning so hard—the WTO, the World Bank, and so on—were treated, by the people who run them, as mere tools to be used or tossed aside at will. The elite see themselves personally as the holders of power, and institutions as their means and modes of power. The activists outside the police barricades, by contrast, see the institutions themselves as the problem. The scene from *The Wizard of Oz* comes forcefully to mind; Dorothy and her friends try to figure out some way to deal with the terrifying apparition of Oz, the Great and Powerful, but never notice the little man behind the curtain.

This is only one form of a pervasive problem in today's progressive politics: the way that identification so often transforms itself into reification. In magical tradition, names are a source of power, since to name something is to give it a context and meaning of the mage's choosing.

In struggles for social change, it's therefore crucial to name what one is fighting; that's identification. But to go beyond this, to forget that every name is an abstraction imposed on a complex reality, and to treat the name as though it's an independent reality lurching around all by itself causing problems—that's reification, and it's fatal.

The economic elite Jones encountered at the World Economic Forum use reification as a form of protective camouflage. The WTO and its like distract protest from the people and interests who shape, operate, and profit from them. The elites could discard any of them in a heartbeat without bringing the world one step closer to progressive goals. But this isn't the only form of reification that gets in the way of effective social change.

Starhawk's essay "A Feminist View of Global Justice" (pp. 45–50) shows another kind of reification at work. Starhawk's a capable mage, and her essay is a good example of name magic. Responding to claims that the world's problems are caused by corporations pursuing their own good under the banner of neoliberal ideology, she argues that corporations and neoliberalism alike are simply forms of patriarchy. By this act of renaming she subordinates anticorporate language and analyses to the feminist philosophy she's defended so ably in her many books.

But what is this thing called "patriarchy"? As feminist philosophers have rightly pointed out, there's nothing in American society or culture that isn't part of the system of privilege subordinating women to men. It's useful to glance a few pages ahead to Betita Martinez's article on racism, which argues that the system of white supremacy (the name she places on racism, in another act of name magic) similarly embraces every institution in American society. If every part of American society is part of the system of patriarchy, and every part of American society is likewise part of the system of white supremacy, are the two systems actually different?

I'd point out that human relations and exchanges in American society (and indeed most others) suffer from systematic inequalities along lines drawn by gender, color, age, ethnicity, social status, sexual orientation, body weight, physical appearance, and many other factors. None of these divisions exists outside the whole system of privilege. It can be good strategy to use labels such as "patriarchy" to focus attention on some particular group suffering under the system, but it's crucial not to fall into the same mistake as those who protest the WTO, and forget that patriarchy is simply one mode of privilege, a manifestation rather than a cause.

Failure to realize this burdened an earlier generation of activists with bitter, divisive, and utterly futile quarrels between men of color and white women as to whether racism or sexism was the "real problem," when the real problem is a system of privilege that treats gender and color, among many other things, as grounds for unequal treatment. But reifying privilege as something separate from society as a whole doesn't advance understanding either. The word "privilege" is merely a way of describing systematic patterns of inequality in the fabric of human relations and exchanges; it doesn't exist outside that fabric, and it can only be changed by changing the fabric thread by thread, weaving it into new patterns of equality and mutual respect.

Of course systematic oppression of women on account of their gender is a reality, and something that any progressive movement worth the name needs to confront. In that Starhawk's essay focuses attention on this, it's performing a valuable service. But it's crucial to remember that many women also suffer oppression and injustice for reasons unrelated to their gender—reasons such as color, ethnic background, and body weight—and that women can also be privileged by social divisions, and inflict oppression and injustice on others. Using a label such as "patriarchy" for the whole problem obscures these issues and, as I'll show a little further on, closes off potential avenues for effective action. Beyond this, insisting that one particular mode of privilege is more important than others is itself a claim of privilege, and—as in the case of the quarrels just mentioned—commonly accompanies attempts to claim that one group's experience of oppression and injustice deserves more attention from the activist community than others.

Reifications are problematic because they can distract progressives from points of access where their actions can make a difference. Consider George Lakey's fascinating account of the Otpor movement against Serbian dictator Slobodan Milosevic in his article "Strategizing for a Living Revolution" (pp. 135–160). One of the tactics Otpor members used to halt police violence against them was to take photos of their wounded and make sure the family members, neighbors, and children of the police got to see them. This was a brilliant bit of magic. The individual human beings who made up that reified abstraction, "the police," were stripped of that identity by a spell of unnaming, and turned back into neighbors, husbands, children, parents: people who were part of civil society, and subject to its standards and social pressures. That couldn't have been achieved if Otpor had reified and protested "police brutality," since that act would have strengthened the reification of police as something other than ordinary members of society.

The same point should be made about one of the most pervasive reifications in *Globalize Liberation*, the reification of the existing order of society itself. David Solnit's otherwise excellent introduction (pp. xi–xxiv) falls headlong into this trap. Solnit confidently proclaims that "the system" is the cause of the world's social and ecological problems, and then goes on to define "the system" as the sum total of those problems: war, economic exploitation, and so on. It's a breathtaking display of circular logic, and invites the retort that "the system" is simply an abstract reification of everything about the world that the progressive community doesn't like.

Again, Lakey's account offers a potent alternative. Otpor strategists recognized that the Milosevic dictatorship wasn't an independent reality imposing itself from above on a passive society. It was simply an arrangement of things within Serbian society, and could only exist with the constant cooperation of millions of ordinary Serbs. The same is true of today's global corporate economy; it exists because people throughout the world, and especially people in America, uphold it by their actions. In effect, we are "the system." If we recognize that fact, instead of reifying "the system" as some force alien to us, we can own and then wield our power over it.

## II. The spell of corporate triumphalism

The notion that "the system" is something outside the society that constitutes it goes hand in hand with the claim that the struggle against "the system" is entering its most desperate phase right now. Patrick, I'm going to pick on you here, mostly because you indicated a willingness to accept scathing criticism; plenty of other essays in the book fall into this same rhetoric. You start your thoughtful essay "Decolonizing the Revolutionary Imagination" (pp. 161–212) with the words: "Our planet is heading into an unprecedented global crisis. The blatancy of the corporate power grab and the accelerating ecological meltdown is evidence that we do not live in an era where we can afford the luxury of fighting merely the symptoms of the problem." Language like "doomsday economy" and repeated insistences that we have no choice except all-out struggle feed this sense of desperation.

There's a strong confirmatory bias at work in discussions of these topics in the activist community, which has resulted in the widespread acceptance of statements that can't be justified by the facts. You comment, for example, that the current ecological transformation is "the sixth great extinction," that it's more rapid than any other, and that it threatens the survival of the Earth's biosphere itself. This rhetoric is extremely common in activist circles these days but it's not actually supported by scientific research into the Earth's past extinction crises, which I'd encourage you to look into. There have been more than twenty great extinctions since the end of the Precambrian Period, not five (or six); many past extinctions were much swifter than the present example (the K-T event that wiped out the dinosaurs was almost instant, since it involved an asteroid smashing into the Earth); and the Earth's biosphere has easily weathered crises much more drastic than anything it's facing now. The current crisis is a reality but it doesn't threaten the survival of life on the planet.

Does this mean that we needn't worry about the ecological and climatic shifts now under way as a result of human blundering? Hardly. Given that global warming alone may well drown every coastal city in the world under rising oceans, wreck the global agricultural system on which six billion people depend for their daily meals, and send tropical epidemics raging through the temperate world, just in the next century, we have plenty to fret about. As James Lovelock has shown, the Earth's biosphere is an intricate, powerful system that responds homeostatically to cancel out imbalances. Our society's inept prodding at the biosphere risks kindling a homeostatic response that could flatten the proud towers of our cities and push *Homo sapiens* to the brink of extinction.

This view of the situation has a solid foundation in science. As a tool for raising questions about the existing order of society and mobilizing individuals and communities, it's likely to work at least as well as the rhetoric of desperation described above. Yet it's received very little attention in progressive circles. Partly that's an effect of the third spell I'll discuss in this essay; partly, it's a rhetorical habit, common on the American left from colonial times to the present, of using apocalyptic rhetoric to prod people into listening (though by this point people are pretty well immunized to it). Partly, though, it's the result of another factor.

This factor is a mythology of corporate triumphalism. Today's global corporate economy presents itself as the inevitable wave of the future, a rising power that will master the destiny of the planet sometime soon if it hasn't done so already. Francis Fukuyama's widely read essay "The End of History" typifies this myth: "liberal democracy" (that is, corporate socialism manipulating the republican systems of an earlier era of politics) is the most efficient and therefore the best possible form of government, and so history defined as the evolutionary clash between competing forms of government is at an end.

Fukuyama's essay is a masterpiece of unintentional comedy, with its implied portrayal of George Herbert Walker Bush as Hegel's "world-historical personality"—am I the only person who thinks that Bush the First talks like Hardy Har Har, the chronically depressed hyena in the old Hanna-Barbera cartoons?—but it also offers a glimpse into the workings of the myth. It starts with a clever reification, turning 6000 years of wildly diverse events into a single process called "history," which by Hegel's definition has one driving force (conflict between forms of government) and one goal (the triumph of the "best," or rather, the most efficient form of government). By this act of name magic, all previous time becomes a process leading inevitably to today's global corporate system, and the total triumph of that system becomes the natural conclusion of everything that's come before: the end of history.

Progressive activists might be expected to challenge this forcefully, and present new ways of seeing the past that either dissolve "history" altogether or redefine it in ways that foster social change. Instead, most modern progressive thought accepts the myth of corporate triumphalism intact, merely changing the moral signs ("good" becomes "bad" and vice versa) and tacking on a final chapter in which, at the last possible minute, the good guys win out anyway. The resulting story makes for good fantasy (it's the basic plot of Tolkien's *The Lord of the Rings*) but bad strategy. Worse, by fitting the social change community into the dramatic role of heroic fighters for a lost cause, it subtly encourages activists to put themselves in positions where they will heroically fail to accomplish their goals, thus playing the part the story defines for them.

As a contrarian thought experiment, imagine that by some accident (a head-on collision between two time machines?) you find yourself holding a history of the world published in San Francisco in the year 3004. You eagerly turn to the pages about the early twenty-first century, hoping to find out how a triumphant, expansionistic corporate system was defeated by a heroic minority of global activists. What you find instead is something quite different…

GETTING BEYOND THE NARRATIVES    127

*By the dawn of the twenty-first century it was clear that the ramshackle structure of economic and political compromises that followed the disastrous Great European War of 1914–1945 was falling apart, and taking Euro-American global hegemony with it. Efforts to expand that hegemony's technological base in the late twentieth century by introducing supersonic transports, large-scale nuclear power, and other dubious advances went nowhere in the face of popular resistance and economic realities, while spectacularly inept handling of currency exchange problems by would-be "global managers" among the governing elites put formidable strains on a faltering system. The triumphant imperialism of the nineteenth century had given way, and the global capitalism that followed it proved too weak to resist the forces of change.*

*From 1970 on, elite groups knew they faced severe resource and energy shortages in the near future, and from 1990 on the catastrophic threat of global climate change could no longer be ignored (though it was publicly denied), but the system they were expected to manage lacked the flexibility and resources to respond to these hard realities. Nor could it cope with the ballooning of a fictive economy built on exotic financial instruments—essentially unpayable IOUs with nothing backing them—which emerged in response to pervasive weakness all through the productive sectors of the economy. Increasingly frantic transfers of jobs, resources, and wealth across nation state borders propped up the system over the short term, but the resulting ecological and economic damage fanned the flames of popular discontent and brought the final collapse steadily closer.*

*The year 2021 marked the beginning of the end. In that year, another fiscal crisis mismanaged by the elites pushed the nation state of Argentina (now part of the Confederacion de Vecindades de America del Sur) into economic and political meltdown. Argentines responded by building new, locally based networks for decision making and exchange, and as these expanded the remnants of national government slowly flickered out. Fiscal and ecological crises elsewhere in Latin America, Asia, and Eastern Europe in 2025, 2028, and 2030 saw more than a dozen nation states start coming apart in the same way. Even in those nation states that managed to hold together through the troubled early decades of the twenty-first century, economic dislocation and political failure drove the growth of new local systems on the Argentine model. As news of these spread over the internet, it fed a growing awareness that the old order's days were numbered.*

> *In the end, the breakup of the West Antarctic ice sheet in 2032 proved to be simply one crisis too many for a beleaguered, malfunctioning, and overloaded system. Faced with rising sea levels and coastal flooding worldwide, hamstrung by an unmanageable burden of unpayable debt from the fictive economy, and targeted by overwhelming popular resentment due to their failure to take preventive action against the global warming crisis, the world's economic and political elites were left without any viable options at all. Most members of the elites were killed outright or fled into hiding. In their absence, the old society fell apart in a matter of months, leaving local networks and neighborhood councils to pick up the pieces.*

Take a moment to think of your own place today in that history of elite failure and collapse. To mimic the effects of confirmatory bias, think of everything you know that fits that vision of the future. Make an effort to experience the world around you as though today's global corporate system isn't a triumphant monster, but a brittle, ungainly, jerry-rigged contraption whose managers are vainly scrambling to hold it together against a rising tide of crises. See the issues that engage your activism in that light, not as though you're desperate, but as though the system is. It's a very different perspective from that of most activists, and reaching it even in imagination might take some work, but give it your best try.

The point I'd like to make, once you've tried on both stories of the future, is that both of them—the story of corporate triumph and the story of corporate failure—explain the past and present equally well. The actions of the IMF and the World Bank in the last decade or so, for example, can be explained as a power grab by a doomsday economy in the driver's seat, but they can equally well be explained as desperation moves by a faltering elite faced with a world situation that's more unsteady and ungovernable by the day. The same is true of the 2003 invasion of Iraq, and anything else from the current-events page you wish to name.

Which of these stories is true? Wrong question. The events that define either story haven't happened yet, and which story people believe could well determine which way the ending turns out. If people believe that the global corporate system is invulnerable, most of them will make their peace with it and come to rely on it, and their actions will give it more power. If people believe that the global corporate system is doomed, most of them will withdraw their support from it and begin seeking alternatives—and that in itself could doom it. Ask yourself, then, which of these stories fosters more hope, gives more encouragement to alternative visions of society, and more effectively cuts at the mental foundations of today's economic and political systems.

Yet of course these aren't the only two choices. Philosophers of science have agonized over the hard realization that any given set of facts can be explained by an infinite number of hypotheses. Mages, by contrast, revel in the freedom this implies. The freedom to reinterpret the world, to abandon a story of desperation for one of possibility and hope, is basic to the worldview of magic. It's a freedom that today's progressive community might find it useful to embrace as well.

## III. The spell of rescue

But the progressive community's embrace of the rhetoric of desperation and the mythology of corporate triumphalism have another source, as I've suggested above. Another spell or, to use a model that's particularly appropriate here, another story keeps these patterns in place.

Patrick, I'm going to pick on you again, though I could as well discuss most of the essays in the book. "Decolonizing the Revolutionary Imagination" tells a story with three characters. One is innocent, helpless, and in need of rescue. The second is sinister, devious, and the cause of the first character's predicament. The third is heroic, idealistic, and the first character's only hope of rescue. The biosphere, the corporate "doomsday economy," and the activist community are the names you give these three characters. Other essays in the book tell the same story but give the characters different names. Still, you know whose story I'm talking about. It's the story of Dudley Do-Right.

On the off chance that you somehow missed out on watching *The Rocky and Bullwinkle Show*, where he originally appeared, I'll summarize. Dudley Do-Right was a Mountie, blond, heroic, and as thick as a brick. His girlfriend Nell Fenwick was always being tied to railroad tracks by the villainous Snidely Whiplash. Dudley rescued her time after time, to the sound of Snidely's trademark line, "Curses, foiled again!" The next episode, though, there's Snidely tying Nell to the tracks again as Dudley gallops to the rescue. The roles of the three characters are as predictable as a corporate press release: Snidely has the active role and gets the action going in each episode, Nell's role is passive (getting tied up and rescued), and Dudley's is reactive (foiling Snidely and rescuing Nell).

Map the story of Dudley Do-Right onto your article and it fits down to the fine details. "The system" has the active role, and it's always tying someone or other to the railroad tracks. The biosphere, in this case, waits passively to be rescued. The progressive community reacts by galloping to the rescue, and Whiplash Petroleum issues a press release saying "Curses, foiled again!" Dudley uses direct (re)action of various kinds—at the point of assumption (he tries to talk Snidely out of tying people to railroad tracks), destruction (he unties Nell from the tracks), production (he flags down the train), and so on. The next episode, though, there's Snidely tying Nell to the tracks again. And again. And again …

What's happened here is another bit of magic gone awry. The magic in question is what the system of magic I practice calls "assuming a godform." For certain kinds of magic, mages in my tradition choose one of the gods or goddesses of ancient Egypt, based on the energy they want to bring into focus—Isis for love, Horus for power, Nephthys for wisdom, and so on—and first visualize, then actively experience themselves as that deity. In its psychological dimension (it has others) assuming a godform is a way of temporarily redefining self-concept. Who you think you are defines what you think you can do, and that sets the limits on what you can do. Assuming a godform allows the mage to step outside the limits of ordinary self-concepts by taking one aspect of human potential and raising it to the power of infinity.

People do this in a less conscious way all the time. Kids assume popular culture "godforms" right and left—look, I'm Spider-Man! Most adults do it a bit more subtly, but if you watch them and know your pop culture you can usually figure out what images they've assumed. You'll also notice, though, that many of them are stuck in a single image, repeating the same role over and over, even when it's counterproductive. I suggest that this is what's happened to the American progressive community; it's gotten stuck in the godform of Dudley Do-Right.

No, I don't think today's activists literally spent too much time watching *The Rocky and Bullwinkle Show* and got mesmerized by Canada's least intelligent Mountie. Like any satire, Dudley Do-Right pokes fun at familiar themes; we laugh at him because we all know the story he's lampooning. The self-concept that the progressive community has embraced is the one Dudley Do-Right makes fun of, the image of the heroic rescuer. Assuming that image in the first place was good strategy: an effective counter to negative images of "protesters," not to mention a way to impose the image of Snidely Whiplash on defenders of privilege. What makes it a problem is that activists got stuck in the role and can't step out of it. They can't see themselves as anything but heroic rescuers. As confirmatory bias comes into play, they inevitably see the world around them in terms of Nells to rescue and Snidelys to vanquish.

The spell of Dudley Do-Right has much to do with the purely reactive stance of the American activist community. When activists define their role wholly in terms of resistance and refusal, of "articulat[ing] a NO to the system" (David Solnit's phrase, p. xv) rather than pursuing a positive ideal, they guarantee that they'll perpetually be scrambling to counter some new assault by the system, trying to maintain an inadequate status quo against the threat of further losses, rather than making the system and its defenders scramble to counter efforts to change the status quo for the better. This reactive stance comes out of the Dudley Do-Right role, since the heroic rescuer is always reactive; it's the Snidelys of the world who get each episode moving by grabbing another Nell and tying her to the railroad tracks.

Dudley also underlies some of the less productive rhetorical habits of the activist community. Patrick, I'm going to use your sidebar "Framing the Climate Crisis" on p. 182 as an example; it's fairly mild compared to some of what we've all seen, but it'll make the point. You argue that "It's up to activists to ensure that people understand that a small cartel of energy corporations and their financial backers knowingly destabilized our planet's climate for their own personal gain. This may turn out to be the most devastating crime ever perpetrated against humanity, the planet, and future generations." Grand rhetoric, but I trust you're aware that it's a fantastic hypersimplification of a hugely complex issue. To be precise, it's a Dudley Do-Right definition, in which activists are Dudley, energy corporations are Snidely Whiplash, and "humanity, the planet, and future generations" are a collective Nell.

Is it a useful redefinition? Depends on what you're trying to achieve. It sounds as though you hope to target the energy companies for destruction by using them as scapegoats for disasters caused by global warming. If that's indeed your intention, it might work, but since global warming's sources go far beyond the mere Snidelyhood of oil companies (and include the actions of the energy-squandering American middle class you skillfully dismiss as "soccer moms"), having oil company CEOs torn to pieces by howling mobs won't actually do much for humanity, the planet, or future generations. In the meantime, the rhetoric of demonization helps guarantee that the issue of global warming will become more fiercely polarized and further from a solution than ever.

An alternative approach might be worth considering. Again, George Lakey's discussion of the Otpor movement is relevant. The Otpor strategists deliberately avoided polarization of the sort that American progressives embrace reflexively. Instead of demonizing the police, they pursued a policy of outreach, building bridges that ultimately reached into the upper levels of the police bureaucracy. That paid off handsomely in the final crisis of the Milosevic regime, when the police stood by and did nothing as crowds seized the Serbian Parliament building. If activists in this country took an Otpor approach to people in the energy companies, instead of painting Snidely Whiplash's long black mustache on them, they could get similar results.

Of course this would require giving up the very real emotional payoffs of the Dudley Do-Right role; the rush of being a rescuing hero is a potent drug, and so is the righteous indignation of knowing your enemies are Satan (or Snidely) incarnate. Letting go of Dudleyhood can also require giving up more tangible payoffs; as Patrick points out in an excellent analysis of the professionalization of dissent (pp. 193–199), significant parts of the activist community have been bought out and turned into junior partners in the corporate system. Playing Dudley Do-Right is among other things an effective way to ignore one's own complicity in arrangements of privilege and exploitation, since everything can be blamed on a Snidely Whiplash of one's choosing (such as "the system").

## *IV. Binaries, ternaries, and shifting levels*

I'd like to shift gears here and talk a little more directly about the magical dimension of all this. One of the interesting things about the spell of Dudley Do-Right is that it's a dysfunctional ternary. James, we've discussed magical number theory at quite some length, but again I don't know how much of that you've shared with Patrick, and if either of you shows this to anyone else the chance that they'll have the least idea of what I'm talking about is pretty slim. So I'll try to sum up the elements of magical philosophy in 500 words or less.

Toward the beginning of this letter I mentioned that the structures of consciousness are tools of magic. In the system of magic I practice, those structures are identified with the numbers from one to ten, understood not as quantities but as abstract relationships. You can experience anything through any number (though numbers above ten denote relationships too complex for the human nervous system to handle). Each number has its strengths and its weaknesses. If you're working deliberately with the structures of consciousness—which is to say, if you're a mage—you choose the structure/number you use based on the effects you want to get. Most of the time, for reasons too complex to get into here, you choose one, two, or three.

Anything seen through the filter of the number one is called a unary. When you see something as a unary, you highlight qualities in it such as wholeness, indivisibility, and isolation. See it through the number two, as a binary, and you'll highlight different qualities such as division, conflict, balance, and complementarity. See it through the number three and still different qualities such as change and complexity will be highlighted. All these have practical implications. If you want people to cooperate and build community, get them to think of themselves as part of a unary; if you want them to quarrel and resist change, convince them they're on one side of a binary; if you want them to make change, make them think of their community and their world as a ternary.

Our society has a persistent habit of always seeing things in binaries. The binary is symbolically masculine—think of the ithyphallic straight line, defined by any two points—so this isn't surprising! Our politics divide up into left and right, our ethics into good and evil, our most popular religions oppose one god and one devil, and so on. Campaigns for social change are no different, and plenty of activists think they can get where they want by opposing something. In a binary, though, every action is balanced by an opposite reaction, so thinking in binaries is very problematic if you want to foster change.

If you're a mage, you respond to dysfunctions of this sort by shifting numbers. The traditional rule here is that numbers always change in a specific order: one becomes two, two becomes three, and three becomes one and shifts to another level. (The reasons for this rule, again, are too complex to go into here.) Thus if you've got a situation that presents itself as a binary, and you want to change it, you can't effectively turn it back into a unary—it'll just pop back into being a binary again—but you can turn the binary into a ternary by redefining the situation in terms of three independent factors, rather than two. This is called neutralizing a binary, and it's a very common bit of magical strategy.

The "good cop/bad cop" routine is a move of this sort. The cops redefine the binary between policeman and suspect by having one officer act friendly, while the other comes on like Attila the Hun. The binary opposition dissolves, and fairly often the suspect talks. The American political establishment uses the same move on the progressive community every four years, with the Democrats playing good cop and the Republicans playing bad cop; activists time and again get sucked into the ternary, and put their time and energy into a candidate whose only claim on their attention is that he's not quite as bad as the other guy. It doesn't help that the two parties switch roles and do the identical move on conservative activists too.

James, you and I have talked at quite a bit of length about ways that activists can take control of this dynamic and use ternaries for their own purposes—for example, by having "good cop" moderate progressives and "bad cop" radicals double-team a corporation or a government. But it's a crucial mistake to oppose "good" ternaries with "bad" binaries, and thus turn the relationship between them into a binary. Every number is appropriate in some places and a waste of time in others, and the Dudley Do-Right scenario is an example of a ternary that's a waste of time. The three characters circle endlessly around one another; you've got action, complexity, and an addictive emotional payoff of self-regarding heroism and self-righteous indignation. What you don't have is a resolution of the problems the progressive community thinks it's fighting.

The magical response to the Dudley Do-Right trap is to shift from ternary to unary, which means recognizing that Dudley, Nell, and Snidely aren't three independent factors at all, but three interdependent elements of a single structure of experience. As long as activists see themselves as heroic Dudleys, they'll inevitably see every problem in terms of Nells to rescue and Snidelys to rescue them from. Any one role defines the other two. Leaving that behind, in turn, involves shifting to a new level of self-awareness. Many activists these days honestly believe that the three roles are out there in the world, that the biosphere really is tied helplessly to the railroad tracks and the board of directors of Whiplash Petroleum really are twiddling their black mustaches and going "nya ha ha" as the train approaches. Banishing the spell requires waking up to the fact that these roles are in the mind of the observer, and that it's possible to define the situation in other ways.

This is one of the reasons why, earlier on, I deliberately proposed several models for the current situation that don't fit the Dudley Do-Right scenario at all. For the biosphere to be a suitable Nell for Dudley to rescue, she has to be helplessly tied to the railroad track; the fact that this particular Nell might actually be an irritated grizzly bear, fully capable of breaking the ropes and tearing Snidely (and Dudley) limb from limb, doesn't fit the story even though it may fit the facts. In the same way, the future history that shows Snidely himself tied to the railroad track, flailing about helplessly as the train approaches, chucks the Dudley scenario out the window. Redefine one role and the entire story changes.

It may be high time for some such redefinition. I'm heartened by the words of the anonymous aboriginal woman quoted on p. 417: "If you come only to help me, you can go back home. But if you consider my struggle as part of your struggle for survival, then maybe we can work together." In the terms I've used here, she's saying that she isn't a helpless Nell awaiting rescue, and progressives from the industrial world aren't heroic Dudleys riding to her help. She's cast a spell of renaming that turns the Dudley Do-Right ternary into a unary of equals working together for survival. Can that same spell be extended to the entire project of social change? I believe so.

## V. Learning new magics

I've put quite a bit of time into critiquing aspects of the activist community in this letter, and for all I know one or both of you may see that as a frontal assault against everything you believe. That's not my intention, though. I've tried, borrowing your language, to apply some direct action at the point of assumption—that is, to challenge some of the inadequately examined assumptions that are hindering a powerful global movement for positive change.

What I see in *Globalize Liberation* generally is a situation in which theory hasn't caught up to practice. Shopworn slogans and reifications long past their pull date jostle new tactics and strategies that the old language doesn't really describe. Patrick, I've lambasted your essay "Decolonizing the Revolutionary Imagination" several times, but it's also in many ways the most impressive and magically sophisticated section of the book. Yes, it suffers from each of the problems I've noted, but it also breaks very promising ground.

I'd like to point out two things it does that put it way past many other attempts to analyze the situation and propose strategies. First, it focuses on the central place of imagination in the making and unmaking of social reality. That's spectacularly important. The politics of reality, as Theodore Roszak pointed out in *Where the Wasteland Ends* (1972), is a politics of the imagination. It's not just that change has to be thinkable before it's possible, though this is true and important; it's also that imagination can change the world by itself. The collapse of Eastern Europe's communist bloc in 1989 happened because people stopped imagining themselves and their societies in ways that made putting up with a bad system reasonable. Remember the dazed expressions on the faces of so many former communist heads of state and secret police chiefs? Their power had always been imaginary; political power always is. What happened in 1989 was that people recognized that, and imagined it out of existence.

The essay goes on to say that "If we want to talk about reality in the singular ... we must talk about ecological reality" (p. 200). Here you're selling your own insights short. I grant that as mental maps go, ecology—with its keen awareness of limits and consequences—is a helluva lot more useful now than the economic models that powered industrial society through the glory days of the Age of Exuberance, but it's still a map, not the territory it tries to describe. If it's allowed to fossilize into a dogmatic ideology, it could become just as toxic as the mental maps it's starting to replace.

If we want to talk about reality in the singular, we haven't yet grasped the power of the imagination, because "reality" is always in flux, shaped by a complex dialogue between the blooming, buzzing confusion of the universe of our experience and the world-defining powers of the imagination—and the result is never quite the same for any two individuals, ever. The Zapatista quest for "a world where many worlds fit" offers more than any one vision of what's real. That being said, I find the idea of Earth-centered politics very useful, since it focuses attention on the raw experience of natural systems. If I may speak briefly from a position wholly within the magical worldview, how trees and stones imagine the world is at least as important as how human beings do so, even if the human beings are ecologically literate.

The second crucial thing "Decolonizing the Revolutionary Imagination" does is encourage self-awareness in the activist community. The edgy discussion of the professionalization of dissent, and the brief but lethal definition of "defector syndrome" in the appendix, challenge two of the most obvious places where activism has become its own reward rather than a means to an end. My comments about the spell of Dudley Do-Right are aimed at another. When activism becomes a masturbatory act of self-gratification, as it sometimes does, it's just another part of the existing order—a pressure valve that allows the disaffected to vent their passions harmlessly.

This is where *Globalize Liberation*, with its focus on Third World activism and experience, has the most to offer American progressives. The essays on Zapatismo and the Argentine experience are among the most promising things I've read in social change literature in the last two decades. They point to powerful redefinitions of activism and the transformation of society, and if activists here in America pay close attention the results could be spectacular. The principles Manuel Callahan cites in his essay "Zapatismo Beyond Chiapas" (pp. 217–228)—refusal, space, and listening—would be worth applying within the activist community, as well as in interactions with the rest of American society. Can you imagine a group of radicals from San Francisco moving to Pittsburgh, and subordinating themselves to the community in the middle of the Rust Belt? If you can't, work on the idea until you can.

I could go on about many other strong points in the essays in *Globalize Liberation*, but this letter has already ballooned to unjustifiable size and I'll limit myself to one: the theme of Marina Sitrin's brilliant piece "Weaving Imagination and Creation: The Future In the Present" (pp. 263–276). The notion of prefigurative politics itself is profoundly magical. Ritual magic, after all, is prefigurative politics on the individual level; the mage works with symbols, and focuses will and imagination through that act to make the symbol prefigure the reality. To do the same thing on the scale of nations and peoples is an immense challenge, but it's also a powerful possibility. It also points toward modes of politics—parapolitics might be a better term—that use the prefigurative power of the imagination to change the world without using anything that looks like politics in any sense we'd recognize today.

What I'm seeing most clearly in *Globalize Liberation* is a movement in transition, partly anchored in tactics and analyses from past decades, partly working with the improvisations of the present, partly reaching out to the new possibilities of the future. It's a promising sight. As I've suggested in talking about the myth of corporate triumphalism, the existing order may not be nearly so solid as it tries to make itself appear.

It can't be repeated often enough that the modern industrial state isn't the natural endpoint (or endgame) of some inevitable historical process. It's what philosophers call a contingent reality; things happened to turn out this way, but they didn't have to, and there are good reasons why the future probably won't be a duplicate of the past. As we move into the twilight of the industrial age, the old bets are off.

So those are my responses. I hope some of this turns out useful. Call me or drop me an email any time if you want to talk about any of it.

With my best as always,

John Michael Greer

# Magic and the end of history

*An inquiry into the shape of time*

*This essay was written for another anthology of essays on magic, XVI— the reference is to the sixteenth Tarot trump, The Tower. It was my first attempt to weave together magic and the broader perspectives of history, a theme I took up in more detail in my book* The Blood of the Earth *and in an assortment of online essays not yet reworked for print.*

Walking the path of a magician in today's world requires either a lively appreciation for irony or a complete blindness to it. The latter is far and away the more popular of the two, for good reason: Irony is explosive stuff, especially when it weaves itself into the unquestioned assumptions of a culture or a subculture.

Nowadays the occult scene is awash in unrecognized irony. Many occultists today see themselves as innovators boldly taking magic where it has never gone before. Many others see themselves as defenders of some unchanging tradition from the past. Both sides claim to be rebels against the existing order of things. The irony begins here, as it's hard to think of a theme more hardwired into the existing order of things than the hackneyed pseudo debate between a supposedly innovative present and a supposedly static past.

In all its many manifestations—and few corners of contemporary culture lack them—this nonquarrel conceals, behind a conventional facade of rebellious originality, an unquestioning allegiance to the basic presuppositions of modern thought. The most important of those presuppositions concern what we may as well call the shape of time.

Philosophers have suggested that deep-ocean fish have no awareness of the water in which they live, since they have nothing with which to contrast it. Whether or not they are right about the fish, this is certainly true about the way most human beings relate to the way time is defined for them by their culture.

In traditional China, for example, time had a circular shape; every rise was followed by a fall, and every fall by a rise; at every moment, the cycles of time lined up like the cylinders in a combination lock, and the combination might be deduced and the lock picked by someone learned in the *I Ching*, the primary Chinese text of time theory. For thousands of years this way of thinking was so deeply ingrained in Chinese society that it rarely had to be mentioned, and it was only when Europeans arrived and imposed their own very different vision of time by force that time lost its shape.

Pass from traditional China to aboriginal Australia and time changes shape completely; Chinese time moves in circles, but aboriginal time doesn't move at all. The time that matters is the Dreamtime, when everything real happened, or happens, or will happen—the Dreamtime exists equally in the past, the present, and the future. Aboriginal bands performed their increase ceremonies to tap into the always-existing Dreamtime for their own benefit and that of the land. According to archeologists, the aboriginal shape of time remained firmly in place for thousands of years, until European ships arrived with a new kind of time and the firepower to make it the only time that mattered.

The same thing happened to shapes of time around the world as Europeans surged out of their crowded peninsula on the west end of Asia and spread themselves at gunpoint around the world. Of all the dubious imports they brought with them—gunpowder, venereal diseases, Christianity—their shape of time may well have caused the most destruction. The shape of time may seem like sheer abstraction, but then water probably seems that way to fish. Flip the fish out of water and the concrete nature of that seeming abstraction becomes brutally apparent.

For millions of people dragged out of their own times and forced into the alien time of the West, the experience was not very different.

This needs to be remembered just now, because time can change its shape for reasons other than the arrival of invaders from overseas. It can also change if the gap between the shape of time defined by a culture and the shape that's experienced by people within that culture becomes too wide to be bridged. The opening of just such a gap is well under way in the modern industrial world; in the decades just ahead of us, it will become impossible to ignore.

\* \* \*

How can a fish learn to be aware of water? This is becoming a crucial question as the certainties of today's industrial cultures crumble beneath them. Most of us have not yet learned to see the shape of time that surrounds us, precisely because it surrounds us so totally.

That unseen shape is also the central myth of our age. To call it that is to run afoul of deeply entrenched biases. The claim that past societies had myths but ours does not is among the credos of contemporary culture. There are even books claiming that "amythia," the pathological lack of myths, causes many of the ills of modernity.[73]

Once again, though, we are deep in irony. Our society's problems have many roots but a myth deficiency is not among them. It is of course true that the myths of Christianity and Judaism no longer command the belief of most people. Even among those who still make weekly trips to churches, myths and symbols that once inspired martyrs to die with prayers on their lips have generally become social fictions maintained from no better motive than sheer nostalgia. Still, this did not happen because people stopped believing in myths; it happened because they abandoned their old myths for a more appealing one, the myth of progress.

Most people nowadays, even when they cling to the symbols of older faiths, believe that human history traces a straight line from the squalor of a primitive past to the grandeur of a Promethean future. Most people assume that by definition, newer opinions are more true and newer practices more effective than older ones, and old ideas and approaches

---

[73] An example is Loyal D. Rue, *Amythia: Crisis in the Natural History of Western Culture* (Tuscaloosa, AL: University of Alabama Press, 1989).

are not just made unfashionable but disproved by the passage of time. Magicians are by no means immune to such logic; as already mentioned, a sizeable subset of today's magical scene likes to think of itself as cutting-edge innovators whose theories and practices are better than the magic of the past, for no better reason than that they are newer.

A thought experiment can help show just how much emotional power the myth of progress wields. Imagine, then, that the contemporary faith in progress turns out to be based on a simple misunderstanding. The triumphs of the last three centuries were made possible, let's say, not by some grand trajectory of progress, but simply by the exploitation of the Earth's fossil fuel reserves. The fantastic amounts of energy mined and pumped from the ground enabled the world to enjoy an unparalleled economic boom, the Age of Exuberance, in which the limits that bound all other societies were temporarily lifted by a glut of cheap fuel.[74]

Today, to continue the thought experiment, all the factors that gave rise to the Age of Exuberance are going or gone, and a massively overpopulated world is rushing to extract what remains of the coal, oil, and natural gas that made industrial society possible. Assume, for the sake of the experiment, that none of the proposed replacements for fossil fuels can make up the difference. The future facing us then is not a vista of endless progress, but a difficult retreat to the world as it was before 1700, with no hope of another Age of Exuberance to come.

Even to imagine this future as a reality is to confront the myth of progress head on. It can be an extremely uncomfortable experience. Take a moment to think it through. Picture our civilization winding down, technologies abandoned because no one can spare the energy and raw materials to keep them working, the scientific discoveries of the recent past reduced to historical curiosities. Imagine crumbling nations and resurgent local cultures burning through the last fossil fuels in an attempt to cushion the descent into a new Middle Ages, as most people return to subsistence farming, craft work, or manual labor to support themselves, while a dwindling intellectual class struggles to market its knowledge to anyone who will keep it fed and clothed. Imagine the footprints on the moon fading into legend. Imagine the stars forever out of reach.

If your first reaction is that this can't possibly happen, set that aside and imagine that it has. If your second reaction is that people will

---

[74] The phrase "Age of Exuberance" is from William Catton, *Overshoot: The Ecological Basis of Revolutionary Change* (Champaign, IL: University of Illinois Press, 1980).

inevitably find some way to get progress back on track, set that aside as well; imagine that rapid technological progress turns out to have been an exotic phenomenon fostered by one set of rare historical conditions, and that the millennia of technological standstill before the Age of Exuberance are matched by millennia more of stasis or slow decline after it.

Think about what the human situation looks like from this perspective. In such a world, people will still live, love, struggle, and practice magic, but they will do so as their ancestors did, in a world tied closely to the rhythms of nature and the harsh requirements of a subsistence economy. Does that destiny make the story of human existence meaningless? For many people nowadays, it does. That is what happens when a myth dies—or, to use the language already proposed in this essay, when time loses its familiar shape.

\* \* \*

What makes this thought experiment even more uncomfortable is that a great deal of evidence suggests that it is not a fantasy. This evidence has been explored at great length in many recent books, and need not be repeated here; the curious can consult the sources listed in the notes.[75]

The core of the case these books make is that fossil fuels contain more cheap, abundant, readily accessible energy that anything else humanity has within reach; they exist in limited quantities; and they are being extracted from the Earth at a breakneck pace, several times the rate at which new deposits are being discovered. No other energy source available to us can replace them in any meaningful sense, and as they run short, a global industrial and technological infrastructure completely dependent on them will grind gradually to a halt.

The alternative technologies now being touted as replacements for fossil fuels, these studies show, are actually dependent on fossil fuels themselves. Nobody uses wind power, for example, to manufacture wind turbines; electricity from coal and natural gas powers the factories, and diesel fuel from oil wells powers the trucks that transport the turbines and the machinery that installs them. For that matter, today's wind turbines cannot be made or operated without plastics

---

[75] See Catton, op. cit.; John Michael Greer, *The Long Descent: A User's Guide to the End of the Industrial Age* (Gabriola, BC, Canada: New Society Publishers, 2008); Richard Heinberg, *The Party's Over: Oil, War, and the Fate of Industrial Societies* (New Society Publishers, 2003); and James Howard Kunstler, *The Long Emergency: Surviving the Converging Catastrophes of the Twenty-First Century* (New York: Atlantic Monthly Press, 2005).

and lubricants derived from petroleum, as well as rare earth elements that can only be mined and processed in useful quantities because vast amounts of cheap energy can be poured into the process. Add up all the fossil fuel inputs that go into wind power, and it's not unfair to call a wind turbine a roundabout way to convert fossil fuels into energy, with a little additional boost from the wind.

You will not hear perspectives like this in the circles where wind power is being touted as the answer to our energy problems. Nor, though the same points could be made about other energy alternatives from solar cells to fusion power, will you hear them raised in those contexts. The working assumption that dominates nearly all discussions of energy today is that the universe has to contain something newer, bigger, and better than fossil fuels, so that progress can continue unchecked. It's unthinkable to many people that fossil fuels may be the best energy source our species will ever know, and that when they are gone, we will have to make do with the same far more limited sources our great-great-grandparents used.

The resulting effort to avoid thinking about the unthinkable has backed important elements of the alternative energy scene into embarrassing corners. Consider the recent ethanol debacle in the United States. Prominent environmentalists hit on ethanol made from American corn as the wonder fuel that would save the day. They found plenty of support, not least from farm state politicians interested in scoring with their constituents and stock market mavens hoping to cash in on the next stock bubble. Nobody took the time to figure out if ethanol from corn would actually make money, or produce more energy than it consumed, and as it turned out, it couldn't do either one.

Across America's farm belt, as a result, abandoned ethanol factories have become another gravestone marking the slow death of the American dream. Meanwhile, biodiesel from algae has replaced ethanol as the fantasy fuel du jour, and money is currently being poured into schemes with economic prospects even more dubious than the failed ethanol plants.[76] When those schemes fail, as they will, there will be others. There have to be others, because the alternative is to accept that

---

[76] See, for example, Krassen Dimitrov's *GreenFuel Technologies: A Case Study for Industrial Photosynthetic Energy Capture* (available at www.nanostring.net/Algae/CaseStudy.pdf), which documents that algal biodiesel using currently available technologies will only make money if diesel fuel costs $800 a gallon.

Nature is under no obligation to hand us a new energy source to replace the fossil fuels we have wasted so profligately over the last 300 years.

All the money and effort being wasted on such pursuits could be put to work cushioning the decline and making sure that at least some of the useful legacies of our age get passed to the future. Excepting a few projects run on shoestring budgets by individuals and groups on the fringes of society, this is not happening. The power wielded by the shape of time shows itself here as well. In any culture, the shape of time determines what people are able to imagine about the future, even when what is imaginable does not include what is happening around them.

*  *  *

The myth of progress is not quite the only force shaping contemporary expectations about time and the future. An older myth, inherited from the culture that modern industrial society supplanted, still has followers of its own. This myth defines the shape of time in its own way, and it also has a clearly defined social role nowadays: In the stereotyped debates between progress and tradition mentioned at the beginning of this essay, it provides the losers.

The alternative myth has roots deep enough in our culture that everyone reading this essay knows it well enough to recite it in their sleep. There was, this myth claims, a time before history when human beings lived at peace with themselves and their world. Then some terrible event ended paradise; history began, and brought all the miseries and evils that have afflicted us ever since. After countless years of suffering, truth burst forth in a redeeming revelation, and a wise and fortunate few gathered around the banner of truth to defend it against the gargantuan powers of a corrupt and dying world. The next act in the drama, which will arrive any day now, is a cataclysmic change in which the old world will be swept away forever, paradise will be restored, history will come to a full stop, and nothing important will ever change again.

The only thing that makes this myth hard to see as a single pattern is that the names of the characters change from version to version. In the Christian version, the original paradise was Eden, the terrible event was Original Sin, the redeeming revelation was the life of Jesus, the fortunate band battling a corrupt world is the Christian church, and the next act in the drama is Armageddon, followed by the Second Coming and the New Jerusalem. In the Marxist version, the original paradise was primitive communism, the terrible event was the invention of private property, the redeeming revelation was Marxism, the fortunate band is the Communist party, and the next act is revolution, followed by socialism and the transition to Communism. In the radical Pagan feminist version, the original paradise was ancient matriarchal society, the terrible event was the invasion of the patriarchal Indo-Europeans, the redeeming revelation was Marija Gimbutas's speculations, the fortunate band is contemporary feminist Paganism, and the next event is the fall of patriarchy and the rise of a "partnership society" in which women will be just that little bit more equal than men, and so on.

The diversity of labels for the elements of the myth do nothing to counter its underlying unity. The shape it gives to time is a straight line segment with a beginning, an end, and half a dozen clearly defined points in between. The present moment is one of those; those who believe that myth and inhabit the shape of time it defines are always living on the eve of the apocalypse, just before the rising spiral of conflict between the chosen few and the corrupt institutions of a doomed but powerful system explodes into its final, fateful, and utterly predictable finale.

Thus it has exercised a potent magnetism on radicals on all sides of the political continuum since the dawn of the industrial age, as it allows them to see their protests against authority, however unimpressive these may be, as the beginning of the ultimate struggle against evil. It also encourages radicals to fulfill the role assigned them by contemporary society, which is to lose. It's worth noting that those radical movements that accomplish their goals, such as the Civil Rights movement of the 1950s and 1960s or the first two waves of American feminism, are consistently those that steer clear of apocalyptic rhetoric. Those movements that embrace apocalyptic rhetoric just as consistently fail.

It's hard to say why insisting that the world will crash into ruin unless your movement gets its way should be the kiss of death for radical movements, but the track record extends to all sides of the political continuum. Consider the abject failure of Christian fundamentalism to force its moral vision on society. Despite half a century of efforts backed up by levels of popular support and funding that dwarf most left-wing movements, the fundamentalists have yet to get any major piece of their agenda enacted into law, or even manage more than occasional delays in points as fatal to their crusade as the legal recognition of gay marriage. It's anyone's guess which way the arrows of cause and effect run between this litany of failure and the fundamentalist obsession with the End Times, but the correlation is hard to miss.

The rapid spread of apocalyptic beliefs throughout the activist left in recent years is thus not a promising sign. Still, there is another and, at least potentially, a far more serious problem with the popularity of such beliefs all through contemporary society. The myth of progress and the myth of apocalypse both impose a distinctive shape on time, and define specific expectations for the future. The problem is that neither of these myths anticipates a future anything like the one we are most likely to get.

\* \* \*

Civilizations fall. This is one of the most predictable things about them. What is too rarely noticed is that every civilization known to history traces the same general trajectory on its way to history's dumpster: a long, ragged process of crisis, contraction, and repeated attempts at partial recovery extending over one to three centuries.[77]

This is not the way most people today expect civilization to end. Hundreds of otherwise forgettable Hollywood disaster epics have taught us that the fall of our civilization will take place in the two-hour window between opening and closing credits, with special effects courtesy of Industrial Light and Magic. The myth of apocalypse in all its many forms assumes the same thing; Jesus or proletarian revolution or some other messianic force shows up with the biggest possible flash and bang, and by the time the rubble stops bouncing the old world is gone forever. The myth of progress assumes that civilization can only get better, but agrees that whatever the future brings, it has to be bigger, brighter, and louder than the past.

As the pressures of resource depletion and environmental degradation have begun to bite in recent decades, these three currents of thinking about the future have interbred with all the coy reluctance of minks in heat. Visit a bookstore of any size and you'll find the results swarming on the shelves. My favorite example just now is Ray Kurzweil, who got the fifteen minutes of fame Andy Warhol predicted the future would

---

[77] Arnold Toynbee, *A Study of History* vols. V and VI (New York: Oxford University Press, 1939), documents this trajectory in exhaustive detail.

give everyone by rewriting Protestant fantasies of the Rapture in the language of bad science fiction.[78] Kurzweil's pop theology centers on the Singularity, the imminent point—like all apocalypses, it's always just about to happen—when science will know everything that matters and human beings become omnipotent. Once this happens, he insists, we'll all upload our identities into immortal robot bodies and go soaring off the planet to enjoy the good life forever in deep space.

Replace space with heaven, robot bodies with the Resurrection, and the Singularity with the Second Coming, and the narrative is instantly familiar; it's precisely Kurzweil's lack of originality that makes him so entertaining. He's not alone in attempting to tell an apocalyptic story using the language of the myth of progress, either. That sort of mingled myth was mapped by a great many people onto the Y2K nonproblem; an entire industry now exists to project it onto the inkblot patterns of the Mayan calendar; when the next baktun begins without incident on 21 December 2012, no doubt, some new target for the mythology will be found.

The end of the Age of Exuberance has provided an ample excuse for the same exercise, and those who read their way through current speculations on peak oil will find their share of sudden evolutionary leaps to a Utopian world, overnight cataclysms that send hordes of zombified urbanites across the landscape to provide target practice to survivalists, and so on. It's interesting to watch the logic of myth that runs all through these accounts, dismissing all the more likely outcomes so that the future can be forced onto the Procrustean bed of our culture's preferred ways of thinking about the future.

Fusing the myths of progress and apocalypse is easier than it looks, because a common theme unites them: Both are myths of *the end of history*. According to the myth of apocalypse, history is what happens between the Fall and the Second Coming, or whatever their equivalents happen to be; once evil is vanquished, history stops and nothing significant ever changes again. According to the myth of progress, in turn, history as we have known it is already over; now that we have outgrown the errors and superstitions of the past, we can expect a future of endless improvement in which even the most overwhelming crisis will

---

[78] Ray Kurzweil, *The Singularity is Near* (New York: Viking, 2005), is as good an introduction as any.

merely speed up the pace of innovation, or at most impose a setback we will soon overcome on our journey to the stars.

Just below the surface of this insistence on history's end, it's not hard to sense the paralyzing dread of the future that drives it. Civilizations in decline very often experience this sort of terror of history; they see time itself as a trap closing around them, and flail about for some means of escape. As classical civilization faltered, mystery cults that promised a salvation outside of time grew strong, and then were swallowed up by a religion that promised an end to time not only for the individual initiate but for the entire world. Where the temples of the Roman gods faced outwards, embracing the community and its history, Christian churches turned inward and knelt behind closed doors as they prayed for time to end.

Religious people like to claim that all prayers are answered, but the only response this one received was a resounding *No*. Neither the Second Coming nor anything else saved the Roman world from its own mistakes. Instead, classical civilization stumbled down the slow arc of descent into history's dumpster, and the barbarian tribes that swarmed in to fill the vacuum founded new nations and histories of their own.

Two thousand years from now, some future essayist may describe the decline and fall of the American empire in similar terms. Long before that happens, though, those who cling to the hope that history will stop are likely to find out the hard way that it will not do so soon enough to keep them from experiencing the future that they most fear.

\* \* \*

The question that will be asked by a great many people then, and may have risen in the minds of some of this essay's readers already, is how to replace the myths with knowledge of the true shape of time. Plausible though it sounds, it's the wrong question to ask. Cultures down through the ages have come up with a dizzying assortment of myths to give shape to time, and each one seems to work about as well, and about as poorly, as any of the others. Our competing myths of progress and apocalypse are no more true than the Chinese myth of time's complex circles or the Aboriginal myth of the eternal Dreamtime of which all earthly events are pallid reflections.

Nor do we even have the option of ridding ourselves of myths and seeing the world "as it is;" human beings think with myths as inevitably as we walk with feet and eat with mouths, and those who believe themselves to be free of myths are simply caught up in the delusion that their myths are literally true. To abandon that delusion is to approach the borders of magic.

In the broadest sense, this entire essay has been about one branch of magic, the branch that masters the symbols with which we make sense of the universe. Dion Fortune used to say that magic is the art and science of causing change in consciousness in accordance with will.[79] Thus magic does deliberately, on a personal scale, what myth does less consciously and on a collective scale. There's a sense, in fact, in which magic is to myth what engineering is to science: the practical application of patterns that span and shape the universe as a whole.

Thus the question that magicians might usefully ask themselves is not what shape time has, but what shape they might be able to give it. If the view of the future offered in this essay is anything like accurate, we face one to three centuries of decline, ending in a world with roughly the same energy resources and technological options as the one our ancestors knew. That future does not define the whole shape of time, and any number of myths could make sense of the curve of decline in their own terms. All that is needed to work magic with time is a recognition that time's shape is up for grabs.

Not that long ago, many occultists knew as much, and defined the shape of time in their own ways. Most practitioners of magic these days have heard of Aleister Crowley's theory of aeonic cycles, in which one dominant spiritual influence after another, proclaimed at intervals by a qualified Magus, holds the planet in thrall.[80] Fewer know that William Butler Yeats, a Golden Dawn alumnus like Crowley, crafted a far more subtle theory of historical cycles as part of his masterpiece of magical philosophy *A Vision*.[81] Other examples are easy to find; all through the magical revival of the late nineteenth century and early twentieth, it was a rare occultist or magical order that didn't have a distinctive vision of time on offer.

It became fashionable some decades ago to dismiss this sort of thing as pointless clutter, a kind of Victorian architectural gingerbread

---

[79] Quoted in W. E. Butler, *Magic: Its Ritual, Power and Purpose* (Wellingborough, UK: Aquarian, 1975), p. 12.
[80] Aleister Crowley, *The Law Is For All* (Tempe, AZ: New Falcon, 1996).
[81] William Butler Yeats, *"A Vision" and Related Writings*, ed. A. Norman Jeffares (London: Arena, 1990).

unsuited to the gleaming Bauhaus constructions of up-to-date magic. Magical narratives of time went into the same dustbin of collective memory as, say, the colorful accounts of Atlantis and other lost continents. The parallel is exact; I have argued elsewhere that the Atlantis myth was resurrected by nineteenth-century occult lodges in a subtle effort—too subtle, one gathers, for more recent mages—to introduce certain ideas about the morality of science and the future of society into the collective conversation of their time.[82]

The same deeper context can be found, with a little effort, in old occult literature about time and the future. It's easy to dismiss the gaudy furniture of rings and rounds and future histories as so much nonsense, not least because the prophecies of the near future included in them have proven far more often than not to be wildly inaccurate. Still, look past the clutter and trace the shape of time outlined in these ornate narratives, and it's often possible to glimpse what the occultists of an earlier age meant to accomplish with them, sometimes hijacking the standard myths of progress or apocalypse, sometimes contradicting them flatly or offering tempting glimpses of other ways of understanding the shape of time.

It may be useful, in other words, to revisit the dusty tomes that so many of us dismissed out of hand in the wake of the Sixties, and learn to see past the ornate forms of an earlier age to the potent tools they embody. Whether or not they choose to draw on these resources, mages and occultists might be wise to scrap the secondhand versions of the end of history that infest today's occult community, and replace them with a livelier sense of the ways that they might ride history's winds, or even shape them. In the process, they might also put some thought into ways in which the rich magical legacies of the present might best be handed on to a future very different from the ones that believers in the end of history have encouraged us all to expect.

---

[82] John Michael Greer, *Atlantis: Ancient Legacy, Hidden Prophecy* (Woodbury, MN: Llewellyn, 2007).

# Asymmetric tactical shock: a first reconnaissance

*My sole contribution so far to the field of military science, this essay evolved out of a series of discussions on my blog* The Archdruid Report. *For some reason, that blog attracted a noticeable readership of active-duty personnel of the armed forces of countries allied to the United States, though (as far as I know) not from those of the U.S. itself; this essay was quietly circulated among several of those readers. This is its first appearance in print.*

## Introduction

The 1993 publication of Robert Drews's *The End of the Bronze Age: Changes in Warfare and the Catastrophe of Ca. 1200 B.C* reframed a critical and poorly understood period in ancient history, and sparked a lively and continuing debate among historians. Its relevance to current military affairs has not received the same degree of attention. This is unfortunate, because Drews's study outlines a military phenomenon that could play a significant role in our own time.

The events Drews chronicles are dramatic enough in their own right. Within a few decades of 1200 BC, most of the states of the eastern Mediterranean littoral underwent a frightful collapse. Dozens of cities, some of them occupied for thousands of years beforehand, were burnt, looted, and abandoned. Causes ranging from earthquakes through migrations to system collapse have been proposed, but none adequately explained the evidence.[83]

Drews made the case that this collapse occurred because several of the less-developed peoples of the time evolved a blend of tactics and technology capable of overwhelming their technologically, economically, and organizationally superior neighbors. In an ironic contrast to current presuppositions, the breakthroughs responsible for this massive military upset were not technological advances, but a retreat to older and cheaper technologies that, combined with novel tactics, targeted weaknesses in the advanced military technologies of the time, and turned the developed nations' reliance on those technologies into a lethal vulnerability.

The overthrow of a previously dominant military power by less sophisticated military technologies used in novel ways is far from unique to the late Bronze Age, and Drews's study is thus relevant to military history as well as current military affairs. I have tentatively named the phenomenon he described *asymmetric tactical shock*. Its application to military history will be left to others; my concern in this paper is to explore the possibility that events of this kind could play a role in the strategic environment of the near future.

## One: the end of the Bronze Age

Despite great differences in technology and social organization, the world of that time resembled the present in certain respects.[84] The eastern Mediterranean at the end of the Bronze Age, like our world, was divided into several tiers of states. Three great powers—the Hittite empire, the Assyrian empire, and Egypt—formed the first tier, each dominating a bloc of second- and third-tier client states. Wars between the great powers were rare; wars involving lesser states were much more frequent, and intervention by one or another great power in the affairs of client states tolerably common.

The military art of that time also had certain similarities to that of the present. Beginning around 1700 BC, a traditional way of making

---

[83] Drews, pp. 33–93, surveys the alternative explanations.
[84] I have drawn primarily on Drews, pp. 97–134, for this summary.

war involving pitched battles between disciplined bodies of infantry using spear and shield, supported by archers, gave way to a new military order based on fast, maneuverable chariot forces, with infantry relegated to siege warfare and the defense of camps and fortifications. To borrow a currently popular taxonomy,[85] a first generation warfare of static infantry was replaced by a third generation warfare of maneuver. (Limits on the catapults of the time forestalled the rise of a second generation warfare of massed firepower.)

By the standards of the time, the war chariot was a sophisticated technology operated by highly trained specialists. Chariot armies were thus relatively small compared to the territory and population of the states that they defended, or to the infantry armies of an earlier age; the Hittite Empire fielded 2500 chariots of its own and another 1000 from its allies to meet a roughly comparable Egyptian army at the battle of Kadesh in 1275 BC, one of the great military contests of the age. Given the cost of building, equipping, manning, and maintaining chariots, a chariot force much larger would have placed a prohibitive burden on even the richest states of the time. The result was a shift in the ratio of front line to rear echelon personnel similar to, though on a much smaller scale than, the equivalent change in twentieth- and twenty-first-century militaries across the industrial world.

Around the periphery of the Mediterranean world, largely outside the network of treaties and power relationships linking the great powers and their client states, were the less developed countries of the late Bronze Age. Some of these peripheral entities imitated the great powers and fielded small chariot armies of their own. Others maintained their own more traditional political and military forms, while interacting with the developed core through trade, raiding expeditions, and service as mercenaries in the armies of the great powers. Several of them, particularly in the Black Sea and Aegean Sea regions, had substantial fishing and trading fleets that could be converted to use as military transports at a moment's notice, but the apparent military dominance of the developed states of the time kept a check on this potential.

It was by way of mercenary service with the armies of the developed states, Drews suggests, that ambitious men in these outlying areas came to realize that the chariot armies of the developed states were vulnerable to asymmetric attack. Any of the contacts between the developed

---

[85] See, for example, Lind, 2004.

and less developed states, however, could have produced the same effect over time. As Arnold Toynbee pointed out, of all the legacies less developed nations absorb from their more developed neighbors, military technique spreads fastest and furthest.[86] The way of making war that would bring down most of the Bronze Age kingdoms thus emerged somewhere on the northern periphery of the Mediterranean, but no more exact location can be traced; the Egyptians, who alone left detailed written records of the fighting, simply called the attackers the "Sea Peoples."

The basis of the new asymmetric tactics was a focus on specific vulnerabilities in the key military technology of the time, the war chariot. While chariot forces could easily overwhelm the static lines of spearmen of the old "first generation" warfare, the chariots could themselves be overwhelmed by swarming attacks from masses of light infantry armed with antichariot weaponry.[87] The weapons these infantry forces used—long sword, round shield, and javelins—were slight modifications on existing technology; what made them novel and effective was the realization that they could be used to overcome the strengths of a chariot army.

In Drews's assessment, the key element in this tactical suite was the javelin, which allowed infantry to attack the chariot horses of their adversaries. Once a relatively modest fraction of the horses of the chariot force were injured or panicked, organized maneuver became impossible, and the weaknesses of a chariot army—its relatively small numerical strength and its dependence on evasive mobility for defense—became fatal. The Sea Peoples combined these tactics with the use of swift oared ships for transport, which allowed them to appear suddenly anywhere near the Mediterranean or Black Sea coasts, annihilate chariot forces sent to stop them, sack and burn palaces and urban centers, and disappear with their plunder before any more effective response could be made.

Paleoecological evidence suggests that sustained crop failures in Greece and the Balkans, driven by topsoil depletion and drought, may have provided the shove that set the catastrophe of 1200 BC in motion.[88]

---

[86] Toynbee, 1954, pp. 16–19.
[87] While Drews does not use the terminology of "swarming attacks," his description is closely comparable to that in, e.g., Edwards, 2000.
[88] See, among others, Betancourt, 1976 and Shrimpton, 1987. More recently, Fuchs, Lang, and Wagner, 2004 have documented severe soil erosion in Greece around 1200 BC from traces in offshore sediment deposits.

Whatever the proximate cause, the effects were swift and devastating. The first few tentative attacks came in the last quarter of the thirteenth century BC, directed against minor states on the northern periphery, notably in Mycenean Greece. Around 1200, raiders sacked and burnt Hattusas, the capital of the Hittite empire, and ravaged the Hittite heartland; the Hittite state, a major power for centuries, vanished from history thereafter. In the two decades that followed, second- and third-tier states along the eastern Mediterranean littoral, as far east as the northern Euphrates river and as far south as the borders of Egypt, suffered the same fate.

At the southeastern corner of the Mediterranean, Egypt was the richest prize of all, but it had the time and imagination to craft a more effective response to the attackers. In 1179 BC, Egyptian forces on land and sea confronted a massive two-pronged assault by the Sea Peoples, and won. Texts and bas-reliefs at Medinet Habu describe the battles, and in passing reveal the reasons behind the Egyptian victory.

Instead of meeting the attackers on land with chariots in the traditional way, the Egyptian military fielded a force of massed infantry, going back to the "first generation" of Bronze Age warfare. This change, matching one asymmetrical tactical shift (and one retrograde technological shift) with another, removed the weaknesses on which the attackers depended, and in their absence, Egypt's superior numbers and military organization proved decisive. Meanwhile, the seaborne wing of the assault was met by a fleet of Egyptian ships packed with infantry. The Sea Peoples' ships were transports rather than fighting platforms and, unprepared to fight at sea, suffered a shattering defeat.

Within a few years of these victories, the era of mass raids was over. The aftermath, however, saw a dark age descend over the eastern Mediterranean world. Levels of literacy, international trade, and economic diversification common before 1200 BC did not recur for three to five centuries thereafter. Large-scale chariot warfare, meanwhile, vanished permanently from the military scene; the armies of the early Iron Age relied once again on infantry armed with spears and bows, with cavalry—an innovation of the post-Bronze Age world—filling what would be its standard role until the fall of Rome, as a scouting force and flank support for massed infantry formations.[89]

---

[89] Drews, pp. 164–173.

## Two: understanding the phenomenon

If Drews's proposal is correct, the catastrophe of the late Bronze Age resulted from a form of military failure not well studied in recent works on the subject. It belongs to the category of asymmetric warfare, in the broad sense of conflict between forces using radically different technological and tactical suites, and also in the stricter sense in which the term is most often used in contemporary military studies, of a way of making war which can enable a weaker competitor to confront and potentially defeat a stronger one.

Most recent discussions of asymmetric warfare have concentrated on those forms of asymmetric warfare that either avoid direct confrontation with conventional military forces or accept tactical losses in such confrontations in order to achieve strategic goals, and pursue wars of attrition or other prolonged strategic models.[90] There is, of course, ample experience in the post-Second World War era to justify this concentration. Drews's analysis of the Bronze Age catastrophe suggests, however, that the spectrum of asymmetric warfare extends beyond this range of options.

The Sea Peoples of the late Bronze Age, according to his account, took asymmetric warfare onto the battlefields of the time, engaged the dominant conventional military forces of the age, and won decisive and strategically effective victories. Adapting that experience to the wider tactical space of contemporary armed conflict, it becomes possible—and arguably necessary—to envision a range of asymmetric warfare methods that engage an opposing force in ways that are tactically decisive, either on the battlefield as conventionally defined or in the wider space of support facilities, supply chains, communications and information networks, and other military assets that play active roles in today's tactical environment. This end of the asymmetric spectrum, embracing decisive tactical actions with substantial strategic impacts, may be usefully termed *asymmetric tactical shock*.[91]

A survey of examples of asymmetric tactical shock in military history, though it would be valuable in exploring the phenomenon, is beyond the scope of a preliminary essay of this kind. Here, I intend simply to outline some of the salient features of asymmetric tactical shock, explore

---

[90] See, for example, Arreguin-Toft, 2005.
[91] The parallel with Nathan Freier's concept of "strategic shock" is deliberate; see Freier, 2008.

some of the factors that make it a potential threat to security arrangements in the contemporary world, and sketch out one way in which that threat might be faced.

From Drews's reconstruction of the late Bronze Age military catastrophe, five core elements may be tentatively identified:

*1. Asymmetric tactical shock emerges as an option in a context of massive disparities in the ability of states to project conventional military force.*

In the late Bronze Age, the military balance between developed and less developed nations seems to have been nearly as extreme as it has become in our own time. Those states that had the wealth and the organizational and technological capabilities to field chariot armies had, by that fact, a massive advantage over more peripheral states and tribal groups that could or did not do so. Lacking the technical and economic resources to compete with the great powers and their client states in conventional terms, the less developed states had every incentive to pursue asymmetric means of conflict. Meanwhile, the developed states seem to have suffered from a false sense of security produced by the effectiveness of chariot warfare against previously encountered threats; it likely never occurred to them that an older and less advanced military technology could target the highly sophisticated chariot and turn it into a liability.

*2. Asymmetric tactical shock becomes a serious threat when major instabilities in the strategic environment bring either the opportunity or the necessity for a high-stakes gamble.*

The knowledge base and technology needed to bring down the chariot armies of the major Bronze Age powers apparently existed for some time before the first tentative raids of the late thirteenth century BC, but attacking a heavily armed major power such as the Hittite empire with a largely untried tactic would have been enough of a gamble to cause even the most megalomaniac barbarian chieftain second thoughts. The subsistence crisis that hit the Balkans and Greek peninsula toward the end of the thirteenth century may well have changed that equation, either by destabilizing the Mycenean Greek states that were among the first victims, or by placing potential invaders in a situation in which a risky invasion was the only alternative to starvation, or both.

*3. Asymmetric tactical shock depends on battlefield "monkeywrenching" of specific, previously untargeted weak points in key military technologies.*

The chariot warfare tactics that defined the battlefield environment of the late Bronze Age depended on the ability of mobile forces to avoid being pinned down into a static "slugging match" form of combat. Fast swarming attacks by very large forces of light infantry played against this advantage, stripping chariot armies of their mobility and crushing them. In order to accomplish this, the Sea Peoples became as specialized as the chariot forces they fought; their victories depended on speed, surprise, and a very close but asymmetric fit between their weapons and tactics and those of their opponents. When the Egyptian command suddenly retooled its forces for a different kind of warfare, the Sea Peoples were unable to adapt in time.

*4. Asymmetric tactical shock succeeds best when opponents rely on previously successful tactics and technologies, and have no alternative in place if those fail.*

The relatively sedate pace of Bronze Age technological innovation stretched out changes in military strategy and tactics over centuries rather than decades, reinforcing the tendency of generals to prepare for the last war rather than the next one. Late Bronze Age armies in the eastern Mediterranean thus relied almost entirely on massed chariot forces for offensive warfare, relegating infantry to a supporting role in besieging cities and protecting camps on the march. The one major exception was Assyria, which maintained a substantial offensive infantry arm to fight campaigns in its mountainous border regions, where chariots could not go. It is probably not an accident that the Assyrian empire survived the catastrophe of c. 1200 BC unscathed, while cities not far from its western borders were sacked and burnt.

*5. Asymmetric tactical shock fails if opponents are able to shift to a different set of tactics and technologies lacking those specific vulnerabilities targeted by the attackers, in such a way that the attackers lack the time and/or resources to adapt in turn.*

The Egyptian response to the Sea Peoples' assault in 1179 BC is instructive here. At that time Egypt had maintained cultural continuity for well over two millennia; it also lay at the far end of the eastern Mediterranean from the Black Sea and Aegean Sea littoral, the apparent launching point for the Sea Peoples' assault. These resources of heritage and time allowed the Egyptian command to reshape its land forces along the lines of a much earlier military system, on the one hand, and to push through a significant innovation at sea on the other. Both shifts changed the tactical balance decisively in Egypt's favor.

It will probably not have escaped the attention of readers that the first three of these five points could readily be applied to the near future of the modern world. Despite differences in technology, as already mentioned, the strategic environment of the late Bronze Age in the eastern Mediterranean had many features in common with its equivalent today. Huge differentials in wealth and technological sophistication separate the United States and its allies from the rest of the world's nations, and any of the latter not willing to accept a subordinate role relative to the declared U.S. objective of "full spectrum dominance" are all but constrained to pursue asymmetric options. Sources of major instability in the strategic environment of the present and near future include anthropogenic climate change, other forms of environmental disruption, the instabilities of the current global economy and international debt system, and the relatively rapid depletion of existing reserves of fossil fuels; any one of these, to say nothing of two or three of them in interaction, could readily back a regional power into a situation where a high-stakes gamble of the kind already outlined might be the only alternative to national collapse.

The nature of current military technology is among the most troubling dimensions of the model here outlined. The chariot armies of the late Bronze Age, as far as the evidence suggests, had one serious vulnerability to asymmetric tactical shock. A contemporary military force has at least dozens of such vulnerabilities, and possibly hundreds. The drive for integration of service branches and technologies in current military operational doctrine has paid off handsomely, but imposes major risks in a confrontation with an opponent that finds a way to cripple one or more of an opponent's key technologies in the midst of combat operations. The sprawling supply chains required by current military units,[92] information technologies, communications, guidance and navigation equipment, and much more—all these may be vulnerable to sudden asymmetric attack, as may key assets on scales from GPS satellites to aircraft carriers.

The hypercomplex militaries of today's industrial nations thus offer a vast range of potential targets to asymmetric tactical shock, and the timescale on which asymmetric methods can be developed and deployed is typically orders of magnitude faster than the timescale of military equipment procurement. For both these reasons, it is effectively impossible to defend against asymmetric tactical shock on a target-by-target basis, much less to wait until a threat emerges and then pursue remedies to it.

---

[92] See Leckie, 2010 for a discussion of the vulnerabilities of current military technology to supply chain disruption.

The two final points sketched out above, however, provide the basis for a more functional response.

To the extent that a contemporary military remains wedded to familiar tactics and technologies, relying on current models of integrated land-sea-air-space operations and on unhindered and effectively limitless flows of materiel to frontline units, and information throughout the tactical and strategic environment, the risk of asymmetric tactical shock will likely increase. Adherence to the mode of combat harshly but perhaps not unfairly described by William S. Lind as "bumping into the enemy and calling for fire,"[93] which relies on the viability of integrated systems extending as much as several thousand miles away from the battlefield, may present a particular vulnerability. It is unpleasantly easy to imagine the results if, for example, a modern military force used to this style of warfare, and unprepared to fight without support, were to be targeted by some ingenious method that stripped it of communications links, air cover or the like, and then faced a massed assault by an opposing force well prepared to fight in a less technologically sophisticated environment.

By contrast, to the extent that a contemporary military embraces greater flexibility, trains units to carry out missions without support and under unfamiliar limitations, and maintains a close watch on conflicts in the Third World in which asymmetric offensive tactics may appear in embryonic form, the risk of asymmetric tactical shock will likely decrease. It may not be excessive to suggest that reserve combat forces, at least, might benefit from training and exercises drawn from before the emergence of today's integrated military systems, so that they could respond with some degree of effectiveness to an asymmetric tactical shock that forces combat units to confront enemy action on their own.

At least in the near future, it seems unlikely that military forces of the world's industrial nations will find themselves forced to repeat the Egyptian experience of 1178 BC, and confront hostile forces with what amounts to the weapons and tactics of an earlier period. Still, the more attention that is paid to the possibility that complex military systems have unexpected vulnerabilities that a clever and desperate opponent can target and cripple, the greater the likelihood that a sudden collapse of military power of the sort that terminated so many of the eastern Mediterranean's Bronze Age states will remain a purely theoretical issue in our own time.

---

[93] Lind, p. 14.

## References

Arreguin-Toft, I. (2005). *How the Weak Win Wars: A Theory of Asymmetric Conflict*. New York: Cambridge University Press.

Betancourt, P. (1976). The end of the Greek Bronze Age. *Antiquity, 50*: 44.

Drews, R. (1993). *The End of the Bronze Age: Changes in Warfare and the Catastrophe of Ca. 1200 B.C.* Princeton, NJ: Princeton University Press.

Edwards, S. J. A. (2000). *Swarming on the Battlefield: Past, Present, and Future*. Santa Monica, CA: Rand.

Freier, N. (2008). *Known Unknowns: Unconventional "Strategic Shocks" in Defense Strategy Development*. Washington, DC: Strategic Studies Institute.

Fuchs, M., Lang, A., & Wagner, G. A. (2004). The history of Holocene soil erosion in the Phlious Basin, NE Peloponnese, Greece, based on optical dating. *The Holocene. 14*(3): 334–345.

Leckie, C. (2010). Lasers or longbows? A paradox of military technology. *Australian Defence Force Journal, 182*: 44–56.

Lind, W. S. (2004). Understanding fourth generation war. *Military Review*, September–October.

Shrimpton, G. (1987). Regional drought and the decline of Mycenae. *Echos du Monde Classique, 31*: 137–176.

Toynbee, A. (1954). *A Study of History, Vol. VIII*. New York: Oxford University Press.

# Fascism and the future

> *In 2014, I posted a three-part discussion of fascism on my blog The Archdruid Report, as a challenge to a habit, pervasive then as now on the leftward end of the political spectrum, of using the word "fascism" as a catchall label for anything the speaker doesn't like. Later that year I was invited to submit an article based on it to* Dark Mountain, *a series of anthologies exploring the future of industrial society, and it appeared in the Spring 2015 issue.*

Whenever our collective conversation about the future turns away from the twin fantasies of perpetual progress and instant apocalypse that provide so much fodder for the modern mind, certain questions come up as reliably as daffodils in April or airport food on a rough flight. One such repeating question that deserves closer attention than it usually gets is whether the future of industrial society will be troubled by a revival of fascism.

That's an issue worth raising, since the fascist movements of the not so distant past were given their shot at power by the political failure and economic implosion of Europe after the First World War, and "political failure and economic implosion" is a fair description of the state of the United States and Europe these days. It's a difficult issue to explore, though, because the subject has become so cluttered with doubletalk and distortions of historical fact. Hard work will be needed to shovel away some of the manure that's piled up in this Augean stable of our collective imagination, and even so, I'm confident that many of the people who read this essay will misunderstand every single word of it.

There's a massive irony in that situation. When George Orwell wrote his tremendous satire 1984, one of the core themes he explored was the debasement of language for political advantage that was common in the tyrannies of his time. That habit found its lasting emblem in the invented language Newspeak, which was deliberately designed to get in the way of clear thinking. Newspeak remains fictional—well, more or less—but the subject of fascism, and the word itself, have both gotten tangled up in a net of debased language and incoherent thinking as extreme as anything Orwell put in his novel.

These days, the word "fascism" functions as what S. I. Hayakawa used to call a snarl word—a content-free verbal noise that expresses angry emotions and nothing else. When activists on the left insist that the current U.S. government is a fascist regime, in other words, they mean exactly what their equivalents on the right mean when they call the current U.S. government a socialist regime: "I hate you."

This debasement of political language goes to absurd lengths. In the 1990s, for example, when I lived in Seattle, somebody went around spraypainting "[expletive] FACISM" on an assortment of walls in a couple of Seattle's hip neighborhoods. My wife and I used to while away spare time at bus stops discussing just what "facism" might be. (Her theory was that it's the prejudice of businessmen who think that employees in front office jobs should be hired for their pretty faces rather than their job skills; mine, recalling the declaration of a vegetarian cousin that she would never eat anything with a face, was that it's the belief that the moral value of a living thing depends on whether it has a face humans recognize as such.)

Beyond such amusements, though, lay a real question: What on earth did the graffitist believe he was accomplishing by splashing that phrase around oh-so-liberal Seattle? Did he think that members of the American Fascist Party who happened to be goose-stepping through town would see the slogan and quail?

To get past such stupidities, it's going to be necessary to rise up out of the swamp of Newspeak that surrounds the subject of fascism—to reconnect words with their meanings, and political movements with their historical contexts. Let's start in the obvious place. What exactly does the word "fascism" mean, and how did it get from there to its current status as a snarl word?

That takes us back to southern Italy in 1893. In that year, a movement among peasant farmers took to rioting and other extralegal actions to break the hold of the feudal gentry on the economy of the region; the armed groups fielded by this movement were called *fasci*, which might best be translated "group." In 1919, a former Socialist newspaperman named Benito Mussolini borrowed the term for his new political movement. The movement soon morphed into a political party and adapted its name accordingly, becoming the Fascist Party, and the paralysis of the Italian political system allowed Mussolini to seize power with the March on Rome in 1922 and make Italy a Fascist state.

The secondhand ideology Mussolini's aides cobbled together for their regime accordingly became known as Fascism—"Groupism," again, is a decent translation, and the ideology was about as coherent as that sounds. Later on, in an attempt to hijack the prestige of the Roman empire, Mussolini identified Fascism with another meaning of the word—the *fascis*, the bundle of sticks around an axe that Roman lictors carried as an emblem of their authority—and that became the emblem of the Fascist Party in its latter years.

Of the totalitarian regimes of twentieth-century Europe, it bears noting, Mussolini's was far from the most bloodthirsty. The Fascist regime in Italy carried out maybe 2000 political executions in its entire lifespan; Hitler's regime committed that many political killings, on average, every single day the Twelve-Year Reich was in power, and in terms of mass murder, Hitler's body count was relatively modest compared to those of Josef Stalin or Mao Zedong. For that matter, political killings in some democratic regimes exceed Italian Fascism's total quite handily. Why, then, is "fascist" the buzzword of choice for anybody who wants to denounce a political system? More to the point, why do so many people say "fascist," mean "Nazi," and then display invincible ignorance about both movements?

There's a reason for that, and it comes out of the vicissitudes of radical politics between the world wars. The founding of the Third International in Moscow in 1919 forced radical parties across Europe to take sides for or against the Soviet regime. Those that joined the International were expected to obey Moscow's orders without question, even when those orders obviously had more to do with Russia's expansionist foreign policy than with the glorious cause of proletarian revolution; at the same time, many idealists still thought the Soviet regime was the best hope for the future. The result in most countries was the rise of competing Marxist parties, a Communist party obedient to Moscow and a Socialist party independent of it.

In the bare-knuckle propaganda brawl that followed, Mussolini's regime was a godsend to Moscow. Since Mussolini was a former socialist who had abandoned Marx in the course of his rise to power, parties that belonged to the Third International came to use the label "fascist" for those parties that refused to join it, as their way of claiming that the latter weren't really socialist, and could be counted on to sell out the proletariat. When the Soviet Union ended up on the same side of the Second World War as its longtime enemies the United Kingdom and the United States, the habit of using "fascist" as an all-purpose term of abuse spread throughout the left in both countries. From there, its current status as a universal snarl word was a very short step.

What made "fascist" so useful long after the collapse of Mussolini's regime was the sheer emptiness of the word. Even in Italian, "Groupism" doesn't mean much, and in other languages it's just a noise. The term "Nazi" has the same advantage: In most languages, it sounds nasty and doesn't mean a thing, so it can be flung freely at any target. The same can't be said about the actual name of the German political movement headed by Adolf Hitler, which is why next to nobody ever mentions national socialism by its proper name.

That phrase isn't simply an invention of Hitler's publicity machine, by the way. The first national socialist party was founded in 1898 in what's now the Czech Republic, and the second was launched in France in 1903. National socialism was a recognized position in the political and economic controversies of early twentieth-century Europe, part of a continuum of political ideas far more diverse than the one that's popular today. In European countries between the wars, political parties existed to support the interests of specific social classes, just as they do today. Conservative parties promoted the interests of the aristocracy and rural landowners; they supported trade barriers, low property taxes, and an economy biased toward agriculture. Liberal parties, by contrast, furthered the interests of the bourgeoisie; they supported free trade, high property taxes, military spending, and colonial expansion, because those were the policies that increased bourgeois wealth and power.

The working classes had their choice of several options. There were syndicalist parties, which sought to give workers direct ownership of the means of production. There were also socialist parties, which generally sought to place firms under some form of government control. Standing apart from the socialists were communist parties, which (after 1919) echoed whatever Moscow's party line happened to be that week; and there were other, smaller movements—distributism, social credit, and many more—which had their own followings and their own answers to the problems of the day.

The tendency of these parties to further the interests of a single class became a matter of public concern by the end of the nineteenth century, and this drove the emergence of parties that pursued, or claimed to pursue, policies of benefit to the entire nation. Many of them tacked "national" onto their names to indicate this shift. Thus national conservative parties argued that trade barriers and agricultural subsidies would benefit everyone; national liberal parties argued that free trade and colonial expansion was best for everyone, and so on. There were no national communist parties, because Moscow didn't allow it, but there were national bolshevist parties—in Europe between the wars, a bolshevist was someone who supported the Russian Revolution but insisted that Lenin and Stalin had betrayed it to establish a personal dictatorship—which argued that violent revolution against the existing order really was in everyone's best interests.

National socialism was a position along the same lines. National socialist parties argued that business firms should be made subject to government regulation and coordination in order to keep them from acting against the interests of society as a whole, and that the working classes ought to receive a range of government benefits paid for by taxes on corporate income and the well-to-do. Those points were central to the program of the National Socialist German Workers Party, and those were the policies it enacted when it took power in 1933.

If those policies sound familiar, they should. That's why next to nobody mentions national socialism by name these days: The Western nations that defeated national socialism in Germany promptly adopted most of its economic policies, the source of much of its mass appeal, to forestall any attempt to revive it. Strictly speaking, in terms of the meaning that the phrase had before the beginning of the Second World War, national socialism is one of the two standard flavors of political economy nowadays. The other is liberalism, and it's another irony of history that in the United States, the party that hates the word "liberal" is a picture-perfect example of a liberal party, as that term was understood back in the day.

Now of course when people think of the National Socialist German Workers Party nowadays, they don't think of government regulation of industry and free vacations for factory workers, even though the Nazi party implemented those policies once it got into power. They think of such other habits of Hitler's regime as declaring war on most of the world and herding millions into death camps. Those are realities, and they need to be recalled. It's crucial, though, to remember that when Germany's National Socialists were canvassing for votes in the years before 1933, they weren't marching proudly behind banners saying VOTE FOR HITLER SO FIFTY MILLION WILL DIE! When those same National Socialists trotted out their anti-Semitic rhetoric, for that matter, they weren't saying anything the average German found offensive or even unusual; anti-Semitism was common in public life all through the Western world until the Holocaust made its implications too uncomfortably clear.

For that matter, when people talked about fascism in the 1920s and 1930s, unless they were doctrinaire Marxists, they didn't use it as a snarl word. It was the official title of Italy's ruling party; many people of goodwill were impressed by the programs enacted by Mussolini's regime, and hoped to see similar policies in their own countries. It took the Second World War and the Cold War to make the complex reality of early twentieth-century fascism vanish into a vast and distorted shadow-image vague enough to be projected onto anything at all.

One consequence of that history is the erasure of the term's actual meaning, as a description of a particular form of government rather than a snarl word. Historians have accordingly argued at length whether there's still a point to talking about fascism in general, and some thoughtful writers have insisted that there isn't—that words such as "dictatorship" cover the ground quite adequately, and the label "fascism" belongs to Mussolini's regime alone. On the other side were those who argued that a certain kind of authoritarian movement is sufficiently distinct from other kinds of tyranny that it deserves its own moniker.

One of those was Ernst Nolte, whose 1968 book *Die Krise des liberalen Systems und die faschistischen Bewegungen* (*The Crisis of the Liberal System and the Fascist Movements*) helped launch the debate just mentioned. Nolte was careful enough not to propose a hard definition of fascism, and offered instead six features common to historical fascist movements. The first three are organizational features: a cult of charismatic leadership, a uniformed party militia, and the goal of totalitarianism.

That last word has been bandied around so freely that it's probably necessary to discuss what it means. A totalitarian political system is one in which the party in power claims the right to rule every sphere of life: political, religious, artistic, scientific, sexual, and so on through all the dimensions of human existence. Plenty of dictatorships aren't totalitarian; in fact, it's common for dictators to spare themselves extra work by focusing on the political sphere, and letting people do what they want in other spheres so long as they don't stray into politics. There are also totalitarian systems that aren't dictatorships—plenty of religions, for example, claim totalitarian authority over every aspect of the life of the faithful.

The totalitarian dimension, though, is central to those regimes that count as fascist by Nolte's criteria. The charismatic leaders and party militias of classic European fascism presented themselves, and in at least some cases honestly saw themselves, as standing in opposition not merely to a political system, but to an entire civilization they believed was rotten to the core. Crusades against "degenerate" art and literature weren't simply the personal vagaries of fascist leaders; they were part of an attempt to reshape entire societies from the ground up.

Much of the discussion that followed the publication of Nolte's book focused on whether the organizational features he noted were sufficiently unique to serve as touchstones, whether more features should be added to the list, and so on. The other three features in Nolte's description, by contrast, were broadly accepted by scholars. This is all the more interesting in that one is almost always rejected, on the rare occasions it slips outside the charmed circle where professional historians practice their craft. These three features are the things that fascist movements consistently rejected. The first is Marxism, the second liberalism, and the third—the hot-button one—is conservatism.

Mention this to anyone in today's left, and you can expect blank incomprehension. It's one of the credos of current political folklore that fascism belongs to the conservative side of the political spectrum. More specifically, it's supposed to be the far end of that side, the thing that's more conservative than the conservatives, just as Communism is supposed to be the far end of the left side of the spectrum, the thing that's more liberal than the liberals.

Compare that linear model to the diversity of pre-1945 politics outlined above, and it's clear that quite a few options have been erased from the picture. One of them, curiously enough, is conservatism, in the original meaning of that word. Anglo-American conservatism—Europe has its own slightly different form—has its roots in the writings of Edmund Burke, whose *Reflections on the Revolution in France* became a lightning rod for thinkers who found the hubris of the radical Enlightenment too much to swallow. At the risk of oversimplifying a complex tradition, traditional conservatism is based on the recognition that human beings aren't as smart as they like to think. As a result, when intellectuals insist that they know how to make a perfect society, they're wrong, and the consequences of trying to enact their fantasies in the real world range from the humiliating to the catastrophic.

To the conservative mind, the existing order of society has an advantage that the arbitrary inventions of world-reformers can't match: it actually works in practice. Conservatives thus used to insist that changes to society ought to be made only when there was very good reason to think the changes will be improvements. The besetting vice of old-fashioned conservatism, as radicals loved to point out, was thus that it tended to defend and excuse traditional injustices; among its great virtues, in turn, was that it defended traditional liberties against the not always covert authoritarianism of would-be reformers.

In America before the Cold War, conservatives thus called for hard limitations on federal power, denounced the nation's moves toward global empire, demanded balanced budgets and fiscal prudence, and upheld local cultures and governments against the centralizing reach of Washington DC. Like every political movement in the real world, it was a complex thing, and combined high ideals and base motives in the same proportions as its rivals. Whatever its faults, though, it was shoved right out of the political dialogue during the middle years of the twentieth century. The ideologues and party hacks who took over the brand name in the Reagan-Thatcher counterrevolution now use "conservative" to refer to policies no traditional conservative would have tolerated for a moment.

During the heyday of fascism, though, conservatism in the original sense of the word was still a major force, and Nolte was quite correct to say that fascists consistently rejected it. Where conservatives saw themselves as the defenders of the old order of Europe—Christian, aristocratic, agrarian, and committed to local custom and local autonomy—fascists wanted to impose a New Order (one of Hitler's favorite phrases) in which traditional hierarchies would dissolve in the orgiastic abandon of "one leader, one party, one people." Fascists hated the conservatives, and conservatives returned the feeling with interest; it's indicative that the most diehard resistance Hitler's regime faced, and the conspiracies that came closest to blowing Hitler himself to smithereens, came straight out of the aristocratic right wing of German society.

The bitter divide between fascists and conservatives, in fact, goes straight back to the origins of both movements. In a teasingly titled book, *Hitler as Philosophe*, Lawrence Birken showed in detail that Hitler's political vocabulary came out of the same radical Enlightenment that Burke critiqued. When Hitler ranted about the will of *das Völk*, for example, he was simply borrowing Rousseau's notion of the general will of the people, which both men believed ought to be free from the pettifogging hindrance of mere laws and institutions. Examples could be multiplied almost endlessly, and matched nearly word for word out of Mussolini's speeches.

Point this out nowadays, though, and you'll get pushback from those who insist that German national socialism was bought and paid for by big business, and thus had to be a conservative movement. That's a very common claim these days, repeated endlessly on the left as though it were proven fact. The only problem is that it doesn't happen to be true.

Two excellent scholarly studies have addressed the issue, Pool and Pool's *Who Financed Hitler?* (1978) and Turner's *German Big Business and the Rise of Hitler* (1985). Both showed that the National Socialist German Workers Party got the vast majority of its financing from its own middle-class membership until the last year or two before it took power, and only then got handouts from business because most German businesses decided that between the two rising powers in the final crisis of the Weimar regime—the Nazis and the Communists—they would prefer the Nazis. In point of fact—and this can be found in any social history of Germany between the wars—German big business by and large distrusted Hitler's party, and bitterly resented the new regime's policy of *Gleichschaltung*, "coordination," which subjected even the largest firms to oversight and regulation by party officials.

So where did the claim that fascism is always a puppet of big business come from? Like the use of "fascism" as a generic snarl word, it's a third-hand borrowing from Soviet propaganda. In the political theology of Marxism, everything boils down to the struggle between capitalists and the proletariat. Everyone that doesn't support the interests of the proletariat as defined by Marxist theory is therefore by definition a tool of the capitalist ruling class, and any political movement that opposes Marxism thus has to be composed of capitalist lackeys. QED!

More broadly, communist parties generally pitched themselves to the public by insisting that all other political movements work out in practice to a vote for the existing order of things. A useful bit of marketing in any context, it became a necessity once Stalin demonstrated just how unpleasant a communist regime could be in practice. Insisting that fascism is simply another name for what we've already got, though, had an enduring downside—it convinced a great many people, in the teeth of the evidence, that fascism by definition defends the status quo. The fact that Italian Fascism and German national socialism both rose to power promising radical change in their respective societies *and delivered on that promise* has been completely erased from modern political memory.

For that matter, the flattening out of political thought into a linear spectrum from "the left" (the labor or liberal party, and the Communists who are presumed to be lurking in its leftward fringe) to "the right" (the conservative party, and the fascists who are presumed to have a similar hideout in its rightward fringe) helps feed the same belief. Once all political thought has been forced onto that Procrustean bed, after all, if the fascists aren't hiding out somewhere on the far end of the Republican half of the spectrum, where else could they be?

It's at this point that we approach the most explosive dimension of the history of fascism, because the unthinking acceptance of the linear model of politics presupposed by that question isn't merely a problem in an abstract sense. It also obscures some of the most important dimensions of contemporary political life. According to that model, the point in the middle of the spectrum—where left and right fade into one another—is the common ground of politics, the middle of the road, where most people either are or ought to be. The further you get from that midpoint, the closer you are to "extremism." (Think about that last word for a moment.) What happens, though, if the common ground where the two major parties meet and shake hands is far removed from the actual beliefs and opinions of the majority?

That's the case today in most of the Western world. The one common belief that unites the fractious populations of the industrial nations is the sense that none of the mainstream political parties offers policies they find appealing or even bearable. Where the major parties reach a consensus, there's a yawning chasm between that consensus and the policies that most people support. Where parties remain at loggerheads, there are normally three positions: the mainstream liberal position, the mainstream conservative position, and the position most people favor, which never gets brought into the political arena at all.

This is a common liability of democratic systems under strain. In Italy before and during the First World War, and in Germany after it, democratic institutions froze up around problems that politicians were unwilling to confront and therefore could not effectively address. Every mainstream political party was committed to the status quo in the face of a rising spiral of crisis that made it brutally clear that the status quo no longer worked. One government after another took office, promising to make things better by continuing exactly those policies that were making things worse, while the opposition breathed fire and brimstone, promising change on every issue except those that mattered—and so, in both countries, a figure outside the mainstream who rejected the failed consensus was able to shoulder his way into power.

In its classic forms, in other words, fascism isn't a right-wing movement, or for that matter a left-wing one. It seizes the abandoned middle ground of politics, takes up the issues other parties refuse to touch, and imposes a totalitarianism of the center. That's the secret of fascism's popularity. It's also the reason why an outbreak of fascism is a frightening possibility as the industrial world stumbles blindly into an unwelcome future, because if something like classic fascism were to emerge today, a great many people who think they oppose fascism probably wouldn't recognize it as such.

That blindness is nothing new. Many avant-garde intellectuals in the Weimar Republic, for example, were convinced that they already lived in a fascist country. They pointed to the blatant influence of big business on politics, civil rights violations perpetrated by governments, and the other abuses of power common to any centralized political system, and they insisted that this amounted to fascism, since their concept of fascism assumed that it must by definition defend the status quo.

As Walter Laqueur showed in his capable survey *Weimar: A Cultural History*, denouncing the Weimar Republic as a fascist regime was quite the lively industry in pre-Nazi Germany. Unfortunately for those who made this claim, history has a wicked sense of humor. Many of the people who insisted that Weimar Germany was a fascist state got to find out, often at the cost of their lives, that there really is a difference between a corrupt, crippled, and failing democracy and a totalitarian state.

It's entirely possible that history's gallows humor could repeat in a similar way. To see how that could take place, let's engage in a thought experiment. Imagine that sometime this spring, you visit some public place in the United States, and encounter a dozen young people dressed identically in bright green T-shirts, surplus black BDU trousers, and army-style boots. They're clean-cut, bright, and enthusiastic, and they want to interest you in a new political movement called the American Peoples Party. You're not interested, and walk on.

A couple of months later you run across another dozen of them, as bright, clean, and enthusiastic as the first bunch. Now the movement is called the National Progressive American Peoples Party, NPAPP for short, and it's got a twenty-five-point program focused on the troubled economy, peak oil, and climate change. You take a copy, mostly to humor the cute young thing who hands it to you. The points aren't especially original, but they make more sense than what either Obama or the Republicans are proposing.

Over the months to come you see more and more of them, handing out flyers, going door to door to invite people to local meetings, and doing the other things that political parties used to do back when they were still serious about grassroots organizing. A news website you follow shows a picture of party chairman Fred Halliot,[94] an Army vet who did three tours in Afghanistan and earned a Silver Star for courage under fire. You glance at his face and then go to something more interesting.

Meanwhile, the economy's getting worse. Two of your friends lose their jobs, and the price of gasoline spikes from its current lows, plunges again, and stabilizes again well above what you can easily afford. The Democrats insists that the recovery is already here and people just need to be patient and wait for prosperity to trickle down to them. The Republicans insist that the only reason the economy hasn't recovered yet is that the rich still have to pay taxes. The media insist that the holiday shopping season is going to be so big that stores may run out of toys and electronic gewgaws to sell; the TV yammers about big

---

[94] Yes, it's an anagram. Work it out yourself.

crowds on Black Friday, but nobody you know has the spare money to buy much. Not until midway through January do the media admit that the shopping season was a disaster and that two big-box chains have just gone broke.

In the spring, Halliot begins a nationwide speaking tour. He travels in a school bus painted green and black, the NPAPP colors, with a Celtic tree-of-life symbol, the party's new emblem. A handful of pundits start talking about Halliot and the NPAPP, making wistful noises about how nice it is to see young idealists in politics again; a few others fling denunciations, though they don't seem to know quite what they're denouncing. Both mainstream parties launch youth organizations with their own t-shirts and slogans, but their lack of new ideas make these efforts a waste of time.

The speaking tour ends in Washington DC with a huge rally, and things get out of hand. Exactly what happened is hard to tell afterwards, with wildly different stories coming from the mass media, the internet, and NPAPP headquarters in St. Louis. The upshot is that Halliot and two aides are arrested on federal conspiracy charges. The trial is a media circus; Halliot gives an impassioned speech justifying his actions on the grounds that the nation and the world are in deep trouble and radical change is needed to keep things from getting much worse. He gets sentenced to four years in prison, and the mainstream parties breathe a huge sigh of relief, convinced that the NPAPP is a flash in the pan.

They're wrong. The NPAPP weathers the crisis easily, and publicity from the trial gives it a major boost. NPAPP candidates enter races across the country in the upcoming elections, seizing much of the limelight from the dreary presidential race between a pair of bland and interchangeable candidates. When the votes are counted, the new party has more than three hundred local positions, forty-three seats in state legislatures, and two seats in the House of Representatives. The major parties try every trick they know to overturn the results of each race, and succeed only in making themselves look corrupt and scared.

Then Halliot gets released from prison, having served only nine months of his sentence. (Word on the internet has it that the point of locking him up was to keep him out of the way during the election—but is that simply a NPAPP talking point? Nobody's sure.) It turns out that he put the time into writing a book, *A Struggle for the Soul of America*. You leaf through a copy in the public library. It's not a great work of literature, and it's written in a folksy, rambling style you find irritating, but it's full of the kind of political notions that Americans swap over beers and pizza: the kind, in other words, that no mainstream party will touch.

The book has an edge that wasn't in NPAPP literature before Halliot's prison term, though. The government of the parties, he insists, must be replaced by a government of the people, guided by a new values consensus that goes beyond the broken politics of special interests to do what has to be done about the economy, peak oil, and climate change. Time is short, he insists, and half measures aren't enough; a transformation of every aspect of American life, a Great Turning, is the only option left. Edgy though his language is, you note, he's the only figure in national politics who takes the economic, energy, and climate crises seriously.

The next autumn, as if on cue, the economy lurches down hard. Petroleum prices spike again, and a big Wall Street bank that had huge derivative bets the other way goes messily broke. Attempts to get a bailout through Congress freeze up in partisan bickering. Over the next two months, despite frantic efforts by the Bush administration, the economy stumbles and the credit markets seize up. Job losses snowball. NPAPP people are everywhere, leafleting the crowds, staffing impromptu soup kitchens, marching in the streets. You would pay less attention, but by spring you're out of a job, too.

The following years are a blur of grim headlines, heated rhetoric, hungry mobs at soup kitchens, and marching crowds in green and black. In the next election, there are rumors, never proved, of NPAPP squads keeping opposition voters away from the polls in critical districts. One way or another, Halliot's party seats six senators and 185 representatives in Congress, and takes control of a dozen states. The three-way split in the House makes it impossible for Congress to get anything done, and the administration copies its predecessors by flailing and fumbling to no noticeable effect. One thing of importance does happen; to get NPAPP support for a stopgap budget bill, the president is forced to grant a federal pardon to Halliot, removing the last legal barrier to the latter's presidential ambitions.

Fast forward to the next round of presidential elections, which are fought out in a flurry of marches, protests, beatings, riots, and charges and countercharges of vote fraud. When the dust has settled, no party has a majority in the electoral college. The election goes to the House of Representatives, and Halliot wins on the forty-second ballot. He is inaugurated on a bitterly cold day, surrounded by NPAPP banners and greeted by marching files of party faithful in green and black. He calls for a constitutional convention to replace the government of the parties with a government of the people, get the country back on its feet, and sweep away everything that stands in the way of the Great Turning that will lead America to a bright new future. The crowd roars its approval.

Later that year, the crowds go wilder still when the new constitution is enacted. Those with old-fashioned ideas find some of its terms objectionable, as it lacks such minor details as checks and balances, not to mention meaningful and enforceable guarantees of due process and civil rights. The media don't mention that, though, because the "new values consensus" is enforced by Party officials—the capital letter becomes standard usage very quickly—and those who criticize the new constitution too forcefully, well, let's just say that nobody's quite sure where they are now, and most people know better than to ask.

And you, dear reader? At what point along that trajectory would you have decided that for all its seeming promise, for all the youth, enthusiasm, and earnestness that surrounded it, the National Socialist German Workers Party and the charismatic veteran who led it were likely to be worse—much, much worse—than the weary, dreary, dysfunctional mess of a political system they were attempting to replace? Or would you end up as part of the cheering crowds along the Unter den Linden in January 1933 in that last scene?

What's too rarely recalled about the fascist movements of Europe between the wars is just how much promise they seemed to hold, and how many people saw them as the best hope of the future. Their leaders were young—Hitler was forty-three when he became chancellor, the same age as John F. Kennedy at his inauguration, and Mussolini was only thirty-nine when he became prime minister of Italy—and much of the rank and file was younger still; Hitler was a huge success among college students long before he had a mass following elsewhere. Both parties also drew heavily on the avant-garde culture of their time; how many people remember that before the Second World War, the swastika was a Pagan symbol of life, redolent of ancient roots and primal vitality, with the same cultural ambience that the NPAPP's Celtic tree-of-life emblem might have today?

The fascist movements of the 1920s and 1930s were thus closely attuned to the hopes and fears of the people, far more so than either the mainstream parties or the established radical groups of their countries. Unlike the imagined "fascism" of current radical rhetoric, they were an alternative to business as usual that positioned itself squarely in the abandoned center of the political discourse. In terms of that discourse, in the context of their own times and places, the talking points of the fascist parties weren't anything like so extreme as they appear to most people nowadays—and we forget that at our deadly peril.

That's what I tried to duplicate in the thought experiment above, by changing certain details of German national socialism so I could give the National Progressive American Peoples Party a contemporary slant—one that that calls up the same reactions Hitler's party got in its own place and time. Anti-Semitism and militarism were socially acceptable in Germany between the wars; they aren't socially acceptable in today's United States, and so they won't play a role in a neofascist movement of any importance. What will fill those roles, of course, are the tropes and buzzwords that appeal to Americans today, and those may well include the tropes and buzzwords that appeal most to you.

There's a deeper issue I've tried to raise here. It's easy and comfortable to define every political conflict in terms of good versus evil. The habit of seeing politics that way is a reliable source of problems, because it's rare for such crude stereotypes to reflect political reality; conflict between the slightly better and the slightly worse, or between the worse in one sense or the worse in another, is considerably more common. The hardest of all political choices, though, comes from conflict between the wretchedly bad and the much, much worse. That's the choice Weimar Germany faced, between a crippled, dysfunctional democratic system riddled with graft and abuses of power, on the one hand, and a shiny new tyranny on the other.

There are no easy answers to that conundrum. Unless we can find some way to step back from the partisan hatreds that bedevil our political life, it's quite possible that the long and ugly list of the world's totalitarian regimes will receive several new additions from today's failing industrial democracies, complete with the usual complement of prison camps and mass graves. As long as the word "fascism" retains its current status as a meaningless snarl word, certainly, that possibility seems far more likely than any of the alternatives.

# THE ROAD AHEAD

# How civilizations fall

### *A theory of catabolic collapse*

*History has been an important interest of mine since childhood; ecology has been another. As the twentieth century gave way to the twenty-first, and the predictions of planetary crisis made and then ignored in the 1970s began to come true, I spent several years reading everything I could find about the decline and fall of civilizations. I came to see that the specific pattern of collapse traced out in* The Limits to Growth—*the most prescient, and thus inevitably the most loudly denounced, of the warnings issued in the 1970s—could be applied to the fall of civilizations more broadly. The following paper, which was completed in 2004, built on that insight; it was circulated fairly widely on the internet, but saw print for the first time as an appendix to my book* The Long Descent.

### Abstract

The collapse of complex human societies remains poorly understood and current theories fail to model important features of historical examples of collapse. Relationships among resources, capital, waste, and production form the basis for an ecological model of collapse in which production fails to meet maintenance requirements for existing capital. Societies facing such crises having depleted essential resources risk catabolic collapse, a self-reinforcing cycle of contraction converting most capital to waste. This model allows key features of historical examples of collapse to be accounted for, and suggests parallels between successional processes in nonhuman ecosystems and collapse phenomena in human societies.

**Keywords:** collapse, ecology, resources, succession

## Introduction

The collapse of complex human societies, while a subject of perennial scholarly and popular fascination, remains poorly understood. Tainter (1988), surveying previous attempts to account for the demise of civilizations, noted that most proposed explanations of collapse failed to adequately describe causative mechanisms, and relied either on ad hoc hypotheses based on details of specific cases or, by contrast, essentially mystical claims (e.g., that civilizations have life spans like those of individual biological organisms). In another recent survey of collapses in history (Yoffee & Cowgill, 1988), contributors proposed widely divergent explanatory models to account for broadly similar processes of decline and breakdown.

Tainter (1988) proposed a general theory of collapse, in which complex societies break down when increasing complexity results in negative marginal returns, so that a decrease in sociopolitical complexity yields net benefits to people in the society. This theory has important strengths, and models many features of the breakdown of civilizations, but it fails to account for other factors, especially the temporal dimensions of the process. Tainter defines collapse as a process of marked sociopolitical simplification unfolding on a timescale of "no more than a few decades" (Tainter, 1988, p. 4), replacing an unsustainably high level of complexity with a lower, more sustainable level. Most of the examples he cites, however, fail to fit this description, but occurred over a period of centuries rather than decades (see Table 1) and involved an extended process of progressive disintegration rather than a rapid shift from an unsustainable state to a sustainable one.

Table 1. Timescales of collapse for selected civilizations (all dates from Tainter, 1988)

| Civilization | Onset of collapse | Time to collapse |
|---|---|---|
| Minoan Crete | c. 1500 BCE | c. 300 years |
| Mycenean Greece | c. 1200 BCE | c. 150 years |
| Hittite empire | c. 1200 BCE | c. 100 years |
| Western Chou empire | 934 BCE | 163 years |
| Western Roman empire | 166 CE | 310 years |
| Medieval Mesopotamia | c. 650 CE | c. 550 years |
| Lowland Classic Maya | c. 750 CE | c. 150 years |

The best documented examples of collapse, such as the fall of the western Roman empire, show a distinctive temporal pattern even more difficult to square with Tainter's theory. Thus, during the collapse of Roman power, each of a series of crises led to loss of social complexity and the establishment of temporary stability at a less complex level. Each such level then proved to be unsustainable in turn, and was followed by a further crisis and loss of complexity (Gibbon, 1776–88; Tainter, 1988; Grant, 1990). In many regions, furthermore, the sociopolitical complexity remaining after the empire's final disintegration was far below the level that had existed in the same area prior to its inclusion in the imperial system. Thus Britain in the late pre-Roman Iron Age, for example, had achieved a stable and flourishing agricultural society with nascent urban centers and international trade connections, while the same area remained depopulated, impoverished, and politically chaotic for centuries following the collapse of imperial authority (Snyder, 2003).

An alternative model based on perspectives from human ecology offers a more effective way to understand the collapse process. This conceptual model, the theory of catabolic collapse, explains the breakdown of complex societies as the result of a self-reinforcing cycle of decline driven by interactions among resources, capital, production, and waste. Previous work on the human ecology of past civilizations (e.g., Hughes, 1975; Sanders, Sanders, & Santley, 1979; Ponting, 1992; Elvin, 1993; Webster, 2002) and attempts to project the impact of ecological factors on present societies (e.g., Catton, 1980; Gever, Kaufman, Skole, &

Vorosmarty, 1986; Meadows, Meadows, & Randers, 1992; Duncan, 1993; Heinberg, 2002) have yielded data and analytical tools from which a general theory of the collapse of complex societies may be developed. This will be attempted here.

## The human ecology of collapse

At the highest level of abstraction, any human society includes four core elements. *Resources* (R) are naturally occurring factors in the environment which can be exploited by a particular society, but have not yet been extracted and incorporated into the society's flows of energy and material. Resources include material resources such as iron ore not yet mined and naturally occurring soil fertility that has not yet been exhausted by the society's agricultural methods, human resources such as people not yet included in the workforce, and information resources such as scientific discoveries which can be made by the society's methods of research but have not yet been made. While the resources available to any society, even the simplest, are numerous, complex, and changing, this conceptual model treats resources as a single variable. This radical oversimplification is acceptable solely because it allows certain large-scale patterns to be seen clearly, and permits one model to be applied to the widest possible range of societies.

*Capital* (C) consists of all factors from whatever source that have been incorporated into the society's flows of energy and material but are capable of further use. Capital includes physical capital such as food, fields, tools, and buildings; human capital such as laborers and scientists; social capital such as social hierarchies and economic systems; and information capital such as technical knowledge. While a market system is a form of social capital, and currency and coinage are forms of physical capital, it should be noted that money as such is a mechanism for allocating and controlling capital rather than a form of capital in its own right. While the capital stocks of every society are diverse, complex, and changing, again, for the sake of exposition, this model treats all capital as a single variable.

*Waste* (W) consists of all factors that have been incorporated into the society's flows of energy and material, and exploited to the point that they are incapable of further use. Materials used or converted into pollutants, tools and laborers at the end of their useful lives, and information garbled or lost, all become waste. All waste is treated as a single variable for the purpose of this conceptual model.

*Production* (P) is the process by which existing capital and resources are combined to create new capital and waste. The quality and quantity of new capital created by production are functions of the resources and existing capital used in production. Resources and existing capital may be substituted for one another in production, but the relation between the two is nonlinear and complete substitution is impossible. As the use of resources approaches zero, in particular, maintaining any given level of production requires exponential increases in the use of existing capital, due to the effect of decreasing marginal return (Clark & Haswell, 1966; Wilkinson, 1973; Tainter, 1988). For the purpose of this model, all production is treated as a single variable.

In any human society, resources and capital enter the production process, and new capital and waste leave it. Capital is also subject to waste outside production—uneaten food suffers spoilage, for example, and unemployed laborers still grow old and die. Thus maintenance of a steady state requires new capital from production to equal waste from production and capital:

$$C(p) = W(p) + W(c) \rightarrow \text{steady state} \qquad (1)$$

where $C(p)$ is new capital produced, $W(p)$ is existing capital converted to waste in the production of new capital, and $W(c)$ is existing capital converted to waste outside of production. The sum of $W(p)$ and $W(c)$ is $M(p)$, maintenance production, the level of production necessary to maintain capital stocks at existing levels. Thus Equation 1 can be more simply put:

$$C(p) = M(p) \rightarrow \text{steady state} \qquad (2)$$

Societies which move from a steady state into a state of expansion produce more than necessary to maintain existing capital stocks:

$$C(p) > M(p) \rightarrow \text{expansion} \qquad (3)$$

In the absence of effective limits to growth, once started, this expansion becomes a self-reinforcing process, because additional capital can be brought into the production process, where it generates yet more new capital, which can be brought into the production process in turn. The westward expansion of the United States in the nineteenth century offers a well-documented example; in a resource-rich environment, increases in human capital through immigration and increases in information capital through development of new agricultural technologies increased production, driving increases in physical capital through geographical expansion, settling of arable land, manufacturing, etc., which increased production again and drove further increases across the spectrum of capital (Billington, 1982). This process may be called an *anabolic cycle*.

The self-reinforcing aspect of an anabolic cycle is restricted by two factors that tend to limit increases in $C(p)$. First, resources may not be sufficient to maintain indefinite expansion. Here the use of "resources" as a single variable must be set aside briefly. Each resource has a replenishment rate, $r(R)$, the rate at which new stocks of the resource become available to the society. For any given resource and society at any given time, $r(R)$ is a weighted product of the rates of natural production, new discovery of existing deposits, and development of alternative resources capable of filling the same role in production. Over time, since discovery and the development of replacements are both subject to decreasing marginal returns (Clark & Haswell, 1966; Wilkinson, 1973; Tainter, 1988), $r(R)$ approaches asymptotically the combined rate at which the original resource and replacements are created by natural processes.

Each resource also has a rate of use by the society, $d(R)$, and the relationship between $d(R)$ and $r(R)$ forms a core element in the model. Resources used faster than their replenishment rate, $d(R)/r(R) >1$, become depleted; a depleted resource must be replaced by existing capital to maintain production, and the demand for capital increases exponentially as depletion continues. Thus, unless all of a society's necessary resources have an unlimited replenishment rate, $C(p)$ cannot increase indefinitely because $d(R)$ will eventually exceed $r(R)$, leading to depletion and exponential increases in capital required to maintain $C(p)$ at any given level. Liebig's law of the minimum suggests that for any given society, the essential resource with the highest value for $d(R)/r(R)$ may be used as a working value of $d(R)/r(R)$ for resources as a whole.

Resource depletion is thus one of the two factors that tend to overcome the momentum of an anabolic cycle. The second is inherent in the relationship between capital and waste. As capital stocks increase, $M(p)$ rises, since $W(c)$ rises proportionally to total capital; more capital requires more maintenance and replacement. $M(p)$ also rises as $C(p)$ rises, since increased production requires increased use of capital and thus increased $W(p)$, or conversion of capital to waste in the production process. All other factors being equal, the effect of W(c) is to make M(p) rise faster than C(p), since not all capital is involved in production at any given time, but all capital is constantly subject to conversion to waste. Increased C(p) relative to M(p) can be generated by decreasing capital stocks to decrease W(c); by slowing the conversion of capital to waste to decrease W(c) and/or W(p); by increasing the fraction of capital involved in production, to increase C(p); or by increasing the intake of resources for production, thus increasing C(p). If these are not done, or prove insufficient to meet the needs of the situation, M(p) will rise to equal or exceed C(p) and bring the anabolic cycle to a halt.

Broadly speaking, a society facing the end of an anabolic cycle faces a choice between two strategies. One strategy is to move toward a steady state in which C(p) = M(p), and d(R) ≤ r(R) for every economically significant resource. Barring the presence of environmental limits, this requires social controls to keep capital stocks down to a level at which maintenance costs can be met from current production, and to maintain intake of resources at or below replenishment rates. This can require difficult collective choices, but as long as resource availability remains stable, controls on capital growth stay in place, and the society escapes major exogenous crises, this strategy can be pursued indefinitely.

The alternative is to attempt to prolong the anabolic cycle through efforts to accelerate intake of resources through military conquest, new technology, or other means. Since increasing production increases W(p) and increasing capital stocks lead to increased W(c), however, such efforts drive further increases in M(p). A society that attempts to maintain an anabolic cycle indefinitely must therefore expand its use of resources at an ever-increasing rate to keep C(p) from dropping below M(p). Since this exacerbates problems with depletion, as discussed above, this strategy may prove counterproductive.

If the attempt to achieve a steady state fails, or if efforts at increasing resource intake fall irrevocably behind rising M(p), a society enters a state of contraction, in which production of new capital does not make up for losses due to waste:

$$C(p) < M(p) \rightarrow \text{contraction} \qquad (4)$$

The process of contraction takes two general forms, depending on the replenishment rate of resources used by the society. A society that uses resources at or below replenishment rate (d(R)/r(R) ≤ 1), when production of new capital falls short of maintenance needs, enters a *maintenance crisis* in which capital of all kinds cannot be maintained and is converted to waste: Physical capital is destroyed or spoiled, human populations decline in number, large-scale social organizations disintegrate into smaller and more economical forms, and information is lost. Because resources are not depleted, maintenance crises are generally self-limiting. As capital is lost, M(p) declines steeply, while declines in C(p) due to capital loss are cushioned to some extent by the steady supply of resources. This allows a return to a steady state or the start of a new anabolic cycle once the conversion of capital to waste brings M(p) back below C(p).

A society that uses resources beyond replenishment rate (d(R)/r(R) > 1), when production of new capital falls short of maintenance needs, risks a *depletion crisis* in which key features of a maintenance crisis are amplified by the impact of depletion on production. As M(p) exceeds C(p) and capital can no longer be maintained, it is converted to waste and unavailable for use. Since depletion requires progressively greater investments of capital in production, the loss of capital affects production more seriously than in an equivalent maintenance crisis. Meanwhile further production, even at a diminished rate, requires further use of depleted resources, exacerbating the impact of depletion and the need for increased capital to maintain production. With demand for capital rising as the supply of capital falls, C(p) tends to decrease faster than M(p) and perpetuate the crisis. The result is a *catabolic cycle*, a self-reinforcing process in which C(p) stays below M(p) while both decline. Catabolic cycles may occur in maintenance crises if the gap between C(p) and M(p) is large enough, but tend to be self-limiting in such cases. In depletion crises, by contrast, catabolic cycles can proceed to *catabolic collapse*, in which C(p) approaches zero and most of a society's capital is converted to waste.

A society in a depletion crisis does not inevitably proceed to catabolic collapse. If depletion is limited, so that decreased demand for resources as a consequence of diminished production brings d(R) back below r(R), the accelerated fall in C(p) may not take place and the crisis may play out much like a maintenance crisis. If the gap between C(p) and M(p) is modest, nonproductive capital may be diverted to production to raise C(p) or preferentially converted to waste to bring down M(p), forcing C(p) and M(p) temporarily into balance in order to buy time for a transition to a steady state. A society in which depletion is advanced and M(p) rapidly increasing relative to C(p), though, may not be able to escape catabolic collapse even if such steps are taken. Cultural and political factors may also make efforts to avoid catabolic collapse difficult to accomplish, or indeed to contemplate.

## Testing the model

These two forms of collapse, maintenance crisis leading to recovery and depletion crisis leading to catabolic collapse, are to some extent ideal types, and form two ends of a complex spectrum of societal breakdown. Most historical examples of collapse fall somewhere in the range between. The limitations of the abstract and extremely simplified model on which the theory is based should also be kept firmly in mind when attempting to apply it to past or present examples. Still, a survey of historical examples shows that many of these have features which support the model proposed in this paper.

Closest to the maintenance-crisis end of the spectrum are tribal societies such as the Kachin of Burma. Kachin communities cycle up and down from relatively decentralized (*gumlao*) to relatively centralized (*shan*) social forms without significant losses of physical, human, or information capital. In this case anabolic cycles lead to the growth of organizational capital in the form of relatively centralized social forms, but the maintenance costs of this organizational capital prove to be unsustainable, leading to maintenance crises, loss of social capital, and the restoration of less resource- and capital-intensive social forms (Leach, 1954).

Essentially the same process on a larger and more destructive scale characterizes the history of imperial China from the tenth century BCE to the end of the nineteenth century CE. Efficient cereal agriculture and local market economies provided the foundation for a series of anabolic cycles resulting in the establishment of centralized imperial dynastic states (Gates, 1996; Di Cosmo, 1999). These anabolic cycles drove increases in population, public works such as canals and flood control projects, and sociopolitical organization, which proved unsustainable over the long term. As maintenance costs exceeded the imperial government's resources, repeated maintenance crises led to the breakup of national unity, invasion by neighboring peoples, loss of infrastructure, and steep declines in population (Ho, 1970; Di Cosmo, 1999). Imperial China's resource base had a relatively high replenishment rate, due largely to the long-term sustainability of traditional Chinese agriculture and the use of human and animal muscle as the primary energy sources, and any significant depletion was made good once population levels dropped (Elvin, 1993). Though resource depletion played a limited role, the maintenance crises of imperial China were self-limiting and resulted in contraction to more modest levels of population and sociopolitical organization, rather than the total collapse of the society.

The collapse of the western Roman empire, by contrast, was a catabolic collapse driven by a combined maintenance and resource crisis. While the ancient Mediterranean world, like imperial China, was primarily dependent on readily replenished resources, the empire itself was the product of an anabolic cycle fueled by easily depleted resources and driven by Roman military superiority. Beginning in the third century BCE, Roman expansion transformed the capital of other societies into resources for Rome as country after country was conquered and stripped of movable wealth. Each new conquest increased the Roman resource base and helped pay for further conquests. After the first century CE, though, further expansion failed to pay its own costs. All remaining peoples within the reach of Rome were either barbarian tribes with little wealth, such as the Germans, or rival empires capable of defending themselves, such as the Parthians (Jones 1974). Without income from new conquests, the maintenance costs of empire proved unsustainable, and a catabolic cycle followed rapidly. The first major breakdown in the imperial system came in 166 CE, and further crises followed until the western empire ceased to exist in 476 CE (Grant, 1990, 1999).

The Roman collapse has an instructive feature which offers further support to the model presented here. In 297 the emperor Diocletian divided the empire into western and eastern halves. Coordination between them waned, and by the death of Theodosius I in 395, the two halves of the empire were effectively independent states. Since the western empire produced one third of the revenues of the eastern empire, but had more than twice as much northern frontier to defend against barbarian encroachments, this placed most of the original empire's vulnerabilities in one half and most of its remaining resources in the other. In terms of the catabolic collapse model, the eastern empire allowed massive quantities of relatively unproductive, high-maintenance capital to be converted to waste, bringing its $M(p)$ below its remaining $C(p)$ and breaking out of the catabolic cycle. The eastern empire's territory decreased further with the Muslim conquests of the seventh and eighth centuries CE; while this was involuntary the effects were the same.

Successfully shifting to a level of organization that could be supported sustainably by trade and agriculture within a more manageable territory, the eastern empire survived for nearly a millennium longer than its western twin (Bury, 1923).

Near the depletion crisis end of the spectrum is the collapse of the Lowland Classic Maya in the eighth, ninth, and tenth centuries of the Common Era. The most widely accepted model of the Maya collapse holds on demographic and paleoecological evidence that Maya populations grew to a level that could not be indefinitely supported by Mayan agricultural practices on the nutrient-poor laterite soils of the Yucatan lowlands. In terms of the present model, the key resource of soil fertility was used at a rate exceeding its replenishment rate, and suffered severe depletion as a result. Mayan polities also invested a large proportion of $C(p)$ in monumental building programs, which raised maintenance costs but could not be readily used for production, and maintained these programs up to the beginning of the Terminal Classic period. The result was a "rolling collapse" over two centuries, from c. 750 CE to c. 950 CE, in which Lowland Maya populations declined precipitously and scores of urban centers were abandoned to the jungle (Willey & Shimkin, 1973, Lowe, 1985, Webster, 2002).

The Lowland Classic Maya collapse is particularly suggestive in that it appears to have been preceded by at least two previous breakdowns. Preclassic sites such as El Mirador and Becan show many of the same artistic and cultural elements as Classic Maya urban centers, but were abandoned in a poorly documented earlier collapse around 150 CE (Webster, 2002). A second episode, the so-called Hiatus between the Early Classic and Late Classic periods (500–600 CE), saw sharp declines in monumental building and evidence for political decentralization (Willey, 1974). Whether these events were maintenance crises preceding the final resource crisis of the Terminal Classic, or whether some other explanation is called for, is difficult to determine from the available evidence.

Features of comparative sociology outside the realm of collapse processes also offer support to the catabolic collapse model. One implication of the model is that societies which persist over extended periods will tend to have social mechanisms for limiting the growth of capital, and thus artificially lowering $M(p)$ below $C(p)$. Such mechanisms do in fact exist in a wide range of societies. Among the most common are systems in which modest amounts of unproductive capital are regularly converted to waste. Examples include aspects of the potlatch economy among Native Americans of northwest North America (Kotschar, 1950; Rosman & Rubel, 1971; Beck, 1993) and the ritual deposition of prestige metalwork in lakes and rivers by Bronze and Iron Age peoples in much of Western Europe (Bradley, 1990; Randsborg, 1995). Such systems have been interpreted in many ways (Michaelson, 1979), but in terms of the model presented here, one of their functions is to divert some of C(p) away from capital stocks requiring maintenance, thus artificially lowering W(c) and making a catabolic cycle less likely.

Such practices clearly have many other meanings and functions within societies. Nor does this interpretation require any awareness within societies that systems of capital destruction prevent catabolic cycles. Rather, if such systems make catabolic collapse less likely, cultures that adopt such systems for other reasons would be more likely to survive over the long term and to pass on such cultural elements to neighboring or successor societies.

### Conclusion: collapse as a succession process

Even within the social sciences, the process by which complex societies give way to smaller and simpler ones has often been presented in language drawn from literary tragedy, as though the loss of sociocultural complexity necessarily warranted a negative value judgment. This is understandable, since the collapse of civilizations often involves catastrophic human mortality and the loss of priceless cultural treasures, but like any value judgment it can obscure important features of the matter at hand.

A less problematic approach to the phenomenon of collapse derives from the idea of succession, a basic concept in the ecology of nonhuman organisms. Succession describes the process by which an area not yet occupied by living things is colonized by a variety of biotic assemblages, called seres, each replacing a prior sere and then being replaced by a later, until the process concludes with a stable, self-perpetuating climax community (Odum, 1969).

One feature of succession in many different environments is a difference in resource use between earlier and later seres. Species characteristic of earlier seral stages tend to maximize control of resources and production of biomass per unit time, even at the cost of inefficiency; thus such species tend to maximize production and distribution of offspring even when this means the great majority of offspring fail to reach reproductive maturity. Species typical of later seres, by contrast, tend to maximize the efficiency of their resource use, even at the cost of limits to biomass production and the distribution of individual organisms; thus these species tend to maximize energy investment in individual offspring even when this means that offspring are few and the species fails to occupy all available niche spaces. Species of the first type, or R-selected species, have specialized to flourish opportunistically in disturbed environments, while those of the second type, or K-selected species, have specialized to form stable biotic communities that change only with shifts in the broader environment (Odum, 1969).

Human societies and nonhuman species cannot be equated in a simplistic manner, but the radical differences in subsistence and production strategies among human societies allow them to be compared to distinct biotic groups in certain contexts. Human societies enter into common ecological relationships such as symbiosis, commensality, parasitism, predation, and competitive exclusion with other societies. Thus processes by which human societies are replaced by others may be usefully compared to succession to see if common features emerge.

The model of catabolic collapse suggests one such common feature. As outlined above, societies differ in their response to changes in resource availability and maintenance costs. The spectrum of response ranges from adjustment to a steady state, through a history of repeated maintenance crises and partial breakdowns followed by recoveries, to severe depletion crisis and total collapse. These differences, according to the model presented here, unfold from differing relationships among resources, capital, production, and waste, especially the relationships between capital production and maintenance, $C(p)/M(p)$, and between use and replenishment rates of resources, $d(R)/r(R)$.

These parallel differences between R-selected and K-selected nonhuman species. A society that maximizes its production of capital, like an R-selected species, prospers in an environment with substantial uncaptured resources but falters once these are exhausted. Its successors are likely to be societies that, like K-selected species, use key resources more sustainably at the cost of decreased production of capital. Nonhuman climax communities also typically display a higher diversity of species, but a lower population per species, than earlier seral stages, and produce notably lower volumes of biomass per unit time (Odum, 1969).

Broadly similar changes often distinguish pre-collapse and post-collapse societies. Thus the collapse of the western Roman empire, for example, could be seen as a succession process in which one seral stage, dominated by a single sociopolitical "species" that maximized capital production at the cost of inefficiency, was replaced by a more diverse community of societies, consisting of many less populous "species" better adapted to their own local conditions, and producing capital at lower but more sustainable rates. Analyses that portray this transformation as pure tragedy miss important aspects, since the Roman collapse enabled other societies to emerge from Rome's shadow, and launched major cultural initiatives such as vernacular literatures in the ancestors of today's Celtic, Germanic, and Romance languages (Wiseman, 1997). As with any succession process, there were gainers as well as losers. If a lapse into fantasy may be excused, were nonhuman biota literate and interested in their past, a history of lake enrichment, known as eutrophication, written by meadow grasses would differ sharply from one written by fish.

Since humans have capacities for change that most species lack, the same human individuals can change from fish to grass, so to speak, composing an "R-selected" production-maximizing society at one time and its "K-selected" sustainability-maximizing replacement at a later time. The example of the Kachin cited above shows that this is not merely a theoretical possibility. However, as other cited examples and the general evidence of history suggest, such a change is not inevitable. The possibility of maintenance crisis needs to be considered whenever a society shows signs of being unable to maintain its existing capital, and the possibility of depletion crisis followed by catabolic collapse cannot be excluded whenever capital production depends on the use of resources at rates significantly above their rate of replacement.

Such assessments of past and present societies, in order to achieve a high degree of analytic or predictive value, require careful quantitative analysis of a sort this paper has not attempted. Since each element in the conceptual model presented here stands for a diverse and constantly changing set of variables, such analysis offers significant challenges, and in many historical examples it may be impossible to go beyond proxy measurements of uncertain value for crucial variables. However, general patterns corresponding to the catabolic collapse model may be easier to extract from incomplete data. Any society that displays broad increases in most measures of capital production coupled with signs of serious depletion of key resources, in particular, may be considered a potential candidate for catabolic collapse.

## References

Beck, M. G. (1993). *Potlatch: Native Ceremony and Myth on the Northwest Coast.* Anchorage, AK: Alaska Northwest.

Billington, R. A. (1982). *Westward Expansion: a History of the American Frontier.* New York: Macmillan.

Bradley, R. (1990). *The Passage of Arms: an Archaeological Analysis of Prehistoric Hoards and Votive Deposits.* Cambridge: Cambridge University Press.

Bury, J. B. (1923). *History of the Later Roman Empire.* London: Macmillan.

Catton, W. R., Jr. (1980). *Overshoot: the Ecological Basis of Revolutionary Change.* Urbana, IL: University of Illinois Press.

Clark, C., & Haswell, M. (1966). *The Economics of Subsistence Agriculture.* London: Macmillan.

Corning, P. A. (1983). *The Synergism Hypothesis.* New York: McGraw-Hill.

Corning, P. A. (2002). 'Devolution' as an opportunity to test the 'synergism hypothesis' and a cybernetic theory of political systems. *Systems Research and Behavioral Science, 19*(1): 3–24.

Di Cosmo, N. (1999). State formation and periodization in inner Asia. *International History Review, 20*(2): 287–309.

Duncan, R. C. (1993).The life-expectancy of industrial civilization: the decline to global equilibrium. *Population and Environment, 14*(4): 325–357.

Elvin, M. (1993). Three thousand years of unsustainable growth: China's environment from archaic times to the present. *East Asian History, 6*: 7–46.

Gates, H. (1996). *China's Motor: a Thousand Years of Petty Capitalism.* Ithaca, NY: Cornell University Press.

Gever, J., Kaufman, R., Skole, D., & Vorosmarty, C. (1986). *Beyond Oil: the Threat to Food and Fuel in the Coming Decades.* Cambridge, MA: Ballinger.

Gibbon, E. (1776–88). *The Decline and Fall of the Roman Empire.* New York: Modern Library.

Grant, M. (1990). *The Fall of the Roman Empire.* London: Weidenfeld & Nicolson.

Grant, M. (1999). *The Collapse and Recovery of the Roman Empire.* London: Routledge.

Hughes, J. D. (1975). *Ecology in Ancient Civilizations.* Albuquerque, NM: University of New Mexico Press.

Heinberg, R. (2002). *The Party's Over: Oil, War, and the Fate of Industrial Societies.* Vancouver, BC, Canada: New Society.

Ho, P.-T. (1970). Economic and institutional factors in the decline of the Chinese empire. In: C. M. Cipolla (Ed.), *The Economic Decline of Empires* (pp. 264–277). London: Methuen.

Jones, A. H. M. (1974). *The Roman Economy: Studies in Ancient Economic and Administrative History.* Oxford: Basil Blackwell.

Kotschar, V. F. (1950). *Fighting with Property: a Study of Kwakiutl Potlatching and Warfare, 1792–1930*. Seattle, WA: University of Washington Press.

Leach, E. R. (1954). *Political Systems of Highland Burma*. Boston, MA: Beacon.

Lowe, J. W. G. (1985). *The Dynamics of Apocalypse: a Systems Simulation of the Classic Maya Collapse*. Albuquerque, NM: University of New Mexico Press.

Meadows, D. H., Meadows, D. L., & Randers, J. (1992). *Beyond the Limits*. Post Mills, VT: Chelsea Green.

Michaelson, D. R. (1979). From ethnography to ethnology: a study of the conflict of interpretations of the southern Kwakiutl potlatch. PhD diss., New School for Social Research, New York.

Odum, E. (1969). The strategy of ecosystem development. *Science*, 164: 262–270.

Ponting, C. (1992). *A Green History of the World: the Environment and the Collapse of Great Civilizations*. New York: St. Martin's.

Randsborg, K. (1995). *Hjortspring: Warfare and Sacrifice in Early Europe*. Aarhus, Denmark: Aarhus University Press.

Rosman, A., & Rubel, P. G. (1971). *Feasting with Mine Enemy: Rank and Exchange among Northwest Coast Societies*. New York: Columbia University Press.

Sanders, W. T., Parsons, J. A., & Santley, R. S. (1979). *The Basin of Mexico: Ecological Processes in the Evolution of a Civilization*. New York: Academic Press.

Snyder, C. A. (2003). *The Britons*. Oxford: Blackwell.

Tainter, J. A. (1988). *The Collapse of Complex Societies*. Cambridge: Cambridge University Press.

Webster, D. L. (2002). *The Fall of the Ancient Maya: Solving the Mystery of the Maya Collapse*. London: Thames & Hudson.

Wilkinson, R. G. (1973). *Poverty and Progress: an Ecological Model of Economic Development*. London: Methuen.

Willey, G. R. (1974). The classic Maya hiatus: a 'rehearsal' for the collapse? In: N. Hammond (Ed.), *Mesoamerican Archeology: New Approaches* (pp. 417–430). London: Duckworth.

Willey, G. R., & Shimkin, D. B. (1973). The Maya collapse: a summary view. In: T. P. Culbert (Ed.), *The Classic Maya Collapse* (pp. 457–501). Albuquerque, NM: University of New Mexico Press.

Wiseman, J. (1997). The post-Roman world. *Archaeology*, 50(6): 12–17.

Yoffee, N., & Cowgill, G. (Eds.) (1988). *The Collapse of Ancient States and Civilizations*. Tucson, AZ: University of Arizona Press.

# The long road down

### *Decline and the deindustrial future*

*By 2005 it had become clear to me that the process of catabolic collapse sketched out in my essay "How Civilizations Fall" was no longer just of theoretical concern. This essay, tracing out how the normal process of decline and fall could be expected to work out in our future, was written that year and published on several online forums. The favorable response it received was one of the main things that convinced me to begin my blog* The Archdruid Report *the following year, in which the themes in this essay ended up being central to eleven years of blogging.*

For more than three decades now, the world has been on notice that the long afternoon of industrial society is drawing to a close. The Club of Rome's epochal report *The Limits to Growth* (1973), the first of many persuasive studies, warned that unrestricted economic growth would collide with hard planetary limits sometime in the early twenty-first century, unless expensive and politically unpopular steps were taken soon. Of course those steps weren't taken at all. A failure of vision and political will on the part of leaders and constituencies alike threw away the decades that could have made a difference. Today we live in the shadow of that failure.

Yet an odd blindness affects attempts to make sense of our predicament. People on all sides of the debate talk as though the future has only two possible shapes: progress or apocalypse, either business as usual for the foreseeable future or a catastrophic slide into savagery and mass death. Whether the topic is global warming, renewable energy, fossil fuel depletion, or anything else, the same claims repeat like a broken record. One side insists that technology will inevitably solve our problems and yield a better life for all, while the other side brandishes worst case scenarios and talks of millions of corpses. It should be obvious that these aren't the only possibilities. The fact that this isn't obvious at all is worth exploring.

Most people would notice something odd if two meteorologists, discussing tomorrow's weather on a wet autumn day, ignored all possibilities except clear weather or a sudden snowstorm. Yet the same sort of illogic goes unchallenged in debates about our future. Thus it's crucial to set aside our assumptions, and look at what actually happens when civilizations run into the limits of their resource base. That's happened many times in the past, but technological spurts and sudden collapses are rare. Far more common is a process nobody thinks about nowadays: decline.

## *The historical parallels*

It's unfashionable to suggest that we have anything to learn from the past. Quite possibly this is because history holds up an unflattering mirror to our follies. Those who recall the 1929 stock market bubble, for example, can find every detail repeated in the tech market frenzy of the late 1990s. The same claims that a "new economy" and new technology made the business cycle obsolete, the same proliferation of investment vehicles (investment trusts then, mutual funds today), the same airy confidence that stock values would go up forever and fundamentals didn't matter: fast forward seventy years, and the follies of 1929 replayed in 1999, cheered on by economists who, of all people, should have known better.

The rise and fall of civilizations offers the same embarrassment on a grander scale. We know beyond the slightest doubt what happens to societies that outrun their resource base: they go under. Clive Ponting's

*A Green History of the World* (1992) documents dozens of past cultures that ended up in history's wrecking yard for exactly this reason. One highly relevant example is the ancient Maya, who flourished on the Yucatan Peninsula of Central America while Europe struggled through the Dark Ages.

Like modern industrial society, the Maya built their civilization on a nonrenewable resource base. In their case it was the fertility of fragile tropical soils, which couldn't support intensive corn farming forever. On that shaky foundation they built an extraordinary civilization with fine art, architecture, astronomy, mathematics, and a calendar more accurate than the one we use today. None of that counted when the crops began to fail. Mayan civilization disintegrated, cities were abandoned to the jungle, and the population of the Mayan heartland dropped by 90%.

The parallels go deeper, for the Maya had other options. They could have switched from corn to more sustainable crops such as ramon nuts, or borrowed intensive wetland farming methods from their neighbors to the north. Neither of these happened, because corn farming was central to Maya political ideology. The power of the *ahauob* or "divine lords" who ruled Maya city-states depended on control of the corn crop, so switching crops or farming systems was unthinkable. Instead, Maya elites responded to crisis by launching wars to seize fields and corn from other city-states, making their decline and fall far more brutal than it had to be.

Even so, the Maya decline wasn't a fast process. Maya cities weren't abandoned overnight, as archeologists of two generations ago mistakenly thought, but went under in a "rolling collapse" spread across a century and a half from 750 to 900. Outside the Maya heartland, the process took even longer. Chichen Itza far to the north still flourished long after cities such as Tikal and Bonampak were overgrown ruins, and Mayan city-states on a small scale survived in corners of the Yucatan right up to the Spanish conquest.

Map the Maya collapse onto human life spans and the real scale of the process comes through. A Maya woman born around 730 would have seen the crisis dawn, but the *ahauob* and their cities still flourished when she died of old age seventy years later. Her great-grandson, born around 800, grew up amid a disintegrating society, and the wars and crop failures of his time would have seemed ordinary to him. His great-granddaughter, born around 870, never knew anything but ruins sinking back into the jungle. When she and her family finally set out for a distant village, the last to leave their empty city, it would never have occurred to her that her quiet footsteps on a dirt path marked the end of a civilization.

## *The Olduvai theory*

This same pattern repeats over and over again in history. Gradual disintegration, not sudden catastrophic collapse, is the way civilizations end. It usually takes somewhere between 150 and 350 years for a civilization to decline and fall. This casts a startling light on today's crisis. It took America two centuries of incremental change to transform itself from an agrarian society to its current status as an aging industrial behemoth. Now, with its resource base failing, it faces the common fate of civilizations. Yet if that fate follows its usual timeline, it could easily take two more centuries of incremental change to transform America to an agrarian society again.

Startling as this seems, it's supported by telling evidence. Consider our dwindling oil resources. The Hubbert Curve, devised by geologist M. King Hubbert in the 1950s, tracks production over time for any oil reserve from a single oil well to a planet. It's a bell shaped curve: oil comes slowly at first, rises to peak production, then falls gradually to zero. The peak arrives when roughly half the oil is gone. The continental U.S. reached peak in 1970, and production has slumped ever since. Many energy scientists put the worldwide peak before 2010. After the peak, according to the Hubbert Curve, global oil production will decline at about the same rate it rose before. With a peak before 2010, production in 2030 will be somewhere around production in 1975 or 1980, or maybe 20 billion barrels. In the 2030s oil will have to meet the needs of a doubled world population and a world in crisis, but 20 billion barrels is still a lot of oil.

To misquote T. S. Eliot, this is the way the oil ends, not with a bang but a trickle. Other fossil fuels are headed the same way, along with uranium for nuclear power, but they can help cushion declining oil production for a while before they hit their own Hubbert peaks. Renewable energy sources can provide only a small fraction of the energy we now get from fossil fuels, but that fraction can help cushion the decline and stretch dwindling oil and coal reserves. The problem we face isn't having no energy at all. It's having to make do with less and less each year, until finally we get down to levels that can be sustained indefinitely.

The logic of the Hubbert Curve provides the framework for Richard Duncan's Olduvai theory,[95] an uncompromising look at a deindustrial future. Duncan starts with White's law, a widely accepted rule that culture evolves as the amount of energy per capita goes up. Globally, energy per capita stood at very modest levels until 1800, when fossil fuels sent it skyrocketing to its all-time peak in 1979. At that point, Duncan shows, two centuries of explosive progress began to unravel.

After 1979, global energy per capita declined as rising population outstripped modest increases in energy production. As energy production itself drops after the Hubbert Curve peaks, the decline accelerates. Follow the curve, and by 2030 global energy per capita is where it was in 1930, around a third of its 1979 value. Duncan argues that the industrial age is a *pulse waveform*, a single, bell-shaped, nonrepeating curve centered on 1979. Since no renewable energy resource can provide more than a small fraction of the immense amounts of fossil fuel energy we've squandered in the recent past, he predicts that the millennia of low tech cultures before the industrial pulse, when nobody knew about the fantastic treasure of free energy locked up in fossil fuels, will be balanced by millennia of low tech cultures after the industrial pulse, when the treasure will be gone forever.

## *The power of myth*

Many people find predictions of this sort extremely upsetting. Believers in progress insist that human ingenuity will get progress going again somehow and lead to a more advanced society than we have today. Believers in apocalypse insist that incremental declines will bring about catastrophe somehow and lead to mass death and a Road Warrior future. The concept of a slow descent to the agrarian cultures of the deindustrial future offends both. In my experience, many believers in either one literally can't fit their minds around a third alternative.

Blind spots of this sort show the hidden presence of myth. Many people nowadays think only primitive people believe in myths, but myths dominate the thinking of every society, including our own. A myth is a story that makes sense of the world. Most ancient cultures took their myths from religion; most modern societies take theirs from science or

---

[95] http://hubbertpeak.com/duncan/Olduvai.htm.

political ideology. Two competing stories provide modern society with its most popular myths. You know them both.

The first is called the *progressivist myth*. According to this story, all of human history is a drama of progress. From primitive ignorance and savagery, according to the progressivist myth, people climbed step by step up the ladder of civilization. Knowledge gathered over generations made it possible for each culture to go further than the ones before it. With modern times, progress went into overdrive, and it's still in overdrive today. The purpose of human existence is to make this upward climb possible so that our descendants can someday reach the stars.

The second is called the *separativist myth*. According to this story, all of human history is a tragic blind alley. Once people lived in harmony with their world, each other, and themselves, but that time ended and things have gone downhill ever since. Vast cities governed by bloated bureaucracies, inhabited by people who have abandoned spiritual values for a wholly material existence, mark the point of no return. Sometime soon the whole rickety structure will come crashing down, overwhelmed by sudden crisis, and countless people will die. Only those who abandon a corrupt and doomed society will survive to build a better world.

Both stories are versions of the much older religious myth of apocalypse, which includes vast disasters followed by a millennium of bliss for the chosen. Sociologist Philip Lamy showed in his book *Millennial Rage* (1996) that most people, including most Christians, now embrace "fractured" versions of the apocalypse myth which focus on one theme out of the complexity of the older myth. The progressivist and separativist myths are good examples, the former stressing the hope of future bliss, the latter the threat of catastrophe.

The mythic nature of these viewpoints shows up clearly when either one is measured against history. Believers in progress insist that human history has always been progressive, but a look at the past challenges this comfortable faith to its core. Between the agricultural revolution and the industrial age, human life changed little; all things considered, the life of a peasant in Egypt under the Pharaohs was not much different from that of a peasant in seventeenth-century France (both even had a Sun King). Industrialization broke the pattern only by tapping into stored energy in the earth to launch two centuries of exuberant growth.

Everything necessary for industrial society, except a way to turn fossil fuels into mechanical energy, existed long before the industrial revolution. Renewable energy sources? Wind power, water power, and biomass were all used extensively in the preindustrial past. Scientific knowledge? The laws of mechanics were worked out in ancient times, and a Greek scientist even invented the steam turbine before the birth of Christ; without fossil fuels it was a useless curiosity. Human resourcefulness and ingenuity? People in past ages were as resourceful and ingenious as we are. Fossil fuels make the one crucial difference between ancient cultures and modern industrial society. As fossil fuels run out and the ecological consequences of their misuse come home to roost, that difference will go away. As for those who simply insist that "we can't go back," that's easy to say, but we no longer have the resources to go forward, and soon we won't even be able to stand still. What other direction do they have in mind?

Believers in apocalypse, for their part, insist that our civilization's end will be sudden, catastrophic, and total. As shown earlier in this essay, history doesn't support that claim. Civilizations take time to fall, the resource base of industrial society is shrinking but it's far from exhausted, the impacts of global warming and other ecological disruptions build slowly over time, and ruling elites and ordinary citizens alike have every reason to hold things together as long as possible. The history of the last century shows that industrial societies can endure tremendous disruption without dissolving into a Hobbesian war of all against all, and people in hard times are far more likely to follow orders and hope for the best than to join the rampaging mobs that play so large a role in survivalist fantasies. The sorry history of the Y2K noncrisis a few years ago may also make a good reminder that risks of catastrophe can be overrated.

Of course it's possible that some ultra-catastrophe is waiting to wipe us all out, just as it's possible that scientists might pull a technological rabbit out of a hat and give industrial society a new lease on life. It's also possible that aliens from space might go zipping through our atmosphere in flying teacups next Tuesday, dropping radioactive vegetables on everyone named Fred. The fact that this last possibility can't be ruled out doesn't make it reasonable to gamble our future on being able to power factories with glow-in-the-dark cabbages!

It's reasonable to consider catastrophe and continued progress as possibilities, but both have to be weighed against the realities of our present situation and the evidence of history. Both require a *deus ex machina* on a grand scale to change the course of events: Ordinary catastrophes aren't enough to bring industrial society down overnight, just as ordinary technological progress isn't enough to get industrial society out of the mess it's made for itself. Without an extraordinary event, our civilization is headed down the well-trodden path of decline. If there's a point in planning for the future at all, it makes sense to plan for the one we're most likely to get.

Both the progressivist myth and the separativist myth have powerful emotional appeal; that's why they're popular. The myth of perpetual progress comforts those people who have made their peace with society as it is, and who want to believe that their lives are part of a process which leads eventually to better things. The myth of imminent apocalypse comforts those people who cannot accept society as it is, and want to believe in a catastrophe that topples the proud towers of a civilization they loathe. Still, the fact that a belief is emotionally powerful and comforting doesn't make it true.

### The course of decline

To see past mythology to the hard realities of the future takes a clear sense of our predicament. More than six billion people live on a planet that can support one billion indefinitely. We can't meet everyone's needs now, and the resources to maintain even today's standards of living are running short. Resource wars have already begun—the 2003 U.S. invasion of Iraq may someday be recalled as the first of the Oil Wars. Meanwhile global warming boosts the cost of natural disasters so fast that one of the world's largest reinsurance firms, Swiss RE, warns that this all by itself will bankrupt the world economy before 2060.

Leave out the *dei ex machina* of progressive and apocalyptic mythologies, map the results onto a scale of human life spans, and a likely future emerges. Imagine an American woman born in 1960. She sees the gas lines of the 1970s, the short-term political gimmicks that papered over the crisis in the 1980s and 1990s, and renewed trouble in the following decades. Soaring energy prices, shortages, economic depressions, and resource wars shape the rest of her life. By age seventy, she lives in a beleaguered, malfunctioning city where half the population has no reliable access to clean water, electricity, or health care. Shantytowns spread in the shadow of skyscrapers while political and economic leaders keep insisting that things are getting better.

Her great-grandson, born in 2030, manages to avoid the smorgasbord of diseases, the pervasive violence, and the pandemic alcohol and drug abuse that claim half of his generation before age thirty. A lucky break gets him into a technical career, safe from military service in endless wars overseas or "pacification actions" against separatist guerrillas at home. His technical knowledge consists mostly of rules of thumb for effective scavenging, cars and refrigerators are luxury items he will never own, his home lacks electricity and central heating, and his health care comes from an old woman whose grandmother was a doctor and who knows something about wound care and herbs. By the time his hair turns gray the squabbling regions that were once the United States have split apart, all remaining fuel and electrical power have been commandeered by the new governments, and coastal cities are being abandoned to the rising oceans.

For his great-granddaughter, born in 2100, the great crises are mostly things of the past. She grows up amid a ring of sparsely populated villages surrounding an abandoned core of rusting skyscrapers visited only by salvage crews who mine them for raw materials. Local wars sputter, the oceans are still rising, and famines and epidemics are a familiar reality, but with global population maybe 15% of what it was in 2000, humanity and nature are moving toward balance. She learns to read and write, a skill most of her neighbors don't have, and a few old books are among her prized possessions, but the days when men walked on the moon are fading into legend. When she and her family finally set out for a village in the countryside, leaving the husk of the old city to the salvage crews, it never occurs to her that her quiet footsteps on a crumbling asphalt road mark the end of a civilization.

## What can be done

People try to sense the shape of the future for much the same reason that drivers watch the road ahead: it's easier to manage crises and take advantage of opportunities if you have enough time to react. So far the two myths already discussed have dominated planning for the future. Believers in progress hold that the best way to face the future is to pour money into research and development, so that new technologies to drive progress will be ready in time. Believers in apocalypse hold that the best way to face the future is to build isolated enclaves stocked with food and weaponry, where those who plan on surviving doomsday can hole up and wait it out.

If we face an age of decline, though, neither of these approaches is worth much. Research and development might be useful if focused on simple, sustainable technologies, but projects of this sort need to be done soon: as decline gets under way, funding for scientific research will be one of the first things cut. As for holing up in a mountain cabin, the slow pace of decline makes this utterly irrelevant. No matter how much canned food and ammo you have, it's not going to last a couple of centuries, and neither are you.

A different future requires a different kind of thinking. The crucial needs that must be met in an age of decline are damage control, cultural survival, and the building of a new society amid the ruins of the old. Political and business interests aren't going to meet these needs, or do anything else helpful; oil is to the modern industrial nations what corn was to the ancient Maya, and the *ahauob* of Washington and Wall Street have turned to war just as their Maya equivalents did. Fortunately, all three needs can be met by individuals and small groups with limited resources, and projects of this kind are being done on a small scale already.

Damage control focuses on ways to keep the impact of decline from costing more than it has to. The great challenge here is that most people in the developed world have no idea how to survive outside the cocoon of industrial society. As technology unravels, infrastructure breaks down, and local disasters hit, people will have to provide what they need for survival by their own efforts, from locally available materials, and yet most people nowadays can't even light a fire to stay warm without matches or a lighter. People will have to learn survival, first aid, and skills of self-reliant living to meet this challenge. Groups can build on this by forming support networks and working out overlapping specialties, so people can draw on a wider range of skills.

The temptation to rely on stockpiles of food, technology, weapons, or precious metals to get through the impact of an age of decline is natural, but fatal. For two centuries machines and their products have been cheaper than skilled human beings. The result is a habit of valuing things over skills and, ultimately, a "prosthetic society" in which we're taught to neglect abilities and then pay for technological replacements: we use day planners instead of training our memories, buy bread machines instead of learning to bake, watch television instead of using our imaginations. That has to be unlearned in a hurry. In hard times, if you have a stockpile, you're a sitting target for other people interested in removing you from your stockpile and enjoying it themselves—but if you have valuable skills you can share and teach, everyone's your friend.

These same principles govern strategies to meet the other two needs. Cultural survival focuses on hanging onto the heritage of the last few thousand years. That's a tall order, because nearly all of it is brutally vulnerable to an age of decline. Nearly all books printed in the last century and a half are on high-acid paper, which gradually turns back to sawdust; librarians are already struggling to preserve collections of disintegrating nineteenth-century books. CDs and DVDs, like other electronic media, have much shorter life spans, and won't be playable anyway in a low tech future. When people are struggling to survive, literature, music, art, and science aren't usually very high on their list of priorities anyway.

Any effort toward cultural survival, in other words, will have to involve ruthless sorting. Today's sprawling libraries will need careful winnowing to sort out collections small enough to be copied by hand if it comes to that. Musical forms that can be passed on as living traditions will be more likely to make it, which means folk music has a better chance than Beethoven's Ninth Symphony. A huge amount will inevitably be lost; the job at hand is to try to make sure that the best possible selection gets through.

One thing that's sometimes been suggested by scientists, a book packed with everything science has discovered so far, is more problematic. History shows that the scientific treatises of one age become the fossilized dogmas of the next, and people in a deindustrial society, given a book with all the answers, could too easily end up thinking that the way to answer any question was to look it up in an old book. That way lies stagnation. Far better would be a textbook on scientific method, treatises on a few useful sciences such as ecology and mechanics, and enough hints and fragments to tantalize future thinkers into launching investigations of their own.

The work of building a new society, finally, will be much easier if the process starts now. During the last two centuries, the quickest way to prosper was to ride the wave of progress, using more energy, more resources, and more technology than your competitors. For the next two centuries, the quickest way to prosper will likely stand this rule on its head. Those who accept the reality of decline and get by on less energy, less resources, and less technology than their competitors will win out. The irony is that now, before the immense knowledge base of industrial society begins to come apart, is the best time to look for ways of living that use less of what we won't have soon.

Organic farming is an excellent case in point. In the last century organic agriculture has made immense strides, to the point that it's now possible to grow a spare but adequate diet year round for one person on less than 1000 square feet of soil, with only hand labor and no fossil fuel inputs at all, and do it while *increasing* the long-term fertility of the soil. These methods may turn out to be our civilization's greatest gift to the future, provided they survive the approaching age of decline. Today they're covered in detail in dozens of books; whether that will be true in 100 years depends on what we do right now.

Scores of other technologies, skills, and traditions of high value to a future low tech society can be found with a little searching. Consider the haybox. If your great-grandmother lived in Europe or North America she probably had one. She brought food to a boil, popped it into a box full of insulating material (such as hay), and left it there to cook by residual heat, saving most of the fuel she would have needed to cook the same dish on the stove. Haybox technology could make a future of energy shortages much more livable, but only if it's brought out of museums and put back into circulation before the information gets lost.

The point to these anecdotes is simple but far-reaching. If people come to terms with the future now, and begin assembling and using skills and lifeways our deindustrial descendants can follow, the approaching age of decline can be made less traumatic than it will otherwise be. Government and business won't help; they'll doubtless cling to the leavings of industrial society the way barbarian chieftains in the Dark Ages clung to the trappings of Roman authority long after the Roman empire was defunct. Yet individuals, groups, and local communities can accomplish much by starting on the long road down to the deindustrial future.

The deindustrial societies of the future need not be condemned to medieval squalor unless we fail to act now. It's possible to have a cultured, literate, humane society with thriving cities and a vigorous exchange economy on a very limited resource basis. During the Tokugawa period (1603–1868), for example, Japan closed its borders to the outside world in a successful bid to stay out of European colonial empires. With a large population and few natural resources, Tokugawa

Japan ran almost entirely on human muscle. Yet this was one of the great periods of Japanese art, literature, and philosophy; literacy was so widespread that the three largest cities in Japan had 1500 bookstores among them, and most people had access to basic education, health care, and the necessities of life. If we get past the distractions of emotionally appealing mythologies, face the future squarely, and start getting ready for it now, future deindustrial societies could achieve as much. That goal is within reach, and it's hard to think of a better gift we can offer the future.

# The falling years

*The unfinished trajectory of Robinson Jeffers's inhumanism*

*In 2010 Paul Kingsnorth and Dougald Hine launched a new journal,* Dark Mountain, *to explore the literary and cultural dimensions of the approaching age of decline. I was delighted to see the journal appear, and even more delighted to learn that the poet Robinson Jeffers, whose verse has been an inspiration to me since my teen years, was among the guiding spirits behind the project. The following essay duly appeared in the first issue of* Dark Mountain; *while it starts with literature, it ends with an exploration of the shape of our future.*

*I*

Robinson Jeffers's name is hardly one to conjure with these days. The odd anthology of American poetry occasionally quotes his less troubling nature poems, and a few tourist shops in Carmel and Monterey have made a minor industry out of him, the way other towns lionize dead rock musicians or football stars. Outside of these limited circles, it's not often one hears of him.

Not until 2001 did a solid collection of his major poetic works appear—try to think of another major twentieth-century poet who was nearly forty years dead when this first happened—and *The Selected Poetry of Robinson Jeffers* set only the quietest ripples in motion. Gone are the days when Jeffers was so controversial that his own publishers put a note in one book of his poems distancing themselves from his views. Those who play at rebelliousness in contemporary letters might take note: make a show of iconoclasm in acceptable ways and you can count on a lasting reputation; stray into actual iconoclasm, rejecting the fashions of the avant-garde along with those of the mainstream, and the world of culture will forget you just as soon as it can.

A few details will put this extraordinary figure in his proper setting.[96] Born in 1887, he belonged to the same generation of American poets as T. S. Eliot and Ezra Pound. Like them, he saw the facile modernist faith in progress refute itself in the cultural sterility of the Gilded Age and the crowning catastrophe of the First World War, and went in search of stronger foundations for his poetry. Eliot found his Archimedean point in a willed acceptance of Christianity; Pound, less successfully, tried to cobble together a tradition of his own from a rag-heap of sources embracing everything from Provençal minstrelsy to Fascist economics. Both turned to Europe for a sense of depth they could not find on American soil.

Jeffers took a more daring approach. In the years just before the First World War, when Eliot and Pound were rising stars in a poetic galaxy rotating around the twin hubs of London and Paris, Jeffers moved to a sparsely settled stretch of the California coastline near Carmel, where he built a house and, later, a stone tower with his own hands.[97] His quest for foundations could not be satisfied at any merely human depth, and finally came to rest in nature itself.

He called his theory of poetry "inhumanism," and sketched it in uncompromising terms: "It is based on a recognition of the astonishing beauty of things and their living wholeness, and on a rational acceptance of the fact that mankind is neither central nor important in the universe; our vices and blazing crimes are as insignificant as our

---

[96] I have used Melba Berry Bennett's *The Stone Mason of Tor House* (New York: Ward Ritchie, 1966) and Arthur B. Coffin's *Robinson Jeffers: Poet of Inhumanism* (Madison, WI: University of Wisconsin Press, 1971) for this brief sketch.

[97] It's a curiosity of poetic history that Jeffers and Yeats, one of the few modern poets Jeffers praised, both built themselves stone towers in the years following the First World War.

happiness. [...] Turn outward from each other, so far as need and kindness permit, to the vast life and inexhaustible beauty beyond humanity. This is not a slight matter, but an essential condition of freedom, and of moral and vital sanity."[98]

Put another way, the core of inhumanism is the principled rejection of anthropocentrism, and the pursuit of what might as well be called an ecocentric standpoint: one in which nature takes center stage, not as a receptacle for human activities, emotions, or narratives, but as itself, on its own inhuman terms. It's an appallingly difficult project, difficult enough that Jeffers himself couldn't always sustain it; critics have pointed out the places in Jeffers's verse where poetry gives way to lecture, or descends into an inverted sentimentality that wallows in images of suffering and despair. When Jeffers achieved the task he set himself, though, the results are stunning: For a moment, at least, the claims humanity loves to make on behalf of its own importance fall silent before a universe that was busy with its own affairs for billions of years before us and won't take the time to notice our absence when we are gone.

Jeffers is thus among the few figures in literature to grasp the core feature of the universe revealed by Darwin and his successors, the perspective that the late Stephen Jay Gould called "deep time"—the sense of human existence as an eyeblink in the long history of the planet. His answer to the spread of suburban sprawl over his beloved Point Carmel is typical:

> It has all time. It knows the people are a tide
> That swells and in time will ebb, and all
> Their works dissolve. Meanwhile the image of the pristine beauty
> Lives in the very grain of the granite,
> Safe as the endless ocean that climbs our cliff.—As for us:
> We must uncenter our minds from ourselves;
> We must unhumanize our views a little, and become confident
> As the rock and ocean that we were made from.[99]

As poetics, this is hard enough. As a program for any more pragmatic engagement with the world, it poses a staggering challenge.

---

[98] From "Preface to *The Double Ax and Other Poems*," in Hunt, ed., op. cit., pp. 719 and 721.
[99] From "Carmel Point," in Hunt, ed., op. cit., p. 676.

Jeffers didn't shy away from the places where poetics and politics intersect; Shelley gave him a sense of the poets' role as the world's unacknowledged legislators,[100] and he addressed the political arena directly in such poems as "Shine, Perishing Republic" and "The Day is a Poem." Still, his politics—like his poetics—found few listeners. Most of the few critics who discussed his work at all slid past the complex political vision that frames much of Jeffers's work with a few comments about "isolationism," and maybe a nod to Spengler and Vico. Jeffers's prophetic ear was exact, but no one else was listening:

> There is no returning now.
> Two bloody summers from now (I suppose) we shall have to take up the corrupting burden and curse of victory.
> We shall have to hold half the earth; we shall be sick with self-disgust,
> And hated by friend and foe, and hold half the earth—or let it go, and
> go down with it.[101]

Still, Jeffers knew as well as anyone that poets' legislation needs time to have its effect. The rising spiral of environmental crises shaping today's headlines marks, I have come to believe, the point where Jeffers's vision becomes a historical fact, and his inhumanism a center of gravity toward which any meaningful response to the predicament of industrial society must move. In saying that, I'm not claiming that responses to our crisis *ought* to move toward inhumanism; I'm saying that they *will* do so, even if those who think they are defending the environment have to be dragged kicking and screaming along that route.

I say that with some confidence because most of the journey has already happened. The anthropocentrism that runs through the environmental movement, even, or rather especially, among those who most bitterly condemn humanity and all its works, seems to me to mark a final, frantic attempt to cling to the illusion of a human-centered cosmos. As today's environmental narratives join the ruins of earlier lines of defense in history's compost heap, it's not easy to imagine any place where anthropocentrism can stake a further claim against the

---

[100] Percy Bysshe Shelley, "A Defence of Poetry;" see also Coffin, op. cit., p. 18.
[101] From "Historical Choice," in Hunt, ed., op. cit., p. 580; this poem was written in 1943.

massed inevitabilities of nature. At that point Jeffers's inhumanism offers a glimpse at the foundations on which human thought will have to rebuild itself.

## II

The environmental movement as a social phenomenon still awaits its historian, though there have been capable histories of the ecological ideas that have inspired it.[102] A first approximation, though, shows three overlapping periods of environmental activism, each with its own distinct narratives and purposes.

The first was the period of *recreational environmentalism*, and ran from the late nineteenth century through the 1960s. Environmental rhetoric in this period focused so tautly on the value of nature as a recreational resource that their opponents, without too much inaccuracy, could accuse conservationists of simply wanting the government to subsidize their vacation spots. Though it's easy to dismiss the period in retrospect, its great achievement—the invention of the national park concept and its deployment over much of the industrial world—marks a historical watershed of some importance. For the first time since the felling of the old Pagan groves, the Western world recognized the point to setting aside space for nature on its own terms.

The second phase, from the early 1960s through the 1980s, was the period of *sentimental environmentalism*. The spark for the transition was Rachel Carson's epochal *Silent Spring*, which brought extinction out of scientific journals and into the public sphere. The results shared far too much with the rest of the popular culture of the time to accomplish much—the baby seals whose Holly Hobby faces made them the mascot of the movement, for example, received far more attention than many more substantive issues—but the underlying shift in awareness is worth noting. For a significant number of people, feelings of loyalty and love once fixed firmly within the human sphere widened to embrace nonhuman nature.

The third phase followed promptly. The first stirrings of *apocalyptic environmentalism* appeared while the age of sentimental environmentalism was barely under way, and once it worked its way out of the fringes,

---

[102] See particularly Donald Worster's *Nature's Economy* (Cambridge: Cambridge University Press, 1994).

it quickly borrowed the same durable tropes about the end of the world that proved their appeal in other contexts. The last two decades have accordingly seen all the usual changes rung on the theme of an imminent Judgment Day, with Gaia pressed into the role more usually filled by an avenging Jehovah.

Surf the web or visit a bookstore and the resulting sermons may be found without too much effort. Alongside claims that a future of ecological horror—sinners in the hands of an angry biosphere!—can be averted if we renounce our wicked ways and get right with Gaia, you can find claims that it's already too late and the wrath of an offended planet will turn sinful humanity into so much compost, upon which the righteous remnant will presumably plant the organic gardens of the New Green Jerusalem. Gospels backstopping these sermons with a giddy range of dubious historical mythologies have flooded the market at nearly the same pace.

It's crucial to recognize the hits as well as the misses of apocalyptic environmentalism. Many of the issues that backstop claims of imminent Ecogeddon are quite real, though some have been exaggerated to the point of absurdity. Where these narratives fail is in forcing the ecological crisis into anthropocentric narratives that falsify far more than they explain.

The function of apocalyptic myth, after all, is to console the unimportant by feeding them fantasies of their own cosmic significance. It's thus no accident that the seedtimes of apocalyptic ideas in Judaism have been epochs when Jews were a powerless minority whose beliefs and hopes were of no concern to anyone but themselves, just as the apocalyptic strain in today's Christianity clusters in the regions and classes most heavily marginalized during the era of economic contraction the media papered over with the euphemisms of "globalization." Apocalyptic environmentalism is partly a reaction to the impact of deep time on our collective sense of self-importance: faced with a planetary history in which geological forces and mass extinctions hold the important roles, we've tried to claim the role of a geological force and a cause of mass extinctions.

That probably couldn't have been avoided. Like the phases before it, apocalyptic environmentalism inevitably got tripped up by the anthropocentricity it tried to escape. Recreational environmentalism reached for the insight that we owe nature space of its own, and fell back to thinking of nature as a resource for outdoor vacations. Sentimental environmentalism reached for the more challenging insight that we owe nature the same bonds of love and loyalty more usually applied to family, community, and nation, and fell back to thinking of nature as a resource for emotional indulgence.

Apocalyptic environmentalism, in turn, reached for the most challenging insight of all: the recognition that we owe nature our existence, and could follow the dodo and the passenger pigeon into extinction if we mess up our relations with the rest of nature badly enough. Like its predecessors, its reach exceeded its grasp, and it fell back to thinking of nature as a resource for narratives that celebrate the supposed uniqueness of humanity just as obsessively as ever. Portraying humanity as the uniquely destructive ravager of nature, after all, is just as anthropocentric as portraying it as the uniquely creative conqueror of nature. The resemblance between the concepts is not accidental; like a spoiled child who misbehaves to get the attention good behavior won't bring, we're willing to see ourselves in any role, even the villain's, as long as we get to occupy center stage.

### III

Still, talking about the anthropocentric obsessions of today's ecological thought in general terms is less helpful than catching sight of those obsessions in their native habitat, in the collective conversation that shapes our world. Nothing is as easy as denouncing an abstract representation of a habit of thought on which one's thinking continues to be based. Think of the way that "dualism" was all but burnt in effigy, a few years back, by a flurry of liberal religious writers who insisted that all religions without exception are either dualist or nondualist, and dualism is absolutely evil while nondualism is absolutely good![103]

No doubt we'll shortly see a critique of anthropocentrism along the same lines: arguing, perhaps, that the habit of anthropocentric delusion is what sets our species apart from the rest of nature and marks us out for some uniquely tragic destiny or other. Thus it's crucial to get past

---

[103] Matthew Fox's *The Coming of the Cosmic Christ* (San Francisco, CA: Harper & Row, 1988) is a particularly embarrassing example; pp. 134–135 includes a handy table of polar oppositions, in which one side is "dualist" and thus evil, and the other "nondualist" and thus good.

the label, and examine specific ways that anthropocentrism distorts the response of today's environmental movement to the incoming tide of ecological crisis.

Compare the recent and continuing furore over anthropogenic climate change to the more muted response to the rapid depletion of the world's remaining petroleum reserves, and one such distortion stands out clearly. Both these problems are unquestionably real;[104] both were predicted decades ago, both could quite readily force modern industrial civilization to its knees, and both are already having measurable impacts around the world.

Yet the response to the two differs in instructive ways. Anthropogenic climate change has become a cause célèbre, splashed across the mainstream media, researched by thousands of scientists funded by lavish government grants, and earnestly discussed by heads of state at summit meetings. Nothing is actually being done to stop it, to be sure, and most likely nothing will be done; not even the climate campaigners who urge drastic action in the loudest voices and most extreme terms have shown any willingness to accept changes in their own lives that would cut carbon dioxide emissions soon enough to matter. Still, the narrative of climate change has found plenty of eager listeners around the world.

None of this has happened with peak oil. The evidence backing the claim that the world has already passed the peak of petroleum production, and faces a future of declining energy and economic contraction, is every bit as solid as the evidence for anthropogenic climate change;[105] the arguments opposing it are just as meretricious, its potential for economic and human costs is as great, solutions are as difficult to reach, and it can feed apocalyptic fantasies almost as extreme as those that have gathered around climate change. Still, no summit meetings are being called by heads of state to discuss the end of the age of oil; there has been no barrage of mainstream media attention concerning it, and precious few government grants. Climate change is mediagenic; peak oil is not.

---

[104] There seems little point here in revisiting the overwhelming evidence backing both humanity's role in climate change and the progressive and severe depletion of accessible oil reserves. Those who already recognize the severity of both problems will need no convincing, while those who disagree with either aren't likely to listen to another review of the facts.

[105] For a good general survey, see Richard Heinberg's *The Party's Over: Oil, War, and the Fate of Industrial Societies* (Gabriola Island, BC, Canada: New Society, 2003).

A core difference between the two crises explains why. Climate change, as a cultural narrative, is a story about human power. We have become so almighty through technological progress, the climate change narrative argues, that we threaten the Earth itself. The only limits that can prevent catastrophe are those we place on ourselves, since nothing else can stop us; and even our own efforts might not be enough to stand in our way. It's nearly a parody of the old atheist gibe: to prove our own omnipotence, we've made a crisis so big not even we can lift it out of our way.

Peak oil as a cultural narrative, on the other hand, is not a celebration of human power but a warning about human limits. At the core of the peak oil story is the recognition that the power we claimed was never really ours. We never conquered nature; we merely stole some of the Earth's carbon and burnt our way through it in three short centuries. All the feverish dreams and accomplishments of that era were simply the results of wasting a vast amount of cheap fuel. Now that the easy pickings are running out, and we have to think about getting by without half a billion years of stored and concentrated solar energy to burn, our fantasies of power are proving unexpectedly fragile, and the future ahead of us involves more humility and less grandiosity than we want to think about.

One rich irony here is that the limits imposed by peak oil are, among other things, limits on our power to destroy the world via climate change. The IPCC projections of climate change assume that the world's nations can increase their coal, oil, and natural gas consumption straight through to 2100. Doubtless they would do so if they could, but the fact remains that they can't. Conventional petroleum production peaked in 2005 and has been declining since then; unconventional petroleum production, even if it recovers from the slump following the crash of 2008, will tip into decline before 2020; natural gas is currently on schedule to reach its peak by 2030, and coal by 2040.[106] As those peaks pass, fossil fuel consumption will decline, not because we want it to decline, but because our ability to extract fuels from the ground runs into geological limits. This awkward reality has not found its way into the climate change debate; nor will it, until the anthropocentric foundations of that debate are seen for what they are.

---

[106] See Richard Heinberg, *Peak Everything* (Gabriola Island, BC, Canada: New Society, 2008) for a detailed discussion of these resource peaks and their consequences.

The same point can be made even more forcefully of the greater irony that surrounds the climate change debate: the fact that the shifts in global temperature painted in doomsday terms in today's media are modest, in scale and speed, compared to those the Earth has experienced many times before. A mere 11,000 years ago, at the end of the last ice age, global temperatures jolted up 15°F. in under a decade[107]—a heat wave more severe than the wildest scenarios in circulation these days. Nor was this anything novel; the Earth's long history is full of such events.

Since the beginning of the Pliocene epoch some ten million years ago, Earth's climate has been in a phase of severe cooling, and for four-fifths or so of the time life has existed on this planet, global temperatures have been far warmer than the IPCC's worst case scenarios imagine. When the Earth's climate is normal, on this inhumanly broad scale, most of its land surface is covered by jungle, and ice caps and glaciers do not exist. A reversion to that normal temperature would obliterate our industrial civilization with the inevitability of a boot descending on an eggshell, and could well push our species over the edge into extinction, but the usual adjustments would soon bring the biosphere into balance, as they have after other climate changes of the planetary past. The fact that we would not be around to see this, if it comes to that, concerns no one but ourselves.

These ironies, furthermore, have direct practical implications. While anthropogenic global warming is a real and serious problem, its consequences are subject to natural limits that current thinking, fixated on images of human triumphalism, is poorly equipped to grasp. Meanwhile, another real and serious problem—the depletion of the nonrenewable energy resources that prop up today's industrial economy and keep seven billion people alive—gets next to no attention, because it conflicts with those same triumphalist obsessions. It's no exaggeration to say that the modern world might solve the global warming crisis and then collapse anyway, because it only dealt with those of its problems that proved congenial to its self-image.

## IV

Sometimes, when sleep keeps its distance in the small hours of the night, I wonder if the grand purpose for which humanity came into

---

[107] This figure, along with supporting research, is cited in Richard B. Alley, *The Two Mile Time Machine* (Princeton, NJ: Princeton University Press, 2000).

being is simply that Earth needed a species good at digging to pull a few billion tons of stored carbon out of the ground and nudge up its thermostat a bit. During daylight hours, I don't actually believe this; if the Earth has conscious purposes, we will almost certainly never know, and if by some chance we do find out, our chances of understanding those purposes are right up there with the chance that a dust mite in Mozart's wig could have understood his music or his marital problems.

It's easy to dismiss reflections such as these as a display of misanthropy. Still, it shows no contempt for an individual to recognize that he or she isn't more important than anyone else in the world. Personal maturity begins, after all, with letting go the infantile self-regard that puts the ego and its cravings at the center of the cosmos. It's arguably time to apply that same insight to humanity as a whole. As Jeffers wrote:

> It seems to me wasteful that almost the whole of human energy is expended inward, on itself, on loving, hating, governing, cajoling, amusing, its own members. It is like a new-born babe, conscious almost exclusively of its own processes and where its food comes from. As the child grows up, its attention must be drawn from itself to the more important world around it.[108]

The environmental crises of the present bid fair to make that shift in attention inevitable, no matter how hard we fight to keep ourselves at the center of our own imagined universe, and in the process most of the presuppositions of human thought will have to change. Crucially, we will be forced to come to terms with the fact that no special providence guarantees our species the fulfillment of its hopes, or even its survival. Sooner or later humanity, like every other species, will become extinct, and it's a safe bet that the history that unfolds between the present moment and that hopefully distant time will be just as sparing of Utopian dreams fulfilled as has human history so far. This doesn't deny us the possibility of improving our lives, our societies, and our relationships with the cosmos that surrounds us; it does mean that those improvements, like everything else in the real world, will take place against a background of hard natural limits that will inevitably restrict what can be attained.

---

[108] Letter from Jeffers to Rudolph Gilbert, in Gilbert's *Shine, Perishing Republic: Robinson Jeffers and the Tragic Sense in Modern Poetry* (New York: Haskell House, 1965), frontispiece.

One consequence is that the faith in perpetual progress that forms the unacknowledged state religion of the modern world faces a shattering disillusionment. Progress as we have known it amounts to little more than the race to find ever more extravagant ways to burn cheap abundant fossil fuels. Those fuels are no longer as cheap or abundant as they once were; in the not too distant future, they will be scarce and expensive, and not all that much further down the curve of history they will be so scarce, and so expensive, that burning them to power what remains of an industrial society will no longer be a viable option.[109]

Nor can we simply count, as too many people are counting, on the hope that some other energy source equally cheap, convenient, and concentrated will come along just as we need it. The fossil fuels we burn so blithely today are the product of hundreds of millions of years of complex ecological and geological processes. At the dawn of our now-receding Age of Excess, they represented the single largest concentration of readily accessible chemical energy in the known solar system. Insisting that an industrial civilization dependent on this vast surplus can thrive on the sparser and less concentrated energy flows the Earth receives from the Sun day by day—which is what most current advocates of sustainability propose—flies in the face of ecological and thermodynamic reality; it's a bit as though someone who won a huge lottery payoff, and spent it all in a few short years, insisted he could keep up the same extravagant lifestyle with the income from a job flipping burgers for minimum wage.

Instead of fantasizing about the kind of future we want humanity to have, in other words, or confusing our daydreams with our destiny, we need to start thinking hard about what kind of future humanity can afford, and taking a hard look at social habits that require levels of energy and resource inputs we won't be able to maintain for much longer. A rethinking of this kind is not optional; if we refuse it, nature will do the job for us. Ecology teaches us that every species either evolves ways to limit the burden it places on nature, or suffers from limits imposed on it by outside factors, and we are no more exempt from that law than we are from the law of gravity.

At this moment in history, only a massive worldwide effort of more than wartime intensity might have even a modest chance of managing a controlled descent from industrial civilization's extravagance to some

---

[109] I have discussed these points in much more detail in my book *The Long Descent* (Gabriola Island, BC, Canada: New Society, 2008).

more durable form of society. The window of opportunity for so staggering a project is narrow, if it has not already closed, and the political will that would be needed to carry it out is nowhere in sight. Thus the same sort of uncontrolled descent that ended the history of so many earlier civilizations has become the most likely future for ours. Certainly this was Jeffers's view:

> These are the falling years,
> They will go deep,
> Never weep, never weep.
>
> With clear eyes explore the pit.
> Watch the great fall
> With religious awe.[110]

Still, it's precisely in the troubled years ahead of us, as our civilization stumbles down the long broken slope toward a future that will make a mockery of our fantasies of progress and cosmic importance, that Jeffers's perspective offers its most important gifts. It's the man or woman who comes to terms with the inevitability of his or her own death that best knows how to grapple with life. In the same way, Jeffers's inhumanist perspective can be a crucial source of strength now, and even more so in time to come. When we realize that human history is nothing unique—from nature's perspective, we're simply one more species that overshot the carrying capacity of its environment and is about to pay the routine price—we can get past the habit of wallowing in a self-blame that's first cousin to self-praise, face up to the hard choices ahead, and make them with some sense of perspective and, at least potentially, some possibility of grace. Humanity cannot and need not bear the burden of being the measure of all things, Jeffers is telling us, for a saner and stronger measure is all around us:

> Integrity is wholeness, the greatest beauty is
> Organic wholeness, the wholeness of life and things, the divine
> beauty of the universe. Love that, not man
> Apart from that.[111]

---

[110] From "For Una," in Hunt, ed., op. cit., pp. 565–567.
[111] From "The Answer," in Hunt, ed., op. cit., p. 522.

# The Next Ten Billion Years

*In 2013, while working on the series of blog posts that turned into my book* After Progress, *I happened to reread an essay by Italian futurist Ugo Bardi titled "The Next Ten Billion Years," in which he deployed the usual rhetoric of progress vs. apocalypse in yet another foredoomed attempt to frighten people into doing something about the crisis of our time. That sent my imagination careening along a very different vision of what the next ten billion years would probably look like. I posted the resulting essay on my blog, where it attracted a great deal of comment, both positive and negative. As a result, I was asked to submit an edited version of it to* Adbusters Magazine, *where it appeared in mutilated form in the May/June 2015 issue. It then appeared intact in the Fall 2015 issue of the* Utne Reader.

Contemporary industrial society loves to preen itself on its rationality, but it's remarkable how brittle the hold of reason really is these days. It's not hard to point to examples of that brittleness; the one I want to explore here is the way that rationality gives way to overt myth as soon as people in the industrial world start talking about the future—not their own, short-term future, but the future of humanity as a whole.

Historians and scientists have learned quite a bit down the years about how civilizations rise and fall, how species evolve and go extinct, and what we can expect from the rest of this planet's long trajectory through time. Typically, though, contemporary visions of the future leave that knowledge untouched. Instead, we get endless rehashes of two stereotyped narratives—the story of perpetual progress leading humanity straight to some simulacrum of godhood, on the one hand, and on the other, the story of overnight apocalypse leading humanity to planetary die-off, with or without a plucky band of survivors to pose while the final credits roll past.

These notions of progress and apocalypse are industrial society's traditional folk mythologies, rather than meaningful ways of understanding the future. Once they're jettisoned, and known details of ecology, evolution, and astrophysics are brought in to fill out the story in their place, the next ten billion years looks very different from either of those overfamiliar scenarios. Here's one version or, if you will, one vision.

### *Ten years from now*

Business as usual continues; the human population peaks at 8.5 billion, fossil fuels and other nonrenewable resources deplete steadily, and the annual cost of weather-related disasters continues to rise. Politicians and the media insist loudly that better times are just around the corner, as times get steadily worse. Among those who recognize that something's wrong, one popular viewpoint holds that fusion power, artificial intelligence, and interstellar migration will shortly solve all our problems, and therefore we don't have to change the way we live. Another, equally popular, insists that total human extinction is scarcely a decade away, and therefore we don't have to change the way we live. Most people accept one or the other, while the last chance for meaningful systemic change slips silently away.

### *A hundred years from now*

It has been a difficult century. After more than a dozen major wars, three global pandemics, repeated famines, and steep worldwide declines in public health and civil order, human population is down to three billion and falling. Sea level is up four meters and rising fast as the Greenland and West Antarctic ice caps disintegrate; fossil fuel production ground to a halt decades earlier as the last economically producible reserves were exhausted, and most of the proposed alternatives turned out to be unaffordable in the absence of the sort of cheap, abundant, highly concentrated energy only fossil fuels can provide. Cornucopians still insist that fusion power, artificial intelligence, and interstellar migration will save us any day now, and their opponents still insist that human extinction is imminent, but most people are too busy trying to stay alive to listen to either group.

## A thousand years from now

The Earth is without ice caps and glaciers for the first time in twenty million years, and sea level has gone up more than a hundred meters worldwide; much of the world has a tropical climate, as it did fifty million years earlier. Human population is one hundred million, up from half that figure at the bottom of the bitter dark age now passing into memory. Only a few scholars have any idea what the words "fusion power," "artificial intelligence," and "interstellar migration" once meant, and though there are still people insisting that the end of the world will arrive soon, their arguments rely more overtly on theology than before. New civilizations are rising in various corners of the world, combining legacy technologies with their own unique cultural forms. The one thing they all have in common is that the industrial society of our era is their idea of evil incarnate.

## Ten thousand years from now

The rise in global temperature has shut down the thermohaline circulation and launched an oceanic anoxic event, the planet's normal negative feedback process when carbon dioxide levels get out of hand. Today's industrial civilization is a dim memory, as far removed from this time as the Neolithic Revolution is from ours; believers in most traditional religions declare piously that the climate changes of the last ten millennia are the results of human misbehavior, while rationalists insist that this is all superstition and the climate changes have perfectly natural causes. As the anoxic oceans draw carbon out of the biosphere and entomb it in sediments on the sea floor, the climate begins a gradual cooling—a process which helps push humanity's sixth global civilization into its terminal decline.

## A hundred thousand years from now

Carbon dioxide levels drop below preindustrial levels as the oceanic anoxic event finishes its work, and the feedback loops that govern Earth's climate shift again: the thermohaline circulation restarts, triggering another round of climate changes. Humanity's seventy-ninth global civilization flourishes and begins its slow decline as the disruptions set in motion by a long-forgotten industrial age are drowned out by older cycles. The scholars of that civilization are thrilled by the notions of fusion power, artificial intelligence, and interstellar migration; they have no idea that we dreamed the same dreams before them, being further in our future than the first Neanderthals are in our past, but they will have no more luck than we did.

## A million years from now

The Earth is in an ice age. Great ice sheets cover much of the northern hemisphere, and sea level is 150 meters lower than today. To the people living at this time, who have never known anything else, this is normal. Metals have become rare geological specimens—for millennia now, most human societies have used renewable ceramic-bioplastic composites instead—and the very existence of fossil fuels has long since been forgotten. The 664th global human civilization is at its peak, lofting aerostat towns into the skies and building great floating cities on the seas; its long afternoon will eventually draw to an end after scores of generations, and when it falls, other civilizations will rise in its place.

## Ten million years from now

The long glacial epoch that began in the Pleistocene has finally ended, and the Earth is returning to its normal status as a steamy jungle planet. This latest set of changes proves to be just that little bit too much for humanity. No fewer than 8,639 global civilizations have risen and fallen over the past ten million years, each with its own unique sciences, technologies, arts, literatures, philosophies, and ways of thinking about the cosmos; the shortest-lived lasted for less than a century before blowing itself to smithereens, while the longest-lasting endured for eight millennia before finally winding down.

All that is over now. There are still relict human populations in Antarctica, and another million years will pass before cascading climatic and ecological changes finally push the last of them over the brink into extinction. Meanwhile, in the tropical forests of what is now southern Siberia, the descendants of raccoons who crossed the Bering land bridge during the last great ice age are proliferating rapidly, expanding into empty ecological niches once filled by the larger primates. In another thirty million years or so, their descendants will come down from the trees.

### One hundred million years from now

Retro-rockets fire and fall silent as the ungainly craft settles down on the surface of the Moon. After feverish final checks, the hatch is opened, and two figures descend onto the lunar surface. They are bipeds, but not even remotely human; they belong to Earth's third intelligent species, distantly descended from the crows of our time, though they look no more like crows than you look like the tree shrews of the Cretaceous. Since you have a larynx rather than a syrinx, you can't even begin to pronounce what they call themselves, so we'll call them corvins.

Earth's second intelligent species, whom we'll call cyons after their raccoon ancestors, are long gone. They lasted a little more than eight million years before the changes of an unstable planet sent them to extinction; they never got that deeply into technology, though their political institutions made the most sophisticated human equivalents look embarrassingly crude. The corvins are another matter. Some twist of inherited psychology gave them a passion for heights; they worked out the hot air balloon before they invented the wheel, and balloons and gliders play the same roles in their earliest epic literature that horses and chariots play in ours.

As corvin technologies evolved, eyes gazed upwards from soaring tower-cities at the Moon, the perch of perches set high above the world. All that was needed to make those dreams a reality was petroleum, and a hundred million years is more than enough time for the Earth to restock her petroleum reserves—especially if that period starts off with an oceanic anoxic event that stashes gigatons of carbon in marine sediments. Thus it was inevitable that, sooner or later, the strongest of the great corvin kith-assemblies would take on the task of reaching the Moon.

The universe has a surprise in store for the corvins, though. Their first lander set down on a flat lunar plain that, a very long time ago, was called the Sea of Tranquility, and so it was that the stunned corvin astronauts found themselves facing the fragmentary but unmistakable remains of a spacecraft that arrived on the Moon in the unimaginably distant past. Those shattered remnants made it hard for even the most optimistic corvins to embrace the notion that some providence guaranteed the survival of intelligent species.

The corvins never learned much about the enigmatic ancient species that left its mark on the Moon. Even so, the stark warning of that ruined spacecraft helped convince the corvins to rein in the extravagant use of petroleum and other nonrenewable resources, though it also inspired expensive and ultimately futile attempts to achieve interstellar migration—for some reason the corbins never got into the quest for fusion power or artificial intelligence. One way or another, the corvins turned out to be the most enduring of Earth's intelligent species, and more than 28 million years passed before their day finally ended.

*One billion years from now*

The Earth is old and mostly desert. The increasing heat of the Sun as it proceeds through its own life cycle, and the ongoing loss of volatile molecules from the upper atmosphere into space, have reduced the seas to scattered, salty basins amid great sandy wastes. Only near the north and south poles does vegetation flourish, and with it the corbicules, Earth's eleventh and last intelligent species. Their ancestors in our time are an invasive species of freshwater clam. (Don't laugh; a billion years ago your ancestors were still trying to work out the details of multicellularity.)

The corbicules have the same practical limb structure as the rest of their subphylum: six stumpy podicles for walking, two muscular dorsal tentacles for gross manipulations and two slender buccal tentacles by the mouth for fine manipulations. They spend most of their time in underground city-complexes, venturing to the surface to harvest vegetation to feed the metafungal gardens that provide them with nourishment. By some combination of luck and a general tendency toward cephalization common to many evolutionary lineages, Earth's last intelligent species is also its most intellectually gifted; hatchlings barely out of creche get fun little logic problems such as Fermat's last theorem for their amusement, and most adult corbicules are involved in some field of intellectual endeavor. Being patient, long-lived, and not fond of collective stupidities, they have gone very far.

Some eight thousand years back, a circle of radical young corbicule thinkers proposed the project of working out all the physical laws of the cosmos, starting from first principles. So unprecedented a suggestion sparked countless debates, publications, ceremonial dances, and professional duels in which elderly scholars killed themselves in order to cast opprobrium on their rivals. Still, it was far too delectable an intellectual challenge to be left unanswered, and the work has proceeded ever since. In the course of their researches, without placing any great importance on the fact, the best minds among the corbicules have proved conclusively that nuclear fusion, artificial intelligence, and interstellar migration were never practical options in the first place.

Being patient, long-lived, and not fond of collective stupidities, the corbicules have long since accepted their eventual fate. In another six million years, as the Sun expands and the Earth's surface temperature rises, the last vegetation will perish and the corbicules will go extinct; in another ninety million years, the last multicellular life forms will die out; in another two hundred million years, the last seas will boil, and Earth's biosphere, at the end of its long, long life, will nestle into the deepest crevices of its ancient world and drift into a final sleep.

## Ten billion years from now

Earth is gone. It had a splendid funeral; its body dissolved in stellar fire as the Sun reached its red giant stage and expanded out to the orbit of Mars, and its ashes were flung outwards into space with the first helium flash that marked the beginning of the Sun's descent toward its destiny. Two billion years later, the gas- and dust-rich shockwave from that flash plowed into a mass of interstellar dust dozens of light-years away from the Sun's pale corpse, and kickstarted one of the great transformative processes of the cosmos.

Billions of years have passed since that collision. A yellow-orange K-2 star now burns cheerily in the midst of six planets and two asteroid belts. The second planet has a surface temperature between the freezing and boiling points of water, and a sufficiently rich assortment of elements to launch another of the great transformative processes of the cosmos. Now, in one spot on the surface of this world, rising up past bulbous purplish things that don't look anything like trees but fill the same ecological function, is a crag of black rock. On top of that crag, a creature sits looking at the stars, fanning its lunules with its sagittal crest and waving its pedipalps meditatively back and forth. It is one of the first members of its world's first intelligent species, and it is—for the first time ever on that world—considering the stars and wondering if other beings might live out there among them.

The creature's biochemistry, structure, and life cycle have nothing in common with yours, dear reader. Its world, its sensory organs, its mind, and its feelings would be utterly alien to you, even if ten billion years didn't separate you. Nonetheless, it so happens that a few atoms that are currently part of your brain, as you read these words, will also be part of the brain-analogue of the creature on the crag on that distant, not-yet-existing world. Does that fact horrify or depress you? Does it leave you cold? Or does it console you to think of yourself as part of the dance by which worlds are born and die?

# The coming of the Post-Axial Age

*I was startled, to use no stronger word, to receive an email from philosopher Richard Polt inviting me to submit an essay to an anthology of original scholarly papers titled* The Task of Philosophy in the Anthropocene, *which was to take Karl Jaspers's famous theory of the Axial Age as a jumping-off point for an exploration of the future of philosophy. Jaspers's theory had been on my mind for some years, and of course the future of industrial society has been a major concern of mine for decades, so I leapt at the chance. (This essay appears here by permission of Rowman & Littlefield International, the publishers of the anthology.)*

It can be difficult to remember at present that not much more than half a century ago, philosophy was routinely discussed in general-interest magazines and the better grade of newspapers, not merely in the academic press. Sartre was an international celebrity; the posthumous publication of Teilhard de Chardin's *Le Phénomène Humaine* received significant media coverage, and Random House's Vintage Books label among others found a market for inexpensive mass-market paperback editions of major philosophical writings from Plato straight through to Nietzsche and beyond.

Though philosophy was never really part of the cultural mainstream at that time, it had the same kind of widespread following as avant-garde jazz or science fiction. Attendees at any reasonably large cocktail party had a reasonable chance of meeting someone who was into philosophy, and those who knew where to look in any big city or college town with pretensions to culture could find at least one bar, bookstore, or all-night coffee shop where philosophy geeks talked earnestly into the small hours about Kant or Kierkegaard. Furthermore, that level of interest in the subject had been common in the Western world for a very long time.

Here in North America, at least—I understand that conditions in Europe are a little less dire at present—we have come a long way since then. These days discussions about philosophy in the North American media usually come from scientific materialists such as Neil deGrasse Tyson who insist that philosophy is nonsense. The occasional work of philosophy still gets a page or two in the *New York Review of Books*, but popular interest in the subject has vanished, and more than vanished: the truculent ignorance about philosophy displayed by Tyson and his many equivalents has become just as common among cocktail party attendees as a feigned interest in the subject was a half century in the past. Largely shut out from the realm of public discourse, philosophy clings to a narrowing niche in the academic world, and current trends do not bode well for the continued existence of the institutional arrangements that give it what grudging support it still receives.[112]

At first glance, then, it may seem out of place to talk about what philosophy has to contribute to the so-called Anthropocene epoch.[113] It is an open question whether philosophy as a living tradition will survive long even under current conditions; furthermore, the cascade of changes that have been set in motion by our species' abuse of the biosphere will not necessarily spare the institutional arrangements that

---

[112] Jacobs, Jane. *Dark Age Ahead*. New York: Random House, 2004.

[113] The term "Anthropocene" implies, through its imitation of the names of geological epochs such as the Pliocene and Pleistocene, that humanity's capacity to affect the planet on a geological scale will endure for a period comparable to other geological epochs—that is, several million years. It seems considerably more likely that the industrial system that enables human beings to have large-scale effects on the planet will be among the early casualties of the ecological crises now in motion. The so-called "Anthropocene" would thus better be termed the *anthropic transition*, a geologically brief interval separating the Holocene from a geological epoch to come. See Greer, John Michael. "Confronting the Cthulhucene." *Dark Mountain*, 13 (Spring 2018).

support the practice of philosophy just now. A glance back over the history of philosophy offers only qualified hope, since philosophy has died at least once in the history of Western philosophy itself, during the dark ages that followed the fall of Roman civilization. Even where classical literature clung to a tenuous existence during that hiatus, as in Byzantium, the living tradition of philosophy was lost, and had to be rekindled from literary remains once conditions changed, first in the Arabic world and then in Europe.

This way of looking at the prospects of philosophy conflicts with certain deeply held modern beliefs about the nature of history. The idea that an era of intellectual sophistication and subtlety can give way to an era of superstition and crude empirical generalization is unthinkable to many educated people today, even though history shows no shortage of examples. The further suggestion that the intellectual and philosophical triumphs of the last several centuries could give way to the sharply narrowed mental horizons of a new dark age is not merely unthinkable to many, but deeply offensive. Behind that reaction lies the metanarrative of progress, the modern world's most widely accepted way of interpreting history.[114]

At the heart of the metanarrative of progress is a rhetorical strategy that assigns certain arbitrarily chosen events of past and present the status of irreversible forward steps in the grand march of humanity, and tacitly assigns a less significant status to events that fail to further movement in whatever direction the grand march of humanity is held to follow. The historical emergence of philosophy in the ancient world, alongside more recent events in the history of the discipline, have been assigned meanings of this kind tolerably often in the three centuries or so since the metanarrative of progress rose to prominence in the Western world.

The enlistment of philosophy under the banner of the metanarrative of progress played a pivotal role in the philosophy of history in the nineteenth and twentieth centuries, in particular, and took many forms in the philosophical writings of that period. It received one of its most distinctive expressions at the hands of Karl Jaspers, who identified the historical emergence of philosophy in ancient times with what he considered the most important turning point in history, the coming

---

[114] I have explored this theme in Greer, John Michael. *After Progress: Religion and Reason at the End of the Industrial Age*. Gabriola Island, BC, Canada: New Society, 2015.

of the Axial Age. To make sense of the very different turning point facing modern industrial culture at this stage of its history, and the ways that this transition can be expected to affect the project and purposes of philosophy, a close look at Jaspers's theory and the realities behind it will be helpful.

### The hinge of history?

Jaspers introduced the concept of the Axial Age in his 1949 book *Vom Ursprung und Ziel der Geschichte* (*On the Origin and Goal of History*). Like most twentieth-century European historiography, it built on the foundations laid by Hegel's philosophy of history, but—also like most twentieth-century European historiography—it also reacted against the ideas of a more controversial figure in German intellectual life, the historian Oswald Spengler.

Hegel famously argued for a theory of history in which the ancient civilizations of Egypt and Mesopotamia, the classical civilizations of Greece and Rome, and the modern civilizations of Europe formed the three stages of a single narrative of human progress, to which the historical experiences of all other societies were mere addenda.[115] That view was widely embraced in scholarship as well as popular culture throughout the nineteenth and twentieth centuries. In his own work, by contrast, Spengler proposed that human history cannot be made to fit any single trajectory, and that the metanarrative of progress in particular represents a drastic falsification of historical fact.[116]

In *Der Untergang des Abendlandes* (*The Decline of the West*), his major work, Spengler argued that each great culture traces out its own historical trajectory, subject to common laws of development and decline, and this history unfolds in a predictable series of stages from birth to death. The intellectual life of a great culture is thus as distinct as its history: "Each Culture has its own new possibilities of self-expression which arise, ripen, decay, and never return. There is not *one* sculpture, *one* painting, *one* mathematics, *one* physics, but many, each in its deepest essence different from the others[.]"[117]

---

[115] Hegel, Georg Wilhelm Friedrich. *Lectures on the Philosophy of History*, trans. H. B. Nisbet. Cambridge: Cambridge University Press, 1975.

[116] Spengler, Oswald. *The Decline of the West, vol. 2: Perspectives of World History*, trans. Charles Francis Atkinson. New York: Alfred A. Knopf, 1928, pp. 23–51.

[117] Spengler, Oswald. *The Decline of the West, Vol. 1: Form and Actuality*, trans. Charles Francis Atkinson. New York: Alfred A. Knopf, 1926, p. 21.

From Spengler's standpoint, as a result, the metanarrative of progress is a twofold falsification. To begin with, our civilization has risen but not yet fallen, and therefore judges its own history as well as that of other civilizations through the distorting lens of an incomplete experience of the historical process. On a deeper level, to Spengler, our idea of progress is simply a reflection of our own civilization's necessarily ethnocentric sense of values. What makes our civilization "more progressive" than others? Simply that we embody, more completely than do other civilizations, the specific set of values our civilization happens to prize. What makes us sure that history is progressive in nature? Our myopic take on our own incomplete history, which has so far traced out only half of the normal cycle of rise and fall.

In the face of this challenge, the metanarrative of progress had no shortage of defenders in twentieth-century European thought, and Jaspers was among these. Central to Jaspers's project in *On the Origin and Goal of History*, accordingly, was the search for a weapon with which to refute Spengler's assault. The intellectual stakes here were high, since Jaspers sought to prove that the rise of modern industrial civilization marked a permanent change in human affairs and not, as Spengler argued, the prelude to the Western world's decline and fall. The concept of the Axial Age was born out of that search.

Jaspers argued that the period between 800 and 200 BC represented an irrevocable turning point in human thought, a hinge of history dividing a lower from a higher realm of cultural and intellectual phenomena. Before the Axial Age, mythic thought, primitive superstition, the timeless repetition of archaic irrationalities; after it, philosophy, reason, revealed religion, humanity set free to pursue its truly human capacities—this, at least, according to Jaspers.[118] Grant that claim, and it becomes reasonable to argue, as Jaspers did, that the further transformations of human thought that drove the rise of modern industrial civilization were equally irrevocable.

Fair enough. Certain questions, though, follow from this claim, and these have to be faced in order to address Jaspers's argument for the irrevocable nature of progress. What exactly was it that appeared with the Axial Age? Can anything be said about the cause of this apparent break with the past? And is Jaspers correct that the change heralded by the coming of the Axial Age is an irreversible event in human history?

---

[118] Jaspers, Karl. *The Origin and Goal of History*, trans. Michael Bullock. New Haven, CT: Yale University Press, 1953, pp. 2–8.

Trying to characterize the diverse cultural and intellectual phenomena that appeared between 800 BCE and 200 BCE in the eastern Mediterranean, India, and China, Jaspers indulged in very broad generalizations: "In this age were born the fundamental categories within which we still think today, and the beginnings of the world religions, by which human beings still live, were created."[119] This is true in a certain sense, but only so long as terms such as "we" and "human beings" apply only to those inhabitants of industrial societies who accept those categories of thought Jaspers considered fundamental, and embrace one of the world religions rather than any of the other religious or irreligious options. This is at least a questionable claim, and requires considerably more justification than Jaspers gave it.

Features of the Axial Age he considers distinctive suffer from a similar narrowness of focus. These include the end of myth, the rise of philosophy, the birth of speculative thought, and the emergence of "the specifically human in man," that is, "what was later called reason and personality."[120] He seems to be correct that philosophy as such first appears with the coming of the Axial Age, and certain kinds of speculative thought appear with it, though others can quite readily be traced as far back as written records go; the rise of quantitative astronomical science in ancient Mesopotamia, enriched as it was with the soaring speculations of ancient astrology, is merely one of the more thoroughly documented examples.

The claim that myth was somehow brought to an end by the intellectual breakthroughs of the Axial Age, on the other hand, cannot be justified at all without special pleading. Unless we agree arbitrarily to define "myth" in such a way that the term only refers to the sacred narratives of religions founded before the Axial Age, and use some other word to talk about the corresponding narratives of religions founded during and after that period, Jaspers's claim simply is not true. Mythic discourse—the mode of explaining the world that relies on narratives of the deeds of superhuman beings—persists in all human societies; what happened with the coming of the Axial Age was simply that, for a time, mythic discourse became unfashionable among a large part of the educated elite, while it retained its hold on other strata of society.

---

[119] Jaspers, op. cit., p. 2.
[120] Jaspers, op. cit., pp. 3–4.

The claim that the Axial Age saw the first appearance of "the specifically human in man," in the same way, depends on a set of entirely personal value judgments about what is or is not "specifically human." Any such judgment risks excluding large numbers of our species, past and present, from the "specifically human." By 1949, when Jaspers wrote, it should have been painfully obvious that this is a very dangerous game to play.

At the same time, as already noted, Jaspers does appear to be correct that philosophy had its origin in the places and times he specifies. Certain other modes of human thought, including logic and formal mathematics, also appear to have had their beginnings in the same places and times. Since these modes of thought have played a foundational role in the most prestigious intellectual currents of our culture, Jaspers's focus on their origin may not be misplaced.

## Literacy and the Axial Age

If we grant Jaspers's claim that the Axial Age is a historical reality, though, the second question brought up above—the question of its cause or causes—cannot be evaded. Jaspers himself recognized this, and discussed a number of factors that might have brought about the Axial Age and its many transformations.[121] Among the possibilities he considered were a common source in Central Asia, the impact of Indo-European invasions, and sociological conditions including the presence of many small states engaged in constant warfare.

He concluded, however, that it is impossible to identify any historical cause for the coming of the Axial Age, while pleading gamely that he was not trying to suggest a supernatural cause for the phenomenon.[122] Whether or not this surrender to the unknowable was an attempt to create an opening for a Christian apologetics of history, along the lines of the famous "God of the gaps" argument—a common enough strategy on one end of twentieth-century historiography[123]—it is by no means required by the evidence.

---

[121] Jaspers, op. cit., pp. 13–18.
[122] Jaspers, op. cit., p. 18.
[123] See, for one example out of many, Barfield, Owen. *Saving the Appearances: A Study in Idolatry*. Middletown, CT: Wesleyan University Press, 1957.

If Jaspers was correct in saying that something genuinely new emerged in the eastern Mediterranean, India, and China at roughly the same period in human history, it would seem reasonable to inquire whether the human cultures in these places had evolved, shortly before the emergence of the core features of the Axial Age, some significant feature bearing on the life of the mind, which did not occur before that time and cannot be found elsewhere until a later date. It so happens that there is one such feature: the expansion of literacy beyond a scribal class.

In a useful study of the roles of literacy in classical Greek, Hellenistic, and Roman culture, William V. Harris differentiates among distinct levels of literacy within a population.[124] He uses the term *scribal literacy* for the possession of literacy solely by a scribal elite associated with palaces and temples, who use writing solely for record-keeping and other practical tasks. This is the context in which literacy existed in the ancient Near East, in Minoan and Mycenean societies, in Egypt until the New Kingdom, and in literate New World societies such as the classical Maya.

*Craftsman's literacy*[125] is Harris's term for the possession of literacy by a significant minority of the male population, including skilled craftspeople, landowners, public officials, and the like, while unskilled male laborers, farmers, the poor, and women generally remain illiterate. This differs, finally, from *mass literacy*, in which the majority of the population is literate, including both genders and most or all social classes.

The transition between scribal literacy and craftsman's literacy is the one that deserves attention here. We live in an age of mass literacy, and from that standpoint it can be difficult to realize just how drastic a change followed the end of the scribal monopoly on writing—a change that was not limited to social and economic effects, but also reshaped the way that language itself was and is experienced.[126]

---

[124] Harris, William V. *Ancient Literacy*. Cambridge, MA: Harvard University Press, 1989, pp. 7–8.
[125] The gender reference in this phrase is deliberate; in societies with craftsman's literacy, literacy is almost entirely restricted to men. Literacy among women only becomes common in societies with what Harris calls mass literacy.
[126] See, among other developments of this theme, Ong, Walter J. *Orality and Literacy: The Technologizing of the Word*. New York: Routledge, 2002; Havelock, Eric A. *The Literate Revolution in Greece and Its Cultural Consequences*. Princeton, NJ: Princeton University Press, 1981; Havelock, Eric A. *Preface to Plato*. Cambridge, MA: Harvard University Press, 1963; and Havelock, Eric A. *The Muse Learns to Write: Reflections on Orality and Literacy from Antiquity to the Present*. New Haven, CT: Yale University Press, 1986.

Consider an act of linguistic communication in an oral society. Lacking writing, every use of language was, and had to be, the performative act of a speaker or a group of speakers, and could not be experienced apart from the whole context of the performance—a context that included gestures, vocal tones, facial expressions, and all the other nonverbal carriers of meaning that play a role in oral performance. In an oral society, language never stands alone.

To a very great extent, that remains the case while literacy is the preserve of a small professional class of scribes. In a society with scribal literacy, written language remains tied to oral performance. The core scribal activities are taking oral dictation from illiterate persons, on the one hand, and reading written documents to illiterate persons, on the other. In a society with scribal literacy, in effect, a written document is a script for an oral performance, which enables that performance to be enacted at a distance in space or time.

With the coming of craftsman's literacy, this condition changes decisively for members of the literate community. When literacy is no longer limited to a professional class but spreads through a significant minority of the population, writing and reading are no longer bound to the context of public performance, and the individual reader, pondering a document in solitude, becomes a recognized phenomenon. One crucial consequence is that for the first time, language can be detached from the other elements of oral communication and experienced in isolation. The meaning of words, rather than the character and intentions of speakers, accordingly becomes central to learned discourse.

The impact of this change can best be understood by observing the difference between mythology, the standard intellectual discourse of oral and scribal societies, and philosophy, the standard intellectual discourse of societies that have achieved craftsman's literacy. Every mythology is a description of the actions and intentions of persons; every philosophy, by contrast, is a description of the properties and relations of abstractions. Mythology thus comes naturally in a society in which every linguistic act is part of a personal performance. Philosophy, in turn, comes naturally in a society in which words have become separated from the other, nonverbal elements of personal communication, and can therefore be experienced and understood on their own, as impersonal markers for abstract ideas.

It is of course controversial to suggest that the rise of craftsman's literacy, rather than some more impressive, elusive, or metaphysical cause, brought about the intellectual phenomena that Jaspers assigns to the Axial Age. The metanarrative of progress assigns these phenomena a place alongside the emergence of modern industrial society as irreversible forward steps in the grand march of humanity from the caves to the stars. To reinterpret them instead as unexpected side effects of a change in the social status of literacy is to challenge the assumption of the irrevocability of progress that lies at the heart of the metanarrative itself—an assumption that underlies a great deal of the rhetoric, and even more of the actions, that have brought humanity to its present impasse.

Examine the vagaries of literacy across historical societies, however, and the suggestion I have made here gains powerful support. In post-Roman Europe, to cite only one of many examples, literacy once again became the preserve of a very small body of religious scribes, and mythology promptly replaced philosophy as the common mode of intellectual discourse. Once literacy spread outside the monasteries, in turn, philosophy rose resurgent, and mythology once again began to lose its grip on the literate classes. The same sequence can be traced wherever a society has moved in either direction across the boundary between scribal and craftsman's literacy.

Thus we can understand the phenomena of the Axial Age as the product of an important shift in the way literate individuals in ancient societies experienced language, and accordingly in the way their habits of thinking were conditioned by their use of language. That shift had sweeping consequences, and Jaspers was entirely correct in claiming that the complexities of modern thought still move in patterns first traced out by those ancient societies that first diffused literacy outside a scribal class. Jaspers meant to claim considerably more for the Axial Age than the side effects of a significant change in communication, to be sure, but a strong case can be made that the facts behind his sweeping generalizations can best be understood along the lines just traced out.

### *The triumph of the Logos*

If the phenomena of the Axial Age resulted from a shift of the kind just described, in turn, one of the most curious habits of thought that came in with craftsman's literacy becomes easier to understand. This is the conviction that the truth about the world consists of ideas that can be expressed in verbal formulae, and that the rest of reality is merely an expression of the truth known in words. Put perhaps too bluntly, it is the belief that words are more real than the experiences they describe.

Beliefs very often appear in their most uncompromising form when first articulated, before time and debate have the chance to force nuance upon them. Thus it is no surprise that the conviction just outlined can be seen in its extreme form at the very dawn of philosophical reasoning, in Presocratic Greek philosophy. When Parmenides placed in the mouth of a goddess that the world known by reason is the true world, and the world experienced by the senses was purely illusory,[127] he sounded the keynote of the Axial Age. The later history of Greek philosophy, in turn, was largely a matter of adding nuance to Parmenides's claim. Plato's concept of the Ideas and Aristotle's application of verbal logic to the nonverbal phenomena of nature can usefully be seen as adaptations of the Parmenidean principle in the service of more thoroughly developed accounts of the world.

The same opposition between a true world known by the powers of the mind and the false world constructed by the senses was even more central to Indian philosophy, which made the illusory nature of sensory reality its keynote from the age of the Upanishads onward. The same theme's importance in the debates that shaped ancient Chinese philosophy is attested by the caution Lao Tsu put at the beginning of the Dao De Jing: "The Way that can be described is not the eternal Way; the names that can be spoken are not eternal names"—a warning that would have been unnecessary had Parmenides not had his Chinese equivalents.

The impact and intensity of the Axial Age's trust in verbal formulae over experienced reality, however, can best be observed by watching its impact on religion. Religion, which relies primarily on mythological rather than philosophical discourse, fills many of the same roles in oral and scribal societies that philosophy fills in societies with craftsman's or mass literacy. In societies that have attained craftsman's or mass literacy, in turn, religion functions in large part as a kind of folk philosophy, using mythological discourse to express the common presuppositions of popular thought. These latter, in turn, tend to reflect the core commitments of learned discourse in a fashion reminiscent of a carnival funhouse mirror: inverted and distorted, to be sure, but still recognizably made in the image of its source.

---

[127] See Curd, Patricia. *A Presocratics Reader: Selected Fragments and Testimonia.* Indianapolis, IN: Hackett Publishing, 2011, pp. 53–63.

Thus in all three of the seedbeds of the Axial Age, in the Mediterranean world as in India and China, the coming of craftsman's literacy and the emergence of philosophy was echoed over the following centuries by the abandonment of an ancient mode of religious discourse and its replacement by a radically different religious language. The mode that was replaced may be described without too much inaccuracy as Paganism: a religious sensibility that made traditional rituals and customs central to religious life, and either had no sacred writings or assigned them a secondary importance. Ancient Greek polytheism, the archaic Hinduism of the Vedas and the great Indian epics, and the scarcely remembered polytheism of classical China all fit this mode, as of course do many other faiths of past and present.

The mode that came in with the Axial Age, by contrast, is the one that most people in the industrial world today associate with religion as a matter of course: a religious sensibility that makes belief in doctrines taught in a sacred scripture central to religious life, and gives to traditional rituals and customs a secondary importance. The outspoken certainty of the Gospel of John—"In the beginning was the Word"—puts the central theme of the Axial Age in stark relief. That same triumph of the Logos is echoed in the scriptures of Christianity and Islam, the principal religious products of the Axial Age in the Mediterranean; in the scriptures of Buddhism, the principal religious product of the Axial Age in India; and, in a fine display of history's wry sense of humor, in the way that the philosophical texts of Lao Tsu and Confucius were taken up and redefined as scriptures by Chinese popular religion, the principal religious product of the Axial Age in China.

Here again, it's revealing to trace what happened when societies that had achieved craftsman's literacy lost that status, and once again relegated literacy to a small scribal elite, as happened in post-Roman Europe. Just as mythology took over from philosophy, a religious sensibility based on ritual and tradition supplanted one based on creeds and theology; where the latter survived, they did so in fossil forms and took on functions far removed from their original context—for example, the creeds and prayers of Catholic Christianity took on the role of magic spells in early medieval Europe.[128] The return of craftsman's literacy, in turn, led in due course to the Reformation and Counter-Reformation,

---

[128] See Flint, Valerie. *The Rise of Magic in Early Medieval Europe*. Princeton, NJ: Princeton University Press, 1996.

which reasserted the primacy of formal verbal statements of belief over ritual rooted in mythic narrative.

The verbal formulae at the heart of Axial Age religions were always contested, both by proponents of alternative formulae and by mystics who challenged the validity of any verbal formulae. Yet the fierceness of the debates that surrounded such issues highlights the importance that verbal understandings of reality were assigned in the wake of the Axial Age. It was only after the Axial Age that adherence to a verbal statement became the acid test of commitment to a religion. An ancient Greek Pagan expressed his or her commitment to traditional Paganism by participating in rituals, celebrating festivals, and engaging in other religious actions, not by uttering some statement of belief. It was only after the Axial Age that rival religious factions turned to schism, persecution, and mob violence over questions of verbal formulae—for example, whether the Holy Spirit proceeded from the Father and the Son, or from the Father alone. Such contentions were unimaginable in Pagan societies; in the wake of the Axial Age, they became all too familiar.

## The end of the dream

Philosophy, to its credit, has generally avoided these extremes of behavior, and it has also varied significantly over time in the degree of animosity with which the defenders of one philosophical position have turned on proponents of antithetical positions. There have been periods in the history of philosophy in which competing schools confronted one another across a rhetorical no-man's-land fortified with the intellectual equivalent of trenches and barbed wire, but there have also been periods in which different schools and thinkers have managed some degree of peaceful coexistence.

This has become increasingly common over the last century. The great philosophical contentions of the nineteenth century had the unexpected result of demonstrating that it was impossible to prove the exclusive validity of any one account of the world to the satisfaction of open-minded individuals who had accepted some other account of the world. Among the many consequences of this demonstration was the undermining of any attempt to apply the metanarrative of progress to the history of philosophy. While philosophy can be said to progress in certain specific senses—for example, by elaborating languages of discourse and working out the implications of claims about the world in increasing detail—it has become increasingly clear that no more general concept of progress makes sense of its history.

A distinction proposed by E. F. Schumacher may be useful here.[129] Problems subject to investigation by the human mind, he suggested, fall generally speaking into two categories. Convergent problems are those in which inquiry, however diverse its starting points may be, converges on a single answer. The classic challenges faced and overcome by science are good examples of convergent problems: there is, for example, precisely one correct answer to the question of what set of numbers best models the movement of any given planet relative to the Sun. The history of that particular theme in planetary astrophysics traces the process by which a sequence of theories—Ptolemaic, Copernican, Keplerian, Newtonian, and Einsteinian—successively yielded improved approximations to the correct answer, as inquiry converged from wildly diverse initial hypotheses to exact mathematical formulae that agreed with every observation.

Divergent problems do not have this characteristic trajectory. The classic challenges faced and not yet overcome by ethics, for example, are good examples of divergent problems. Different ethicists grappling with the same issue may come to widely differing conclusions, not because one ethicist is more accurate than the other, but because each builds an argument starting from a different set of presuppositions, and no argument favoring one such set over another has convincing force to those not already predisposed to accept it.

The intellectual history of the nineteenth century demonstrated with tolerable clarity that the central concerns of philosophy are divergent rather than convergent problems. The inability of philosophy to converge on a final answer to the problems of existence thus became a central theme in twentieth-century thought, and received a great deal of thoughtful attention. The work of Michael Polanyi, as set out in *Personal Knowledge* and neatly summarized in *The Tacit Dimension*, is among the most useful explorations of this theme.[130]

Polanyi showed decisively that every human being knows things that cannot be communicated in words—the knowledge that enables each of us to recognize the faces of family members and friends is an

---

[129] Schumacher, E. F. *A Guide for the Perplexed*. London: Jonathan Cape, 1977.
[130] Polanyi, Michael. *Personal Knowledge: Toward a Post-Critical Philosophy*. Chicago, IL: University of Chicago Press, 1962; Polanyi, Michael, *The Tacit Dimension*. Garden City, NY: Doubleday, 1966.

obvious example. He proceeded to show that every verbal statement of knowledge depends on a substructure of tacit, personal knowledge which cannot be communicated in verbal form. Attempting to reduce this tacit knowledge to words requires dependence on an even wider range of tacit knowledge, resulting in an infinite regression.

Thus the old dream of an explicit philosophical account of the entirety of the world, the final expression of the old faith in the truth of verbal formulae, falls at last. Along with it falls the hope of a final philosophy to which all lines of inquiry will eventually converge—a hope that always depended on the assumption that a wholly explicit verbal statement of the nature of the world, relying on no tacit underpinnings, was possible. Polanyi's work, and those of the many other twentieth-century philosophers who contributed to the same recognition of the divergent nature of philosophical questions, thus has a role in the history of philosophy comparable to that of Kurt Gödel in the history of logic.

Gödel's famous theorem, it bears remembering, did not bring about the end of logic. It simply drew a line under certain directions in which logical investigation had proceeded, so that further work could proceed along avenues not yet foreclosed. In the same way, the work of Polanyi and his peers shows that certain pretensions to which philosophers have occasionally been prone can no longer be defended. No final philosophy, no all-encompassing and wholly explicit synthesis embracing the fundamentals of human thought, will ever exist, and attempts to justify philosophy in terms of its movement toward some such synthesis, along the lines of the metanarrative of progress discussed earlier, are misguided at best.

Yet it's a mistake to see this as a denial of the value of philosophy. Many things in the universe of our experience—sex, literature, and the enjoyment of beauty are among the obvious examples—cannot be said to progress in any sense that matters, but this hardly deprives them of their value and significance for human life. A comparable case can be made for the value of philosophy. Such a case, however, would need to be built on the basis of a clear sense of what exactly philosophy is *for*—a clearer sense, arguably, than most philosophers have demonstrated up to the present time.

## The meaning of philosophy

The vision of the Axial Age offered by Karl Jaspers defines the value and meaning of philosophy in very different terms, to be sure. For Jaspers, even though the achievements of the Axial Age were the product of a small number of individuals and influenced only a minority of the people living in the three regions where the Age had its initial manifestations, even though the bulk of the population remained comfortably settled in its earlier primitive and mythic consciousness and promptly returned to earlier ways of doing things once the initial stimulus had worn off, what happened in the Axial Age marked an enduring transformation for all human beings everywhere. Those societies that had no part in the original transformation, he insisted, were doomed either to perish or to embrace the new reality.[131]

This sort of triumphalist rhetoric was common enough in nineteenth- and twentieth-century European intellectual culture, which was beset by a congenital inability to notice that every wave of the future inevitably breaks and rolls back out to sea. It was particularly common in projects of the sort Jaspers was pursuing. In defending the metanarrative of progress against such challenges as Spengler among others leveled against it, finding some way to privilege this or that historical event as an irreversible forward step in the grand upward march of humanity was a gambit that saw heavy use.[132]

If the phenomena Jaspers identified as the hallmarks of the Axial Age were simply the cascading intellectual side effects of the expansion of literacy outside a scribal elite, as this essay has proposed, his claims regarding them require considerable reassessment. Fortunately, history is well stocked with comparable examples of modest changes that set immense consequences in motion. One such example offers a particularly useful lesson in the present context.

Cultivating grains for human food is not that different, all things considered, from cultivating other plant crops, and plenty of human cultures had learned the trick of planting gardens long before the first grain-growing societies emerged in the Middle East.[133] What made grain growing significant, though, was the fact that grains can be transported and stored for long periods without spoilage, and this allowed modes of economic centralization no earlier form of human subsistence had made possible.

---

[131] Jaspers, op. cit., pp. 7 and 19.
[132] See, for one example out of many, Barfield, op. cit., which privileges a different set of historical events in the same manner to support a different historical metanarrative.
[133] Tudge, Colin. *Neanderthals, Bandits, and Farmers: The Origins of Agriculture.* New Haven, CT: Yale University Press, 1998.

While societies that planted and harvested other, less durable crops stayed at the village level of organization, accordingly, grain-growing societies created the first cities, and evolved the city-state model of social organization, in which urban centers maintain complex economies with extensive division of labor, with craftspersons, religious professionals, government officials, artists, and scribes all getting their subsistence from grain raised by farmers in the surrounding agricultural hinterland. The entire suite of practices, technologies, and possibilities we now term "civilization" thus had its origin from the homely act of putting a different kind of seed in a patch of well hoed ground.

Over time, grain agriculture and the city-state economic and political model that emerged out of it spread over those portions of the globe that were well suited to it. The historical narratives of an earlier time liked to portray this as yet another irreversible forward step in the grand upward march of humanity, but research less rigidly constrained by the metanarrative of progress has revealed a far more nuanced tale. There are indeed parts of the world in which grain agriculture and the city-state system, once established, became an enduring reality. There are towns in the Mediterranean basin, India, and China, the heartlands of Jaspers's Axial Age, that have been continuously inhabited for millennia, and still support themselves largely from the produce of their surrounding agricultural hinterlands.

At the same time, there are also a great many places where agriculture and the city-state system failed. In some of those places, it returned after an interval, with or without improved techniques to stave off a second failure, while in others, no return took place, and archeologists there busy themselves today unearthing the remnants of long-abandoned buildings from beneath desert sands or tropical jungle growth.[134] The failures as well as the successes deserve attention in any meaningful understanding of the consequences of grain growing.

I suggest that the same approach might usefully be applied to the consequences of expanded literacy, philosophy among them. Like the practice of growing grain, the practice of diffusing literacy beyond a scribal elite opened up possibilities no one imagined in advance, and set in motion a cascade of consequences that laid the groundwork for a great deal of modern culture. In both cases, those possibilities and

---

[134] Ponting, Clive. *A Green History of the World: the Environment and the Collapse of Great Civilizations*. New York: St. Martin's, 1992.

consequences emerged promptly whenever the underlying practice became sufficiently widespread.

Neither the practices nor their results were irreversible; there have been a significant number of cases in which, for various reasons, the practices have gone out of use, and their results went out of existence thereafter. Neither the practices nor their results, for that matter, were inevitable: There have always been human societies that, for various reasons, did not adopt one or both of them, and did without the results. A strong case can be made that, barring some event drastic enough to abolish either practice and put their recovery out of reach, both grain agriculture and more-than-scribal literacy, with all their consequences, represent enduring additions to the range of possibilities open to human societies and individuals. Getting from that claim to the notion that agriculture or philosophy must be privileged as steps in the inevitable onward march of progress, though, requires a conceptual leap for which no adequate justification has yet been offered.

This way of thinking implies, in turn, that human history is not a convergent problem. The metanarrative of progress presupposes that all of humanity is proceeding along a single line of development toward a single goal; this is what lies behind Jaspers's otherwise odd claim that the intellectual habits resulting from the coming of the Axial Age, limited as they are to minorities even in today's industrial nations, somehow amount to "the specifically human in man." If philosophy and the other products of the Axial Age are understood as possibilities rather than destinies, then human history presents no single line of progress. Instead, it offers a smorgasbord of options from which individuals and societies are within their rights to pick and choose, without that act of choice somehow making them less than specifically human.

## *The Post-Axial Age*

Another lesson that can be drawn from the history of grain agriculture, though, has much to offer philosophers as our species moves deeper into a challenging future. As already noted, some regions are well suited to grain agriculture while others are not. Even at present, when vast supplies of nonrenewable resources can temporarily be lavished on the project of growing grain in areas poorly suited to such projects, there are large portions of the Earth's land surface on which grain agriculture is not an option. As current stocks of fossil fuels, groundwater, topsoil, and other necessities are exhausted, the areas suited to agriculture can be expected to shrink considerably, forcing human societies in those areas to choose between retooling their subsistence strategies or going extinct.[135]

In past eras, when resource depletion and other challenges have forced reconsideration of overenthusiastic projects for expanding the global footprint of civilization, those civilizations that have survived have done so in large part through a process of discernment in which those commitments that made sense in the context of the time were set apart from those that did not. It was by such a process, for example, that the Roman empire bought itself an extra millennium of life by jettisoning its vulnerable western half and falling back on a more sustainable empire centered on Constantinople.[136]

A similar project on a more abstract plane presents itself as an essential project for today's philosophers, and those of tomorrow, should philosophy as a living tradition survive the troubles of the near future. The legacy of the Axial Age, and in particular its obsession with verbal abstractions as distinct from other aspects of human experience, has proven to be a profoundly mixed blessing in recent centuries. Some part of the responsibility for the rising spiral of crises now besetting the industrial world, in fact, might reasonably be assigned to habits of thought that fixate on such abstractions as the metanarrative of progress, and ignore gritty realities such as the dependence of changes arbitrarily singled out as "progressive" on the rapid depletion of nonrenewable resources and the wholesale dumping of poisonous wastes into the biosphere. At the same time, the extraordinary development of abstract reflection and philosophical thought set in motion by the Axial Age has yielded much that may turn out to be of value to the human societies of the far future.

Thus one of the most significant tasks toward which philosophers might choose to devote their time and effort just now is the act of reassessing the heritage of philosophy from the Axial Age to the present, sorting out those ventures that proved to be productive from those that turned out sterile, those that taught useful ways of thinking from those that encouraged people to lose themselves in dysfunctional habits of

---

[135] See Greer, John Michael. *Dark Age America: Climate Change, Cultural Collapse, and the Hard Future Ahead*. Gabriola Island, BC, Canada: New Society, 2016.
[136] Gregory, Timothy E. *A History of Byzantium*. Malden, UK: Wiley-Blackwell, 2010.

mind, and so on. Such a reassessment is a divergent problem rather than a convergent one, to return to Schumacher's dichotomy, for the terms I have just used in setting out the project—"productive," "sterile," "useful," "dysfunctional"—are not objective properties toward which inquiry will necessarily converge; they are value judgments, and thus irreducibly dependent on context. The reassessment I am proposing thus does not aim at a final synthesis of philosophy, but a diverse set of explorations from which the future will make its own choices.

Consider, as an example of the reassessment I have in mind, the dichotomy I have borrowed here from Schumacher. Is it true that questions by and large fall into two categories, those that converge on a single answer, and those that diverge toward many answers? No doubt the point could be debated at length, but in the present context—the context of a discussion about what philosophers might do in the face of the converging crisis besetting modern industrial society—such a debate seems unhelpful to me. I suggest instead approaching the dichotomy as a tool rather than a truth, and exploring the uses and consequences of, say, recognizing this or that set of questions as divergent instead of convergent. Nietzsche's critique of the pursuit of truth in the first section of *Beyond Good and Evil* is relevant here: The tempters and attempters whose importance to the philosophy of the future he proclaimed would be well suited to the work I have sketched out.[137]

Another worthwhile project relevant to the future of philosophy is the presentation of core philosophical ideas in forms suited to the ordinary literate public. As noted earlier, it is an open question whether current trends in North America and elsewhere will permit the survival of philosophy as a living discipline in the academy as presently constituted, and crises of the sort that can be expected in the near and middle future raise serious questions about whether the academy as an institutional phenomenon will long survive. It was largely in the form of summaries, encyclopedias, and popularizations written in late Roman times that philosophical thinking survived in the West after the fall of Rome, and it was from these sources that philosophy was rekindled as scribal literacy and gave way to craftsman's literacy in the Muslim world and medieval Europe.

---

[137] Nietzsche, Friedrich. *Beyond Good and Evil: Prelude to the Philosophy of the Future*, trans. Walter Kaufmann. New York: Vintage, 1966; see especially section 42.

The same thing might be worth aiming for as industrial civilization moves deeper into crisis, with an eye toward the rekindling of philosophy as a living tradition after the deindustrial dark ages ahead. The same principle that led botanists to establish a seed bank on the Arctic island of Svalbard might inspire philosophers to create an idea bank; ideas, fortunately for such a project, can be stored in much more compact form than seeds, and do not require refrigeration to stay viable for the long term.

A third project, more challenging in some ways than the ones already mentioned, would involve sustained reflection on the incongruity between the mass literacy, universal education, and claims to intellectual superiority of contemporary industrial civilization, on the one hand, and the remarkable futility of attempts to turn contemporary industrial civilization from a self-destructive course by rational means. The failure of environmental activism to gain more than lip service from political institutions, even when the evidence of imminent crisis was overwhelming and the costs of inaction catastrophic, is a sobering lesson in the limits of reason.

This same failure also poses a stark challenge to the metanarrative of progress. According to that metanarrative, the necessary sequel to the industrial civilization of our time must be some even more scientific, technologically complex, and intellectually rich civilization in the future, with yet more superlative examples of the same sort of civilization waiting in the wings. This faith is doubtless comforting for those capable of believing it, just as it would no doubt be comforting to children in the first days of fall to convince themselves that summer must be followed by an even sunnier and more pleasant season, and that by a season sunnier and yet more pleasant still. As a fair approximation of the first frosts of autumn spread through the industrial world, however, choosing imagined futures on the basis of their comfort value may not be the wisest option.

As our political, economic, and intellectual institutions consistently fail to respond to imminent crises that are quite capable of ending the project of industrial civilization, belief in the inevitability of progress is hard to sustain on any reasonable basis. If the future follows Spengler's model rather than Jaspers's, and the future of industrial civilization tracks the ordinary process of decline and fall rather than the supposedly unstoppable march of progress from the caves to the stars, what remains of the grand faith of the Axial Age in the power of abstract reason?

What of the conviction that verbal formulae created by human minds were truth itself, and nature merely their imperfect reflections?

History is replete with discoveries that, while useful, turned out to be less so than their discoverers and promoters originally thought. The discovery of abstract thinking set in motion in the Axial Age may turn out to be an example of this kind. From Plato's time down to the present, philosophers have been nonplussed by the discovery that the world is less amenable to rational interpretation and management than it appeared at first glance. This does not make philosophy useless. It simply means that more work needs to be done to differentiate those aspects of human life that can be understood and guided through reasoned exploration of abstract concepts from those that cannot.

The human civilizations that built on the legacy of the Axial Age have witnessed a remarkable development of one narrow aspect of human capacity. Once the spread of literacy turned attention away from language as an act of individual performance to language as a sequence of conceptual abstractions, the abstract intellect and all that depends on it took center stage, and became crucial in the unfoldment of many of the transformations that followed. The failure of intellectual considerations to turn industrial civilization away from self-inflicted calamity, though, suggests that the one-sided development of the abstract intellect may have passed its point of diminishing returns quite some time ago.

Just as the human capacity for abstract thought remained largely undeveloped until the accident of more-than-scribal literacy refocused attention on it, furthermore other regions of human experience—the mythic, the religious, the emotional, the aesthetic, and others—may well conceal other capacities capable of equally remarkable development given the same sort of focused attention. It is impossible to know in advance whether or not these include the capacities that could have guided our species away from the rising spiral of self-inflicted environmental disasters it now faces. Since the abstract intellect clearly is not up to the task, however, it makes sense to look elsewhere.

The impetus of the Axial Age has thus taken the project of human civilization as far as it can. That recognition might easily be fitted into some familiar metanarrative about the future, whether this is based on the currently popular folk mythology of progress or some other narrative structure, but that act of attempted normalization seems unhelpful to me. Instead, I suggest that the age before us might best be understood simply as a Post-Axial Age, a period not yet amenable to any more substantive definition, in which attempts to make sense of the intellectual legacies of the Axial Age will have to grapple with the failure of our time to make good on the apparent promise of abstract reasoning.

Projects of the sort already sketched out, should they yield results that survive the impending crises of our future, may well turn out to be helpful sources of raw material to the intellectual ventures of the Post-Axial Age, just as equivalent ventures in late Roman times provided great assistance to the philosophers of the high Middle Ages and the Renaissance. If that potential is to be realized, though, a great deal of effort will be needed, and soon. Time is short, and the labor needed is not small.

# Toward the deep future

> *In 2016 I was invited to submit an essay to the* Dark Mountain *website on an issue relevant to the future. I had been brooding for some time about the frankly weird way that contemporary ideas about the future have been foreshortening into "the present, just a little more so," and this essay was the result. To my mind, it makes a suitable summing-up of the themes discussed in this volume.*

One of the oddest features of contemporary industrial society, it seems to me, is the profound ambivalence it displays toward the future. It's hard to think of any society in human history that has made so much noise about the future, or used images and ideas of the future so relentlessly as rhetorical ammunition in its political and cultural controversies. In all the tumult and shouting about alternative tomorrows, though, one rarely encounters the sense that the future might be different from the present in any way that genuinely matters.

That wasn't always the case. As recently as the 1970s, imaginary tomorrows that went zooming off at right angles to the conventional wisdom were commonplace. In the decades since then, however, a curious sort of conformism has squeezed the collective imagination of our era into an increasingly narrow rut. Take any randomly chosen portrayal of the future nowadays, and rather more often than not, you'll find two and only two differences from the present: on the one hand, technology extends its current trajectory straight out to the horizon; on the other, the attitudes and customs of this or that affluent group in today's industrial societies become more generally accepted. Nothing else is allowed to change.

So narrow a view of the future isn't limited to the vague mumblings of politicians and pundits, or for that matter such bargain-basement pop culture phenomena as the *Star Trek* franchise. It's pervasive even in science fiction, which used to be far more open to alternative tomorrows. I'm thinking here, among other examples, of Neal Stephenson's otherwise intriguing 2008 novel *Anathem*, which is set on an alternate Earth some 3400 years after the equivalent of our time.

Mind you, Stephenson is better at pushing the boundaries than most. His alternate world features an intriguing scientific monasticism that invites comparison with the scholarly monasticism of Hermann Hesse's *The Glass Bead Game*, to the extent that I've wondered more than once if some of Stephenson's inspiration might have come from the subtle ambiguities of Hesse's novel. Yet the inhabitants of his alternate world, living in the equivalent of 5400 AD, wear t-shirts, eat energy bars, and text each other and access the internet on what, despite a change in name, are pretty obviously iPhones. Worse, they talk, think, and act in ways indistinguishable from their t-shirt-wearing, energy-bar-ingesting, iPhone-using equivalents in 2016.

It's no exaggeration to say that Stephenson could have taken his entire story—plot, characters, dialogue, and all—and set it in an upscale San Francisco neighborhood today without the least sense of incongruity. It's very much as though an ancient Roman science fiction writer penned an adventure set in the twentieth century, in which everyone still wore togas, ate stuffed dormice, wrote on wax tablets, and had the same interests, attitudes, and habits as intellectuals at the court of Augustus Caesar—as though the future had no other options to draw on.

At that, as already noted, Stephenson's vision went further than most. A great deal of science fiction these days is still stuck rehashing the shopworn trope of Man's Future in Space, ringing changes on a handful of imagined futures that were already old hat in the 1960s. Year after year, the technologies become more elaborate but the underlying ideas become more tightly focused on the concerns of the present moment, and tales that span entire universes fail to conjure up the rush of strangeness and wonder that authors once achieved with a trip to the Moon.

I submit that something has gone far astray here. It's the same thing that leads Pentagon officials to publish projections of the military environment in 2035 based on the assumption that the only significant change between then and now will be the arrival of new technologies, and convinces affluent liberals that their carbon-intensive lifestyles don't conflict with their environmentalist beliefs in any way that really matters. A great many people these days have lost track of the fact that the future really can be different from the present.

\* \* \*

There's a tremendous irony here, in that modern industrial society belongs to the minority of societies that pays attention to the reality of historical change. Far more common among human cultures is the belief that the true order of things was set forth once and for all at some point in the past, and any departure from that true order is an error waiting for correction. That's very widespread among those peoples sufficiently comfortable with their environments that they don't need to insert complex technological suites between themselves and the natural world—yes, that's pronounced "primitive societies" in our tribal jargon—but it's not only found there. Ancient Egypt and classical Japan, among many other complex literate civilizations, revered narratives that explained how the principles of right living were set out at the beginning of time.

Among the minority of human cultures that have seen history as a dynamic process, rather than a continual reaching back to the First Time, far and away the most common vision of time is cyclic rather than linear. From within the traditional Hindu or the classic Maya worldview, for instance. the future is the past; all things have happened before and will happen again, and while historical change takes place, there's nothing genuinely new about it. That's one of many reasons why the people who pinned their hopes of Utopia, apocalypse, or some fusion of the two on a nonexistent Mayan prophecy four years ago were barking up the wrong stump. The classic Mayan vision of time has no room for such things, since in that worldview, the rollover of the thirteenth baktun has happened and will happen countless times in the spinning circles of eternity.

It's interesting to speculate on why it was that tribal peoples in one corner of the long peninsula stuck on the western end of Asia—yes, that would be Europe—broke away from those standard options and began to think about time as a straight line. The curious thing is that while the straight lines of history that dominate the imagination of our time lead ever upwards, the oldest known version pointed the other way. We know that because a bitter old man named Hesiod, who lived on a hardscrabble farm in Boeotia during the last century or so of the Greek dark ages, put the tale into one of the oldest surviving works of Greek literature.

There had been a golden age in the past, Hesiod tells us, when people lived without labor and suffering, and the gods walked among men. There had been a silver age of harmless folly after that, and then a bronze age of war. Then had come the time of heroes, and finally the iron age of suffering and destitution, in which Hesiod believed he lived—and not without good reason. Eventually infants would be born with their hair already gray, and then Zeus would send the last wretched remnants of humanity tumbling down into darkness and silence forever.

Christianity, Islam, and a baker's dozen or so of their mostly forgotten rivals rebelled against that vision without actually changing it. Their solution to the terrible vision of a world in permanent decline involved the prophecy of a *deus ex machina* at the end of the tale, to lift up the faithful remnant to inscrutable heights. This was only after the scientific revolution of the seventeenth century, and the first stirrings of the industrial revolution of the eighteenth, to give rise to the modern vision of history as a process of perpetual improvement, a vast journey up from the darkness and squalor of the prehistoric past to the luminous possibilities of an imagined future.

For a good long time, too, "imagined" was the operative world. Once the idea of progress found its initial foothold among eighteenth-century intellectuals, imagining the future that progress would bring became a growth industry. The resulting images extended from the highly practical to the highly absurd—I'm thinking here especially of Charles Fourier, who predicted (and apparently believed) that when humanity passed beyond Civilization to the supreme state of Harmony, the oceans would turn to lemonade and wars between communities would be replaced by competitive orgies—but the most popular visions provided anchors for the hopes of millions.

Not so long ago, this was still true. The question I want to raise is why that was replaced with the present habit of thinking of the future as just like the present, only a little more so. I have an answer to propose, too: The reason so few people spend their time imagining a future of perpetual progress is that so few people actually believe in it any more.

* * *

Gregory Bateson, one of the twentieth century's most versatile intellects, pointed out many years ago the role of double-binds in the origins of schizophrenia. The pattern he traced out works like this. Imagine a child growing up in a family in which there's one set of overt, verbally expressed rules for behavior, and another, covert set of rules that contradict the first. If the child breaks the overt rules by obeying the covert ones, he gets a negative verbal response, but a covert emotional reward; if the child breaks the covert rules by obeying the overt ones, he gets punished on some other pretext. If the child attempts to bring the contradiction out into the open, finally, he gets a reaction intended to terrify him into never mentioning the matter again.

It's the last element, Bateson found, that makes the double-bind so lethal. If the child can talk to one other person who understands what's happening, and can thereby get some confirmation of the fact that there really is something profoundly tangled going on, the double-bind breaks down and the child can shrug and say, "I guess mom and dad are just kind of crazy." It's when the child has no such option—when he has to confront an apparently crazy pattern of behavior without any way of knowing whether the craziness is in his family or in himself—that he's likely to give up on reality altogether, and take refuge in madness.

Bateson's theory of the double-bind has been on my mind of late, because much the same pattern has taken shape in modern industrial society in relation to technological progress. The overt, verbally expressed rules concerning progress can be summed up in a straightforward way as "whatever's newer is by definition better." Listen to media pundits and the chattering classes generally, and you can count on hearing words like "innovative," "advanced," "progressive," and their countless equivalents constantly being deployed as synonyms for "good."

The problem with this habit is that rather more often than not these days, the innovative, the advanced, the progressive, and so on are no longer good in any sense that matters. Calvin Trillin got a nervous general laugh recently with an essay suggesting that the most frightening word in the English language is "upgrade." Less humorous and more pervasive are the innovative pharmaceuticals and medical treatments that have side effects worse than the conditions they are supposed to treat, the advanced technologies that never quite do what they're supposed to do, the progressive political and economic policies that routinely hurt far more people than they help. Every time a new round of products hits the shelves labeled "new and improved," the odds go up that if they're actually new, they won't have been improved.

It's reached the point that the automatic equation of progress with improvement is starting to fray even in public. Recent discussions of driverless trucks and artificial intelligence in the media have admitted up front that these technologies, once they reach the market, will cause tens of millions of people to lose their jobs—this at a time when a soaring number of people across the industrial world have already been pushed out of the workforce with next to no provision for their survival, and the reaction has sparked a populist backlash that already has political establishments running for cover. The Brexit vote, the election of Donald Trump, and the recent Italian referendum are straws in the wind; if the mindless pursuit of progress continues on its present track, as I expect, that wind will likely become a hurricane.

The core of the crisis of our time is that technological progress, which was once industrial society's principal source of solutions, has become its principal source of problems. It's not at all hard to see why this should be so. The law of diminishing returns applies just as forcefully to technological innovation as it does to so many other things; as time goes on, on average, each new generation of technology requires more resources, produces more waste, and yields fewer benefits than the ones that came before it. Keep going, and you inevitably get to the point at which the burdens of each new generation of technology outweigh the benefits. A case could be made that industrial society passed that point some years ago.

The difficulty here is that until recently, you couldn't mention this in public—not without fielding much the same sort of response a child in a dysfunctional family gets if he tries to bring up the double-bind that's literally driving him insane. As it becomes increasingly common to challenge the equation of progress with improvement, a good many of us may finally be able to have the conversations that let us know that there really is something profoundly tangled going on, and get to the point of shrugging and saying, "I guess our society is kind of crazy."

\* \* \*

Our society prides itself on its sense of deep time—its slowly earned recognition of the sheer shattering immensity of the prehuman past. The pride's not misplaced, but it's one-sided. A vast number of people today who think they're comfortable with the abysses of the past turn pale and talk about something else when it comes time to look out on the abysses of the future.

As I've suggested, that's largely driven by the dawning recognition that the future is not going to be anything like the grand upward journey to the stars we thought we were going to get. The thinner the rhetoric of progress has become, and the more obvious it is that the future ahead of us isn't going to fulfill the promises loaded upon it, the more two-dimensional the collective image of the future has become. At this point it's simply a placeholder, a cheery and increasingly flimsy image meant to give people something to look at, so they don't have to notice the future that's actually looming up in front of us.

Comforting though that placeholder is, I don't think it's wise, or for that matter psychologically healthy, to keep staring at it. To the contrary, it's past time to take down the painted screen that shows people like us living lives like ours in a future that's still stocked with its familiar quota of t-shirts, energy bars, iPhones, and contemporary chatter, hang it somewhere else as a memento of a departing age, and lift our eyes toward the deep future.

The truism that we can't actually know anything about the future, like most thought stoppers of the same kind, doesn't happen to be true. Just as an astronomer can observe a newly discovered exoplanet and, after a few observations, predict where it's going to be found a day, a week, or a thousand years later, enough is known about the behavior of civilizations, species, and planets to be able to predict with some certainty the trend of events in the deep future.

Among the things that aren't subject to doubt are certain impossibilities. We're not going to colonize deep space or the other worlds in the solar system, for example, because the Earth is the only rocky planet this side of Proxima Centauri with a magnetic field strong enough to ward off the streams of hard radiation pouring off the vast unshielded fusion reactor 93 million miles away from us. Space scientists have known about this for decades, and have been trying with an increasing sense of panic to find some way around it, without result; human beings simply didn't evolve in a high-radiation environment like space, and it's not a suitable habitat for us.

The grandiose mythic vision of humanity's future in space, in other words, is going to have to be folded up and put away in whatever museum awaits our society's dead dreams. It's popular these days to insist that human beings can accomplish anything they can imagine, but this is another truism that doesn't happen to be true; anyone who wants to make that claim, it seems to me, is obliged to present the world with a working perpetual motion machine. Some things just aren't physically possible; some aren't practically workable; some aren't economically viable—and those are constraints that our species is going to have to learn to live with for the rest of whatever time span we have ahead of us.

Then there are the constraints that follow from the choices we've already made. Our immediate descendants, for example, are going to inherit a planet stripped of nearly all its fossil fuels and most of its nonrenewable resources, and wracked by a wildly unstable climate. Until the coming thermal maximum peaks and levels off, maybe five centuries from now, we can expect wild swings in rainfall and temperature over most of the planet, and sudden upward surges in sea level—when ice caps break up, as glaciologists have learned in recent decades, much of the melting takes place in massive meltwater pulses that can send sea level up five meters or more in a decade or two. It's going to be a very rough half millennium, and I don't imagine it will be any consolation to the survivors to reflect on the fact that we did it to ourselves.

On the far side of the era of climatic chaos, to judge by the evidence from previous greenhouse events and global temperature spikes, the climate will stabilize again, following patterns sharply different from the ones that shape it today. Plants will recover fastest, as they always do after extinction crises, sprouting from buried seeds and spreading in the usual ways from sheltered refugia. The generalist animal species that get through the bottleneck of the current extinction crisis—rats, cats, feral pigs, crows, and many others—will begin expanding into new ecological niches, launching a burst of speciation that will populate the biosphere with a new fauna.

* * *

And human beings? We're also a generalist species, and a highly adaptable one. Even before the industrial revolution, humans spread to every continent except Antarctica, adjusting without too much difficulty to environments as varied as the Arctic tundra, the Sahara desert, the great inland steppes and prairies of the Old and New World, and the island chains of the Pacific. That said, we have a bottleneck to get through, too, and the global population at the bottom of the coming decline will thus likely be only a few per cent of current figures.

Beyond that lies territory that's rarely been explored, even in the pages of science fiction. I've suggested elsewhere that modern industrial society will likely turn out to be merely the first, not to mention the most primitive and wasteful, of a kind of human ecology we can call *technic societies*—that is to say, societies that get a majority of their energy supply from sources other than human and animal muscle. The technic societies of the deep future won't have fossil fuels to draw on, but they will have renewable energy resources: sun, wind, water, biomass, and perhaps others that we haven't thought of yet. They won't have the nonrenewable raw materials we waste so freely, except to the extent that they can extract them for a while from our landfills and ruins, but they will have renewable materials in abundance. The technologies they create using these resources will not be like ours, and will very likely be put to uses we can't even imagine today.

The technic societies of the future will likely be more geographically restricted than today's industrial society. Even today there are regions of the planet that are arguably better suited for hunting and gathering, for nomadic herding, and for village agriculture than they are for the kinds of settlement and economy that we've imposed on them. In the deep future, that's likely to be even more true—as true, for example, as it was back at the beginning of the eighteenth century, when fossil fuels still provided a negligible share of the world's energy. In human terms, the Earth will be a bigger planet than it is today, far bigger and more diverse than the galactic monocultures so often portrayed by today's science fiction authors.

The technic societies of the deep future, furthermore, will be no more eternal than our society is turning out to be. Some of them, for that matter, may manage to mess up the planetary biosphere the way we've done, and pay something like the same dire cost, though I suspect that our fate will be discussed in hushed tones for millennia to come, and that this may provide a certain degree of immunization against a repeat. Other societies will rise and fall according to the normal life cycle of civilizations, and to judge by the evidence of history, each of those future societies will be as different from one another as they are from us, exploring realms of human possibility that, again, we can't even imagine today.

Though we're not going to the stars, in other words, our species will nonetheless be journeying to worlds stranger than any of our dreams. Instead of traveling through space, humanity has launched itself on a journey through time at the dizzying speed of sixty seconds every minute, and the destinations ahead will more than likely be entirely free of t-shirts, energy bars, iPhones, or the increasingly dreary and dysfunctional conventional wisdom of our age. To me, at least, that's an enticing prospect; while none of us can expect to see the worlds of deep time that await our species, we are at least free to dream—and perhaps even to take steps to see that as many of the useful legacies of our time make it through the impending crises of our age to the waiting hands of the deep future.

# *INDEX*

acolyte, 89. *See also* hidden church of Golden Dawn
active imagination, 112
Adeptus Exemptus, 90–94. *See also* hidden church of Golden Dawn
Adeptus Major, 90. *See also* hidden church of Golden Dawn
aeonic cycles, theory of, 150. *See also* magic and end of history
Age of Exuberance, 136, 142, 148. *See also* magic and end of history
Alley, R. B., 222
alternative spiritual traditions, 61
amythia, 141. *See also* magic and end of history
anabolic cycle, 188–191. *See also* civilization collapse
ancient Maya, 201
Ancient Order of Druids (AOD), 22–23
Blake, W., 24–25
Ancient Order of Druids in America (AODA), vii, 61, 87. *See also* Druids, ancient
consecration, 87
grove, 63
initiation rituals, 63
Sphere of Protection, 64–65
Anderson, A. O., 35
Anderson, M. O., 35
Anglo-American conservatism, 172
Anthropocene, 236. *See also* Post-Axial Age
anthropocentrism, 216–217, 219–220. *See also* literary and cultural dimensions of approaching age of decline
anthropogenic climate change, 220–221
anthropogenic global warming, 222
Anthropos quaternio, 66–67. *See also* fourth quaternion
anti-Semitism, 170
AOD. *See* Ancient Order of Druids

Aphrodite, 79
apocalypse, 205
apocalyptic beliefs, 147. *See also* magic and end of history
apocalyptic environmentalism, 217–218, 219. *See also* environmental activism
Arreguin-Toft, I., 158
artificial spirits, 110–111. *See also* place of mingled powers
astronomical theory of religion, 10
asymmetric tactical shock, 153, 158
   Drews's analysis of Bronze Age catastrophe, 154–157, 158
   end of bronze age, 153, 154–157
   new asymmetric tactics, 156
   understanding, 158–162
authenticity, 45
Axial Age, 238. *See also* Post-Axial Age
   features of, 240
   literacy and, 241–244
   phenomena of, 244
   principal religious product of, 246
   vision of, 249

Bagley, R. W., 49
*Barddas* myth, 33–35. *See also* myth
Bardic
   creation myth, 46
   literature, 49
Bardic alphabet. *See* Coelbren of the Bards
Bardon, F., 52
Bateson, G., 263
Bateson's theory of double-bind, 263. *See also* future portrayal
Beck, M. G., 194
beliefs, 245
Betancourt, P., 156
Billington, R. A., 188
binaries, 133
Birken, L., 173
bishop, 90–94. *See also* hidden church of Golden Dawn
Blake, W., 19
   Ancient Order of Druids, 24–25
   as Chosen Chief of Druid order, 20
   Druidism, 25, 29
   Druids and oaks, 26
   The Four Zoas, 29
Bonwick, J., 5
Bradley, R., 194
Bronze Age
   catastrophe, 154–157, 158
   end of, 153, 154–157
Burke, E., 172
Bury, J. B., 193

Calder, G., 14
capital, 186. *See also* civilization collapse
Carson, R., 217
catabolic collapse, 192. *See also* civilization collapse
   model of, 195
   theory of, 183
Catton, W., 142, 143
Catton, W. R., Jr., 185
Cherokee script, 44
Christian church, holy orders of, 87. *See also* hidden church of Golden Dawn
Christianity, 7, 140. *See also* hidden church of Golden Dawn
   Christian Mass, 12
   connection with zodiac signs, 80
   fundamentalism, 146
   holy orders of church, 87
   Jesus's birthplace and ritual, 80–81
   Morgan, O., 78
   myth and history, 81–82
   mythic narratives, 80
   and Paganism, 75
   paradise and Original Sin, 145
   prayers, 149
   reconnecting with origins, 82–83
   in religious literature, 12
   as solar myth, 11
civilization, 147–149, 239, 251. *See also* magic and end of history; Post-Axial Age
civilization collapse, 183. *See also* industrial society

anabolic cycle, 188–191
apocalypse, 205
capital, 186
catabolic collapse, 183, 192
 of complex human societies, 183
 core elements of human society, 186–191
 depletion crisis end of spectrum, 193
 Early and Late Classic periods, 193
 general theory of collapse, 184
 human ecology of collapse, 186–191
 human societies and nonhuman species, 195
 Lowland Classic Maya collapse, 193
 maintenance crisis, 190, 191
 Maya collapse, 201
 model of catabolic collapse, 195
 mystical claims, 184
 process of contraction, 189
 production, 187
 resource depletion, 188
 resources, 186
 rise and fall of civilization, 200
 rolling collapse, 201
 as succession process, 194–196
 testing the model, 191–194
 timescales of, 185
 waste, 186
 western Roman empire, 185, 192, 195–196
Clark, C., 187, 188
Cleland, J., 12
cleric, 88. *See also* hidden church of Golden Dawn
Coelbren, 44
 according to Iolo's account, 46
 Bardic creation myth, 46
 Bardic literature, 49
 practicalities of, 49–51
 symbolism of, 51–57
 traditional history of, 45–48
 uses of, 57–59
Coelbren of the Bards, 43
 A, 52

Abcedilros, 47
B, 54
C, 54
D, 54
E, 53
ebill, 49
Ff, 56
G, 55
I, 53
L, 55
M, 55
Mabcednilros, 47
N, 55–56
O, 53–54
Ogham letters of medieval Irish tradition, 58
P, 56
peithynen, 50
R, 56–57
S, 57
sound symbolism, 52
T, 57
Williams, E., 43
communication, linguistic, 243
communist parties, 169, 174
confraternities, 98–99
conjuring spirits, 112
conservatives, 168, 172
Constantine, M.-A., 32, 35, 43
contemporary industrial society, 227, 259. *See also* future portrayal
convergent problems, 248
Corbin, H., 112
corvin technologies, 231
Cowgill, G., 184
craftsman's literacy, 242, 243. *See also* Post-Axial Age
Crowley, A., 15, 150

Darmestetter, J., 36
daughter myths, 39. *See also* myth
Davies, E., 5
deacon/Adeptus Minor, 90. *See also* hidden church of Golden Dawn

272   INDEX

Decolonizing the Revolutionary Imagination, 129, 135
deep time, 215
　sense of, 265
defector syndrome, 137
deindustrial societies of future, 210–211. *See also* industrial society
deities, 107–108. *See also* place of mingled powers
Demeter, 79
demigods, 80
de Mille, R. W., 45
de Saussure, F., 52
Di Cosmo, N., 191
dictatorship, 170. *See also* fascism
divergent problems, 248
doomsday prophecy, 262. *See also* future portrayal
doorkeeper, 89. *See also* hidden church of Golden Dawn
Dreamtime, 140. *See also* magic and end of history
Drews, R., 153. *See also* end of bronze age
Druidical Society of Anglesey, 22
Druidism, 25
　The Four Zoas, 29
Druid movement, modern, 77
Druid Revival, 3, 19. *See also* Morgan, O.
　ancient Druids, 4
　Christianity and ancient Druids, 7
　Coelbren of the Bards, 57–58
　Davies, E., 5
　eighteenth-century antiquarians, 14
　feminine principle, 6
　gorseddau, 4
　gorsedd of Pontypridd, 4–5
　literature, 12
　magnum opus of Pontypridd Druidism, 5
　phallic religion in, 3
　to religious truths, 28–29
　symbolism, 58
　Williams, E., 23–24, 31
Druidry
　Ancient Order of Druids, 22–23
　Druidical Society of Anglesey, 22
　Stukeley's Dragon Temple, 27
　tradition, 27–28
　world of early modern, 20
Druids
　ancient Druids, 20–21
　cultural property, 22
　Greek or Roman account of, 21
　and oaks, 26
　stereotypes, 22
　Stukeley, W., 22
Druids, ancient, 4, 20–21. *See also* Ancient Order of Druids in America
　Ancient Order of Druids, 22–23
　Togodubeline, 23
Druid writers, 32
dualism, 219
Dudley Do-Right, 129–132
Duncan, R., 203

Early and Late Classic periods, 193. *See also* civilization collapse
Earth's climate, 222
Earth's future, 227
　corvin technologies, 231
　Earth's second intelligent species, 231
　hundred thousand years from now, 230
　hundred years from now, 228–229
　million years from now, 230
　one billion years from now, 232–233
　one hundred million years from now, 231–232
　Sea of Tranquility, 232
　ten billion years from now, 233–234
　ten million years from now, 230–231
　ten thousand years from now, 229
　ten years from now, 228
　thousand years from now, 229
ebill, 49
ecological relationships, 195

ecology, 224
Edwards, S. J. A., 156
ego, 65
Egypt, 157. *See also* end of bronze age
Einigan myth, 38. *See also* myth
Eliot, T. S., 75, 214
Elvin, M., 185, 192
end of bronze age, 153, 154–157. *See also* asymmetric tactical shock
    core elements, 159
    eastern Mediterranean at, 154
    Egypt, 157
    empires, 154
    era of mass raids, 157
    new asymmetric tactics, 156
    Sea Peoples, 156, 158, 160
    swarming attacks, 156
    war chariot, 155, 161
    weapons, 156
environmental activism, 217. *See also* literary and cultural dimensions of approaching age of decline
    apocalyptic environmentalism, 217–218, 219
    recreational environmentalism, 217, 218
    sentimental environmentalism, 217, 218–219
environmental movement, 217. *See also* literary and cultural dimensions of approaching age of decline
era of mass raids, 157. *See also* end of bronze age
ethnographic scripts, 44–45
exorcist, 89. *See also* hidden church of Golden Dawn
extinction crises, 266–267. *See also* future portrayal

fascism, 165
    avant-garde intellectuals, 175
    Benito Mussolini, 167
    common features of fascist movements, 171
    conservatism, 172–173
    debasement of political language, 166
    etymology, 167
    Fascist Party, 167
    Fascist regime in Italy, 167
    fascist rejected features, 171
    fascists and conservatives, 173
    New Order, 173
    Newspeak, 166
    political conflict, 176–180
    political killings, 167
    snarl word, 166, 170
    totalitarian political system, 171
Fascist Party, 167
Fascist regime in Italy, 167
feminine principle, 6
Fortune, D., 76, 109, 150
fossil fuels, 202, 224
fourth quaternion, 61
    Anthropos quaternio, 66–67
    AODA grove, 63
    AODA initiation rituals, 63
    ego, 65
    four quaternios, 65–70
    goal of Jungian therapy, 66
    Juliet Ashley and Carl Jung, 62–64
    Jungian symbolism in sphere of protection, 61–62
    Lapis quaternion, 70, 71
    masonic lodge, 63
    Paradise quaternion, 68–69
    psyche, 65
    Shadow ouaternio, 67–68
    Sphere of Protection, 64–65, 70–72
    the Self, 65
Fox, M., 219
Frankenstein effect, 111
Frazer, J., 79
Freemasonry, 99
Freier, N., 158
Fuchs, M., 156
Fukuyama, F., 126
future portrayal, 259
    Bateson, G., 263

Bateson's theory of double-bind, 263
contemporary industrial society, 259
doomsday prophecy, 262
after extinction crises, 266–267
generalist species, 266–267
history and culture, 261
humanity's future in space, 265–266
imaginary tomorrows, 259
journey through time, 268
narrow view of future, 260
primitive societies, 261
sense of deep time, 265
Stephenson's vision, 260–261
technic societies, 267–268
technological progress as problems, 264
future, visions of, 228

Gates, H., 191
generalist species, 266–267. *See also* future portrayal
Gever, J., 185
giant Ymir, 36. *See also* myth
Gibbon, E., 185
Gleason, W., 51
*Globalize Liberation*, 119
  Age of Exuberance, 136
  binaries, ternaries, and shifting levels, 132–135
  Decolonizing the Revolutionary Imagination, 129, 135
  defector syndrome, 137
  Dudley Do-Right, 129–132
  history, 126
  learning new magics, 135–138
  magic, 120–121
  open letter to activist community, 119–121
  oppression of women, 123
  patriarchy, 122
  pervasive problem in politics, 121
  politics of reality, 136
  privilege, 123

spell of corporate triumphalism, 124–129
spell of reification, 121–124
spell of rescue, 129–132
spells, 121
white supremacy, 122
Zapatista quest, 136
Gödel, K., 249
God of the gaps argument, 241
gods or goddesses of ancient Egypt, 130
Golden Dawn, 85. *See also* hidden church of Golden Dawn
rituals, 106
Yeats, W. B., 150
*Golden Legend* of Jacobus de Voragine, 38. *See also* myth
gorsedd, 4
  of Pontypridd, 4–5
grades of Gold-und Rosenkreutz, 86. *See also* hidden church of Golden Dawn
Grant, M., 185, 192
Greek religion, 79
Greer, J. M., vii–viii, 43, 115, 138, 253
  finding spiritual home, 77
Gregory, T. E., 253
groupminds, 109–110. *See also* place of mingled powers
Gwrn (Urn), 6

Harris, W. V., 35, 242
Haswell, M., 187, 188
Hawkes, J., 4
Hayakawa, S. I., 166
Hegel, G. W. F., 238
Hegel theory of history, 238. *See also* Post-Axial Age
Heinberg, R., 186, 221
Heracles, 80
Hermetic doctrine of macrocosm and microcosm, 101. *See also* place of mingled powers
hidden church of Golden Dawn, 85
  acolyte/Philosophus, 89

bishop/Adeptus Exemptus, 90–94
cleric/neophyte, 88
deacon/Adeptus Minor, 90
doorkeeper/Zelator, 89
exorcist/Practicus, 89
grades of Gold-und Rosenkreutz, 86
holy orders of Christian church, 87
major orders/inner order grades, 89–90
minor orders/outer order grades, 88
priest/Adeptus Major, 90
reader/Theoricus, 89
subdeacon/Portal, 90
Hinton, L., 52
history, 126. *See also* future portrayal
and culture, 238, 261
Hegel theory of, 238
of logic, 249
Hitler, A., 168. *See also* fascism
political vocabulary, 173
holy orders of Christian church, 87. *See also* hidden church of Golden Dawn
Ho, P.-T., 191
Hubbert Curve, 202
Hubbert, M. K., 202
Hughes, J. D., 185
human ecology of collapse, 186–191. *See also* civilization collapse
humanity's future in space, 265–266. *See also* future portrayal
humanity's role in climate change, 220
human society. *See also* civilization collapse
core elements, 186–191
and nonhuman species, 195
Hurle, H., 22

imaginary tomorrows, 259. *See also* future portrayal
Indo-European tradition myth, 35–38. *See also* myth
industrial society, 199. *See also* civilization collapse

ancient Maya, 201
apocalypse, 205
catastrophes, 205–206
contemporary, 227
course of decline, 206–207
decline and deindustrial future, 199–200
deindustrial societies of future, 210–211
fossil fuels, 202
historical parallels, 200–202
Hubbert Curve, 202
Olduvai theory, 202–203
organic agriculture, 210
power of myth, 203–206
progress and industrialization, 204
prosthetic society, 208
renewable energy sources, 202
rise and fall of civilizations, 200
rolling collapse, 201
scientific treatises, 209
steps to be taken, 207–211
traditional folk mythologies, 228
inhumanism, 213–217. *See also* literary and cultural dimensions of approaching age of decline
inner order grades, 89–90. *See also* hidden church of Golden Dawn
intelligent species, Earth's second, 231
investment vehicles, 200
Ioan Culianu, 120
Iolo Morganwg. *See* Williams, E.

Jaspers, K., 237–238, 239, 242, 244. *See also* Post-Axial Age
Jeffers, R., 213. *See also* literary and cultural dimensions of approaching age of decline
falling years, 225
inhumanism", 214–217
quest for foundations, 214
Jenkins, G. H., 32, 43
Jones, A. H. M., 192
Jones, V., 121

Jung, C., 62, 65. *See also* fourth quaternion
active imagination, 112
Anthropos quaternio, 66–67
Lapis quaternion, 70, 71
Paradise quaternion, 68–69
Shadow ouaternio, 67–68
Sphere of Protection, 64–65, 70–72
Jungian therapy, 66

Kaufman, R., 185
Knight, R. P., 8, 13. *See also* phallic religion
Kotschar, V. F., 194
Kurzweil, R., 148

Lamy, P., 204
Lang, A., 156
Lao Tsu, 245
Lapis quaternion, 70, 71. *See also* fourth quaternion
Laqueur, W., 175
Layton, B., 113
Leach, E. R., 191
Leadbeater, C. W., 88
Leckie, C., 161
Lévi, É., 100
liberal parties, 168
Lincoln, B., 36, 39
Lind, W. S., 155, 162
linguistic communication, 243
literary and cultural dimensions of approaching age of decline, 213
 anthropocentrism, 216–217, 219–220
 anthropogenic climate change, 220–221
 anthropogenic global warming, 222
 apocalyptic environmentalism, 217–218, 219
 core of inhumanism, 215
 deep time, 215
 dualism, 219
 environmental activism, 217–219
 environmental movement, 217
 fossil fuels, 224
 function of apocalyptic myth, 218
 inhumanism, 214
 Jeffers, R., 213
 Jeffers's inhumanism, 213–217
 misanthropy, 222–223
 peak oil, 221
 recreational environmentalism, 217, 218
 sentimental environmentalism, 217, 218–219
Logos, 244–247. *See also* Post-Axial Age
Lomer, G., 52
Lowe, J. W. G., 193
Lowland Classic Maya collapse, 193. *See also* civilization collapse

magic, 97, 120, 150. *See also* Globalize Liberation
 Ioan Culianu, 120
 modern, 97
 spells, 121
 storytellers, 120
magical lodge, 98–100. *See also* place of mingled powers
 basic structure, 103–104
 confraternities, 98–99
 historical origins of, 98
 inner lodge, 105–106
 non-magical lodge, 104
 outer lodge, 102–105
 spiritual beings in, 97–98
magical mesocosm, 100–102. *See also* place of mingled powers
magical narratives of time, 151. *See also* magic and end of history
magical robots, 110
magic and end of history, 139
 Age of Exuberance, 142, 148
 amythia, 141
 apocalyptic beliefs, 147
 civilizations, 147–149
 competing myths of progress and apocalypse, 145–149
 Dreamtime, 140
 inquiry into shape of time, 139

magical narratives of time, 151
myth of apocalypse, 147
myth of progress, 145
original paradise, 145–146
partnership society, 146
pop theology, 148
prayers, 149
radical movements, 145–146
theory of aeonic cycles, 150
view of future, 150
maintenance crisis, 190, 191
major orders, 89–90. *See also* hidden church of Golden Dawn
mandala symbolism, 63
Mannus, 39. *See also* myth
Marxism, 174
masonic lodge, 63
mass literacy, 242. *See also* Post-Axial Age
McPherson, J., 32
Meadows, D. H., 186
Meadows, D. L., 186
metanarrative of progress, 239
metaphysical symbolism, 9–10
Michaelson, D. R., 194
minor orders, 88. *See also* hidden church of Golden Dawn
misanthropy, 222–223
modern Druid movement, 77
modern magic, 97
Morgan, O., 4, 5, 34, 78. *See also* Druid Revival
  about Christianity, 7
  Druid philosophy and theology, 78
  masculine and feminine principles of nature, 6
  Pagan nature worship, 13
  phallic Druidism, 7–8, 13–14
  phallic theology, 6–7
  planet-god Saturn, 6
  primal divinities of system, 7
  solar and phallic theories of religion, 11–12
  solar-phallic Druidry, 13
  work and influence, 15–16
Mussolini, B., 167. *See also* fascism

myth, 31, 203, 240. *See also* magic and end of history
  of apocalypse, 147, 218
  in Babylonia, 36
  in *Barddas*, 33–35
  daughter, 39
  of Einigan, 38
  giant Ymir, 36
  *Golden Legend* of Jacobus de Voragine, 38
  in Indo-European tradition, 35–38
  Mannus and Yemos, 39
  mythological bricolage, 38
  mythological parallels, 37
  in non-Indo-European cultures, 36
  Oinogenos, 35
  origins of, 32–33
  origins of origin myth, 38–41
  power of, 203–206
  of progress, 145
  progressivist, 204
  repeating mythic pattern, 36
  separativist, 204
  *Shah-namah* of Firdausi, 36
  Vendidad, 36
  Williams, E., 31, 39, 40
  Yama, 36
mythic discourse, 240
mythological bricolage, 38. *See also* myth
mythological parallels, 37
mythology, 243

national bolshevist parties, 169
National Museum of Wales, 44
National Progressive American Peoples Party (NPAPP), 176
national socialism, 168, 169
National Socialist German Workers Party, 169, 170
  financing, 173
national socialist party, 168, 169
Nazi, 168. *See also* fascism
neophyte, 88. *See also* hidden church of Golden Dawn
New Order, 173. *See also* fascism

Newspeak, 166
Nichols, J., 52
Nichols, R., 15, 20
Nietzsche, F., 254
Nolte, E., 170–171
non-magical lodge, 104. *See also* place of mingled powers
NPAPP. *See* National Progressive American Peoples Party

OBOD. *See* Order of Bards, Ovates and Druids
O'Brien, H., 12
Odd Fellows, 100
Odum, E., 194, 195
Ogham letters of medieval Irish tradition, 58
Ohala, J. J., 52
Oinogenes. *See* Oinogenos
Oinogenos, 35
old Paganism, 83
Olduvai theory, 202–203. *See also* industrial society
Orchard, A., 36
Orden des Gold-und Rosenkreutz, 85
Order of Bards, Ovates and Druids (OBOD), 3
    fortieth anniversary of founding of, 3
organic agriculture, 210
original paradise, 145–146. *See also* magic and end of history
Orwell, G., 166
Ossianic poems, 32–33
Otpor movement, 123, 132
outer order grades, 88. *See also* hidden church of Golden Dawn

Pagan, 79
Paganism, 75, 246
    old, 83
Pagan nature worship, 13
Pan, 79
Paradise quaternion, 68–69. *See also* fourth quaternion
Parsons, J. A., 185

partnership society, 146. *See also* magic and end of history
patriarchy, 122
peak oil, 221
peithynen, 50
phallic Druidism, 7–8. *See also* Druid Revival; Morgan, O.
phallic religion, 8
    ancient and Eastern erotic art, 10
    ancient Greece and modern India, 9
    astronomical theory of religion, 10
    Christianity, 12
    Knight, R. P., 8, 9
    metaphysical symbolism, 9–10
Philosophus, 89. *See also* hidden church of Golden Dawn
philosophy, 235–238, 243, 247. *See also* Post-Axial Age
    inability, 248
    meaning of, 249–252
    Presocratic Greek, 245
Piggott, S., 14
place of mingled powers, 97
    artificial spirits, 110–111
    deities, 107–108
    Freemasonry, 99
    groupminds, 109–110
    Hermetic doctrine of macrocosm and microcosm, 101
    inner lodge, 105–106
    interacting with spiritual beings, 111–112
    macrocosm and microcosm, 102
    magical lodge, 98–100
    magical mesocosm, 100–102
    modern magic, 97
    outer lodge, 102–105
    powers, 108–109
    practical example, 112–116
    rituals, 106
    spiritual beings, 106–107
    spiritual beings in magical lodge, 97–98
planet-god Saturn, 6
Pliocene epoch, 222
Plummer, J. P., 94

Polanyi, M., 248
political killings, 167
Ponting, C., 185, 200, 251
pop theology, 148. *See also* magic and end of history
popular culture "godforms", 130
Poseidon, 79
Post-Axial Age, 235, 252–257
  Anthropocene epoch, 236
  Axial Age, 238
  beliefs, 245
  civilization, 239
  convergent problems, 248
  craftsman's literacy, 242, 243
  divergent problems, 248
  end of dream, 247–249
  features of Axial Age, 240
  Hegel theory of history, 238
  hinge of history, 238–241
  history and culture, 238
  history of logic, 249
  linguistic communication, 243
  literacy and Axial Age, 241–244
  mass literacy, 242
  meaning of philosophy, 249–252
  metanarrative of progress, 239
  myth, 240
  mythic discourse, 240
  Paganism, 246
  phenomena of Axial Age, 244
  philosophy, 235–238
  problems subject to investigation by human mind, 248
  religion, 245
  religious product of Axial Age, 246
  scribal literacy, 242, 243
  triumph of Logos, 244–247
  verbal formulae, 245, 247
  vision of Axial Age, 249
Pound, E., 214
powers, 108–109. *See also* place of mingled powers
Practicus, 89. *See also* hidden church of Golden Dawn
prayers, 149. *See also* magic and end of history

priest, 90. *See also* hidden church of Golden Dawn
primitive societies, 261. *See also* future portrayal
privilege, 123
problems in investigation by human mind, 248
production, 187. *See also* civilization collapse
progressive activists, 126
progressivist myth, 204
prosthetic society, 208. *See also* industrial society
psyche, 65

radical movements, 145–146. *See also* magic and end of history
raids, era of mass, 157. *See also* end of bronze age
Randers, J., 186
Randsborg, K., 194
Raoult, M., 5
RDNA. *See* Reformed Druids of North America
reader, 89. *See also* hidden church of Golden Dawn
recreational environmentalism, 217, 218. *See also* environmental activism
Reformed Druids of North America (RDNA), 77
Regardie, I., 92
religion, 245
  astronomical theory of, 10
  core of, 78
  mystery, 81
  old Paganism, 83
renewable energy sources, 202
resources, 186. *See also* civilization collapse
  depletion, 188
rolling collapse, 201
Roman collapse, 192
Roman empire, western, 185, 192, 195–196. *See also* civilization collapse

Rosman, A., 194
Rubel, P. G., 194

Sanders, W. T., 185
Santley, R. S., 185
Scholem, G., 91
Schumacher, E. F., 248
scientific materialists, 236
scribal literacy, 242, 243. *See also* Post-Axial Age
Sea of Tranquility, 232
Sea Peoples, 156, 158, 160. *See also* end of bronze age
seasonal and sexual religious interpretation, 79
Senner, W., 45
sentimental environmentalism, 217, 218–219. *See also* environmental activism
separativist myth, 204
sexual dimension of religion, 8
Shadow ouaternio, 67–68. *See also* fourth quaternion
*Shah-namah* of Firdausi, 36. *See also* myth
shape of time, 139. *See also* magic and end of history
Shimkin, D. B., 193
Shrimpton, G., 156
Skole, D., 185
snarl word, 166, 170. *See also* fascism
Snyder, C. A., 185
socialist parties, 169
solar interpretations of mythology, 10
solar-phallic Druidry, 13
Solnit, D., 119, 124, 131
sound symbolism, 52
spell, 121
    of corporate triumphalism, 124–129
    of reification, 121–124
    of rescue, 129–132
Spengler, O., 238
Sphere of Protection, 64–65, 70–72. *See also* fourth quaternion
spiritual beings, 106–107. *See also* place of mingled powers

active imagination, 112
conjuring spirits, 112
interacting with, 111–112
in magical lodge, 97–98
spiritual tradition, 31
Stephenson's vision, 260–261. *See also* future portrayal
storytellers, 120
Stukeley, W., 22
    Dragon Temple, 27
subdeacon/Portal, 90. *See also* hidden church of Golden Dawn
swarming attacks, 156. *See also* end of bronze age
syndicalist parties, 169

Tainter, J. A., 184, 185, 187, 188
technic societies, 267–268. *See also* future portrayal
technological progress as source of problems, 264. *See also* future portrayal
Tengwar script, 46
Theoricus, 89. *See also* hidden church of Golden Dawn
the Self, 65
Togodubeline, 23
Tokugawa period, 210–211
Tolkien, J. R. R., 10, 29, 38–39, 46
totalitarian political system, 171
Toynbee, A., 147, 156
Tyson, N. deGrasse, 236

UGC. *See* Universal Gnostic Church
unary, 133
Universal Gnostic Church (UGC), 86
Urn. *See* Gwrn

validity, 45
Vendidad, 36. *See also* myth
verbal formulae, 245, 247. *See also* Post-Axial Age
Vico, G., 52
visions of future, 228
Vorosmarty, C., 185

Wagner, G. A., 156
war chariot, 155. *See also* end of
    bronze age
waste, 186. *See also* civilization collapse
Webster, D. L., 185, 193
western Roman empire, 185, 192,
    195–196. *See also* civilization
    collapse
Weston, J., 113
Wilkinson, R. G., 187, 188
Willey, G. R., 193
Williams ab Ithel, J., 34, 35, 46, 49,
    51, 58
Williams, E., 4, 23–24, 31, 43
    Bardic lore, 31–32
    Bardic synthesis, 43
    Coelbren of the Bards, 44
    creation myth of, 33
    dismissal as forger, 39, 40
    forgery, 32
Williams, H., 46
Williams, T., 44, 46
Wiseman, J., 196
women oppression, 123

Yama, 36. *See also* myth
Yeats, W. B., 150, 214
Yemos, 39. *See also* myth
Yoffee, N., 184

Zalewski, P. J., 93
Zelator, 89. *See also* hidden church
    of Golden Dawn
Zeus, 79

Printed by Printforce, United Kingdom